Large-Scale Scrum

Large-Scale Scrum

More with LeSS

Craig Larman
Bas Vodde

✦✦Addison-Wesley

Boston • Columbus • Indianapolis • New York • San Francisco • Amsterdam • Cape Town
Dubai • London • Madrid • Milan • Munich • Paris • Montreal • Toronto • Delhi
São Paulo • Sydney • Hong Kong • Seoul • Singapore • Taipei • Tokyo

For information about buying this title in bulk quantities, or for special sales opportunities (which may include electronic versions; custom cover designs; and content particular to your business, training goals, marketing focus, or branding interests), please contact our corporate sales department at corpsales@pearsoned.com or (800) 382-3419.

For government sales inquiries, please contact governmentsales@pearsoned.com.

For questions about sales outside the U.S., please contact intlcs@pearson.com.

Visit us on the Web: informit.com/aw

Library of Congress Control Number: 2016941974

ISBN-13: 978-0-321-98571-2

ISBN-10: 0-321-98571-0

Text printed in the United States on recycled paper at LSC Communications in Crawfordsville, Indiana.

2 16

Contents

FOREWORD

by Stephen Denning

Large-Scale Scrum or *LeSS* continues the major discoveries that are transforming the world of management by showing how to implement Agile and Scrum at scale.

In the 20th Century, hierarchical bureaucracy enabled large groups to work together to achieve extraordinary improvements in productivity. Then the world changed. Deregulation, globalization, the emergence of knowledge work and new technology, particularly the Internet, transformed everything. Competition increased. The pace of change accelerated. Computer software enabled huge gains in productivity but in turn generated immense complexity. As power in the marketplace shifted from seller to buyer, the customer, not the firm, became the center of the commercial universe. These shifts required fundamentally different management that could mobilize the talents of everyone in the organization—and beyond—to meet the new and more difficult challenge of delighting customers. The changes went far beyond fixes to existing management practices. Agile and Scrum offer explicit alternatives to seemingly long-held, obvious, self-evident management assumptions.

LeSS shows how to handle large and complex development. Self-managed teams are not just tiny curiosities. They can manage vast international operations of great technical complexity. The practices are not only scalable, unlike bureaucracy, they are scalable without sclerosis.

LeSS continues the process of fundamentally reinventing management by incorporating the hard-won lessons of experience over more than a decade in scaling the management methods of Agile and Scrum. It shows how to cope with immense complexity by creating simplicity.

LeSS is deliberately incomplete. It leaves space for vast situational learning. It doesn't offer definitive answers. Nor does it try to satisfy 20th Century longings for formulaic answers or for apparently safe and disciplined approaches that offer a comforting illusion of predictable control. LeSS focuses on the minimal essence required when scaling, including continuous attention to technical excellence, and a mindset of continuous experimentation. It involves forever trying new experiments in an effort to improve. Like Scrum itself, LeSS strives for a balance between abstract principles and concrete practices.

And like Scrum, LeSS is not a process or a technique for building products. Rather, it is a framework within which processes and techniques can be adapted to meet the needs of the particular situation. It aims to make clear how product management and development practices can enable continuous improvement that adds value to customers.

Rather than providing fixed answers, LeSS provides the starting point for understanding and adopting its deeper principles. Instead of asking, "How can we *do Agile* at scale in our complex hierarchical bureaucracy?" it asks a different and deeper question is, "How can we simplify the organization, and *be Agile*?"

LeSS strives to achieve this balance for larger product groups. It adds more concrete structure to Scrum, while maintaining radical transparency and emphasizing the inspect-and-adapt cycle so that groups can continuously improve their own ways of working. It addresses the basic question: How do we take what works really well at the individual team level and make that happen at a much wider level in the organization?

Much remains to be learned and done in terms of scaling Agile and Scrum. This book is both a progress report and a guide to the future. At present, many organizations are not doing a good job having multiple teams working in sync on various aspects of products and platforms. Surveys show that most Agile and Scrum teams today report tension between the way their team operates and the way the rest of the organization is run. This book provides a practical, step-by-step guide to resolving this tension.

Stephen Denning
Author of *The Leader's Guide to Radical Management*
April 27, 2016

PREFACE

All great truths begin as blasphemies.
—George Bernard Shaw

Welcome to this portal into the world of LeSS, where simpler structures replace organizational complexity by focusing on people and their learning. To some people, LeSS might seem romantic and hopelessly idealistic. Not so, it is the reality for many product groups today!

Why This Book?

While reflecting on the feedback that our previous two books on LeSS presented too many ideas with too few starting points, Craig asked Bas if he wanted to write another book. Bas declined as he was eagerly awaiting the arrival of his second son. A relentless Craig convinced Bas this book was going to be an easy one. Craig was wrong.

Our initial intent was to write a primer for the previous LeSS books. We ended up with a very different book as our exploration in concrete starting points led to a pursuit for the minimum essentials for scaling. The result? The LeSS rules, the LeSS guides, and this book.

The LeSS rules and guides are important, but they are not the only considerations when scaling. Before diving into LeSS, we want to explicitly highlight two other important points: *continuous attention to technical excellence* and the *experimentation mindset*.

Audience

This book is for everyone in product development. The only prerequisite to this book is basic Scrum knowledge. If you don't have that, we recommend you start with reading through the Scrum Guide (*scrumguides.org*) and the Scrum Primer (*scrumprimer.org*). We start every chapter with a quick Scrum refresher related to that topic.

Chapter Structure

Each major chapter has the following structure:

> **One-team Scrum**
> Summarize one-team Scrum, to set the stage for learning LeSS.

> **LeSS**
> Covers the basic LeSS framework. This section is structured as:
>
> > Introduction and related LeSS principles.
> >
> > LeSS rules.
> >
> > LeSS guides.

> **LeSS Huge**
> Structured the same way as the LeSS section.

Style

We decided on the following style choices:

> LeSS and Scrum terms are capitalized, such as: Sprint, Product Backlog, Team. Note: **Team** is the role in LeSS whereas **team** is the general concept of a team.

> Throughout the book we use *you* to refer to you, the reader. We assume you are involved in a LeSS adoption and we pretend your role relates to the topic of the chapter. For example, in the Product Owner chapter, **you** are a Product Owner.

> We use italic, bold, and boxes to emphasize important points.

> The book is intentionally shallow in bibliographic references. For more thorough references, please refer to our previous books which have extensive bibliographies.

Organizational Terms

Most terms are defined when first used. However, we've struggled with organizational terms as different companies use different terms. Therefore, here we introduce the terms we use throughout the book, which will be obvious for some readers, yet obscure for others.

> **Product group**
All people involved in the product. Companies often use *project* to refer to all people involved in the development, but this book avoids the term *project* as it strives to emphasize product development. Hence, product group.

> **Line organization**
The formal organization usually depicted in an org-chart. Line organization is typically involved in evaluation, hiring, firing, and competence development. Companies might also have a matrixed project organization (this should not exist in LeSS) and staff or support organization.

> **Line manager and first-level manager**
A manager you report to in the line organization. The first-level manager is the direct line manager you report to.

> **Senior manager or executive**
Managers who work near the top of the organization. In a large organization, they tend to be outside the product group.

> **Product management or product marketing**
The function in product organizations that explore the market and decide on the content of the product. This is normally **not** in a line relationship with the teams.

> **Head of the product group**
The manager who heads the product group to which all people in the product group report in a line relationship.

> **Project/program manager**
Role traditionally responsible for the schedule of a release. This is normally **not** a line relationship with the team as it has a short-term temporary focus. These roles should not exist in a LeSS organization.

> **Functional organization**
Line organization for a functional skill such as development, test, or analysis. Should cease to exist in a LeSS organization.

Acknowledgments

We've had a huge number of reviewers for this book. Those who commented on more than one chapter are listed below.

Janne Kohvakka, Hans Neumaier, Rafael Sabbagh, Ran Nyman, Ahmad Fahmy, Mike Cohn, Gojko Adzic, Jutta Eckstein, Rowan Bunning, Jean-marc Gerber, Yi Lv, Steve Spearman, Karen Greaves, Marco Seelmann, Cesario Ramos, Markus Gärtner, Viktor Grgic, Chris Chan, Nils Bernert, Viacheslav Rozet, Edward Dahllöf, Lisa Crispin, Mike Dwyer, Francesco Sferlazza, Nathan Slippen, Mika Sjöman, Tim Born, Charles Bradley, Timothy Korson, Erin Perry, Greg Hutchings, Jez Humble, Alexey Krivitsky, Alexander Gerber, Peter Braun, Jurgen De Smet, Evelyn Tian, Sami Lilja, Steven Mak, Alexandre Cotting, Bob Schatz, Bob Sarni, Milind Kulkarni, Janet Gregory, Jerry Rajamoney, Karl Kollischan, Shiv Kumar Mn, David Nunn, Rene Hamannt, Ilan Goldstein, Juan Gabardini, Mehmet Yitmen, Kai-Uwe Rupp, Christian Engblom, James Grenning, Venkatesh Krishnamurthy, Peter Hundermark, Arne Ahlander, Darren Lai, Markus Seitz, Geir Amsjø, Ram Srinivasan, Mark Bregenzer, Aaron Sanders, Michael Ballé, Stuart Turner, Ealden Escañan, Steven Koh, Ken Yaguchi, michael james, Manoj Vadakkan, Peter Zurkirchen, Laszlo Csereklei, Gordon Weir, Laurent Carbonnaux, Elad Sofer.

And then a special thanks to Bernie Quah for the art and Terry Yin for support on nearly anything requested. And to Chris Guzikowski from Addison-Wesley for his patience during this longer than intended book project.

MORE WITH LESS

The cheapest, fastest, and most reliable components are those that aren't there.
—Gordon Bell

• Why LeSS? •

Why did Scrum adoption explode during the last decade? This is the question we toyed with at a hawker center in Singapore, over a beer.

Some say it was due to the simplistic certification model. Perhaps. But another agile method, DSDM, provided certification before Scrum yet never became as widespread.

Others say the availability of Scrum Master courses made the difference. Ken Schwaber's original Scrum Master course has indeed had a strong influence. Yet, Extreme Programming had the XP Immersion course first and isn't as common.

Perhaps it's the simplicity of Scrum that made the difference? Compared to XP, Scrum provides a simpler framework. Yet, even simpler agile methods such as Crystal never really took off.

After some more discussion and thought, Craig suggested:

> **Scrum hits an ideal balance between
> abstract principles and concrete practices.**

That concluded the discussion and we had another beer.

These concrete practices emphasize *empirical process control*—a core Scrum principle. Empirical process control distinguishes Scrum from other agile frameworks. The *Scrum Guide* puts it well:

Scrum is not a process or a technique for building products; rather, it is a framework within which you can employ various processes and techniques. Scrum makes clear the relative efficacy of your product management and development practices so that you can improve.

Meaning? With empirical process control we neither fix the scope of the product *nor the process of how to build it*. Instead, in short cycles we create a small shippable slice of the product. We inspect *what* we have and *how* we created it, and adapt the product and the way we create it. This clear inspection is enabled by the built-in mechanisms for transparency.

Principles sound good but are not obviously actionable. It is the small simple set of concrete *practices* that make it easy to start with Scrum: the clear roles, artifacts, and events.

These practices get you started, but are intentionally "incomplete" so that groups have the *space* to continuously learn and improve within the Scrum framework, recognizing that you are working in domains of high complexity where defined process recipes are too simplistic.

> **The concrete practices of Scrum provide the starting point for adopting its deeper principles. A perfect balance.**

Large-Scale Scrum (LeSS) achieves the same balance for larger product groups. It adds a bit more concrete structure to Scrum, whose purpose is to maintain transparency and emphasize the inspect-adapt cycle so that groups can continuously improve their own ways of working.

Like Scrum, LeSS is deliberately incomplete; it leaves space for vast situational learning. It doesn't offer many definitive answers. It won't satisfy those looking for formulaic answers or for apparently safe and disciplined approaches that offer a comforting illusion of predictable control via defined processes. These approaches destroy the principle of empirical process control, and feeling *ownership* of processes and practices.

A less defined process leads to more learning. More with less.

Contents

a large story map in initial PBR in LeSS

LeSS

> *There are two ways of constructing a [design]:*
> *One way is to make it so simple that there are obviously no deficiencies,*
> *and the other way is to make it so complicated that there are no obvious deficiencies.*
> —C.A.R. Hoare

ONE-TEAM SCRUM

Scrum is an empirical-process-control development framework in which a cross-functional self-managing *Team* develops a product in an iterative incremental manner.[1] Each timeboxed *Sprint*, a *potentially shippable product increment* is delivered and, ideally, shipped. A single *Product Owner* is responsible for maximizing product value, prioritizing *items* in the *Product Backlog*, and adaptively deciding the goal of each Sprint based on constant feedback and learning. A small *Team* is responsible for delivering the Sprint goal; there are no limiting single-specialized roles. A *Scrum Master* teaches why Scrum and how to derive value with it, coaches the Product Owner, Team, and organization to apply it, and acts as a mirror. There is no project manager or team lead.

Empirical process control requires *transparency*, which comes from short-cycle development and review of shippable product increments. It emphasizes continuous learning, inspection, and adaptation about the product and how it's created. It's based on understanding that in development things are too complex and dynamic for detailed and formulaic process recipes, which inhibit questioning, engagement, improvement.

In the *Scrum Guide* and *Scrum Primer*, the emphasis is for one Team; the focus is not many Teams working together. And that naturally leads to thinking about *large-scale* Scrum.

---

1. Please read the *Preface* for why chapters start with this section, the repeating major structure in each chapter, definition of some key terms, and style points.

LeSS

> LeSS is Scrum applied to many
> teams working together on one product.

see Adoption

LeSS is Scrum—Large-Scale Scrum (LeSS[1]) isn't new and improved Scrum. And it's not *Scrum at the bottom for each team, and something different layered on top*. Rather, it's about figuring out how to apply the principles, purpose, elements, and elegance of Scrum in a large-scale context, as simply as possible. Like Scrum and other truly agile frameworks, LeSS is "barely sufficient methodology" for high-impact reasons.

Scaled Scrum is not a special scaling framework that happens to include Scrum only at the team level. Truly scaled Scrum is *Scrum scaled*.

see Organize by Customer Value

...applied to many teams—Cross-functional, cross-component, full-stack feature teams of 3–9 learning-focused people that do it all—from UX to code to videos—to create done items and a shippable product.

see Coordination & Integration

...working together—The teams are working together because they have a common goal to deliver one common shippable product at the end of a common Sprint, and each team cares about this because they are a feature team responsible for the *whole*, not a part.

see Product

...on one product—What product? A broad complete end-to-end customer-centric solution that real customers use. It's not a component, platform, layer, or library.

• Background •

In 2002, when Craig wrote *Agile & Iterative Development*, many believed that agile development was only for small groups. However, we both (Craig and Bas) became interested in—and got increasing requests—to

---

1. *LeSS* suggests both Large-Scale Scrum and simplifying when scaling—*less*.

apply Scrum to large, multi-site, and offshore development. So, since 2005 we have teamed up to work with clients to scale up Scrum. Today, the two LeSS frameworks (smaller LeSS and LeSS Huge) have been adopted in big groups worldwide in disparate domains:

> telecom equipment — Ericsson & Nokia Networks[1]

> investment and retail banks — UBS

> trading systems — ION Trading

> marketing platforms and brand analytics — Vendasta

> video conferencing — Cisco

> online gaming (betting) — bwin.party

> offshore outsourcing — Valtech India[2]

In terms of *large*, what's a typical LeSS adoption case? Perhaps five teams in one or two sites. We've been involved in adoptions of that size, of a few hundred people, and up to a LeSS Huge case of well over a thousand people, far too many development sites, tens of millions of lines of C++, with custom hardware.

More LeSS Learning

To help people learn and based on our experiences with clients, in 2008 and 2010 we published two books on scaling agile development with the LeSS frameworks:

1. *Scaling Lean & Agile Development: Thinking and Organizational Tools for Large-Scale Scrum* — explains the thinking, leadership, and organizational design changes.

2. *Practices for Scaling Lean & Agile Development: Large, Multi-site & Offshore Product Development with Large-Scale Scrum* — shares hundreds of concrete *experiments* for LeSS, based on our experience with clients; experiments in product management, architecture, planning, multi-site, offshore, contracts, and more.

---

1. Nokia Networks is *not* the mobile phone firm acquired by Microsoft.
2. See the case studies at *less.works* for more examples.

This book—*Large-Scale Scrum: More with LeSS*—is the third in the LeSS series, a prequel and primer. This book synthesizes, clarifies, and highlights what's most important.

Besides these books, see *less.works* for online learning resources (including book chapters, articles, and videos), courses, and coaching.

• Experiments, Guides, Rules, Principles •

The first two LeSS books emphasized: *There are no such things as best practices in product development. There are only practices that are adequate within a certain context.*

Practices are situational; blithely claiming they are "best" disconnects them from motivation and context. They become rituals. And pushing so-called best practices kills a culture of learning, questioning, engagement, and continuous improvement. Why would people challenge *best*?

Therefore, the earlier LeSS books shared *experiments* we and our clients have tried, and we encouraged—and encourage—this mindset. But over time we noticed two problems with the only-experiments mindset:

> Novice groups made unskillful decisions to their detriment, adopting LeSS in ways not intended, with obvious problems; e.g. groups created Requirement Areas with one team each. Ouch!

> Novice groups asked, "Where do we start? What's most important?" They understandably couldn't see the key basics.

Based on this feedback we reflected and returned to the *Shu-Ha-Ri* model of learning: *Shu*—follow rules to learn basics. *Ha*—break rules and discover context. *Ri*—mastery and find your own way. In a Shu-level LeSS adoption, there are a few *rules* for a *barely sufficient* framework to kick-start empirical process control and whole-product focus.[1] These rules define the two **LeSS frameworks** that are introduced soon.

To summarize and build on these points, LeSS includes:

---

1. Scrum also has a few rules for its framework, for the same reasons as LeSS.

> **Rules**—A few rules to get started and form the foundation. They define the key elements of the **LeSS frameworks** that should be in place to support empirical process control and whole-product focus. e.g. *Hold an Overall Retrospective each Sprint*.

> **Guides**—A moderate set of guides to effectively adopt the rules and for a subset of experiments; worth trying based on years of experience with LeSS. Guides contain *tips*. Usually helpful and are an area for continuous improvement; e.g. *Three Adoption Principles*.

> **Experiments**—Many experiments that are very situational and may not even be worth trying; e.g. *Try... Translator on Team*.

> **Principles**—At the heart, a set of principles—extracted from experience with LeSS adoptions—that inform the rules, guides, and experiments; e.g. *whole-product focus*.

> The LeSS guides and experiments are optional. Guides will probably be helpful and are recommended trying. But bypass or drop those that limit further improvement or just don't fit.

A good way to look at LeSS is visualized in the *LeSS complete picture*:

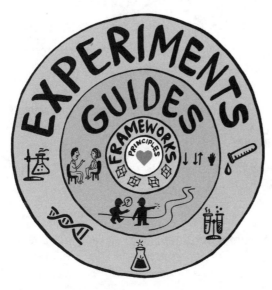

The LeSS complete picture will order the way we introduce LeSS:

1. LeSS **principles**, up next
2. LeSS **frameworks** (defined by the **rules**), in the rest of this chapter
3. LeSS **guides**, in the following chapters of this book
4. LeSS **experiments**, already available in the first two LeSS book

• LeSS Principles •

The LeSS rules define the LeSS framework. But the rules are minimalistic and don't answer how to apply LeSS in your specific context. The LeSS *principles* provide the basis for making those decisions.

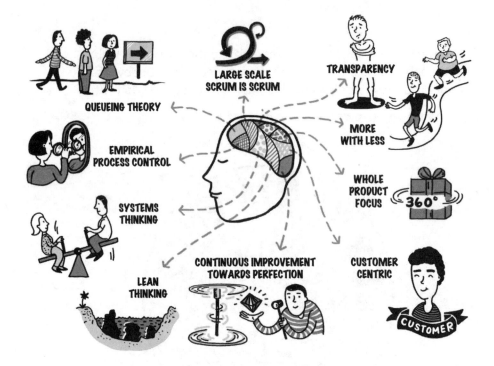

Large-Scale Scrum is Scrum—It isn't new and improved Scrum. Rather, LeSS is about figuring out how to apply the principles, rules, elements, and purpose of Scrum in a large-scale context, as simply as possible.

Transparency—Based on tangible "done" items, short cycles, working together, common definitions, and driving out fear in the workplace.

More with less—We don't want **more roles** because more roles leads to less responsibility to Teams. We don't want **more artifacts** because more artifacts leads to a greater distance between Teams and customers. We don't want **more process** because that leads to less learning and team ownership of process. Instead we want **more responsible Teams** by having less (fewer) roles, we want **more customer-focused Teams building useful products** by having less artifacts, we want **more Team ownership of process and more meaningful work** by having less defined processes. *We want more with less.*

Whole-product focus—One Product Backlog, one Product Owner, one shippable product, one Sprint—regardless if 3 or 33 teams. Customers want valuable functionality in a cohesive product, not technical components in separate parts.

Customer-centric—Focus on learning the customers real problems and solving those. Identify value and waste in the eyes of the paying customers. Reduce wait time from their perspective. Increase and strengthen feedback loops with real customers. Everyone understands how their work today directly relates to and benefits paying customers.

Continuous improvement towards perfection—Here's a perfection goal: Create and deliver a product almost all the time, at almost no cost, with no defects, that delights customers, improves the environment, and makes lives better. Do endless humble and radical improvement experiments toward that goal.

Lean thinking—Create an organizational system whose foundation is managers-as-teachers who apply and teach lean thinking, manage to improve, promote stop-and-fix, and who practice Go See. Add the two pillars of respect for people and continuous challenge-the-status-quo improvement mindset. All towards the goal of *perfection*.

Systems thinking—See, understand, and optimize the whole system[1] (not parts), and use systems modeling to explore system dynamics. Avoid the local sub-optimizations of focusing on the efficiency or productivity of individuals and individual teams. Customers care about the overall concept-to-cash cycle time and flow, not individual steps, and locally optimizing a *part* almost always sub-optimizes the *whole*.

Empirical process control—Continually inspect and adapt the product, processes, behaviors, organizational design, and practices to evolve in situationally-appropriate ways. Do that, rather than follow a prescribed set of so-called best practices that ignore context, create ritualistic following, impede learning and change, and squash people's sense of engagement and ownership.

Queuing theory—Understand how systems with queues behave in the R&D domain, and apply those insights to managing queue sizes, work-in-progress limits, multitasking, work packages, and variability.

• Two Frameworks: LeSS & LeSS Huge •

Large-Scale Scrum has two frameworks:

> > **LeSS**. 2–8 Teams

> > **LeSS Huge**. 8+ Teams

The word *LeSS* is overloaded to mean both Large-Scale Scrum in general and the smaller LeSS framework.

The Magic Number Eight

Actually, *eight* isn't a magic number, and if your group can successfully apply the smaller LeSS framework with more than eight teams, great! But we haven't seen that... yet. It's just an upper-limit empirical observation. And in some cases, such as varied complex goals with multi-site inexperienced foreign-language-only teams, it could be less than eight.

In any event, at some point, (1) the single Product Owner can no longer grasp an overview of the entire product, (2) the Product Owner can't balance an external and internal focus, and (3) the Product Backlog is so large that it becomes difficult for one person to work with.

---

1. The *system* is everyone and everything from concept to cash, and all its dynamics in time and space, primarily from the customer and user perspective.

When the group hits that tipping point, it may be time to change from the smaller LeSS framework to LeSS Huge. On the other hand, we suggest first trying to get better, smaller, and simpler, before getting *huger*.

Common Across the Frameworks

The LeSS and LeSS Huge frameworks share common elements:

> one Product Owner and one Product Backlog

> one common Sprint across all teams

> one shippable product increment

The following two sections of this chapter explain the frameworks; the smaller LeSS framework is next, and LeSS Huge starts on p. 33.

LeSS Framework

• LeSS Framework Summary •

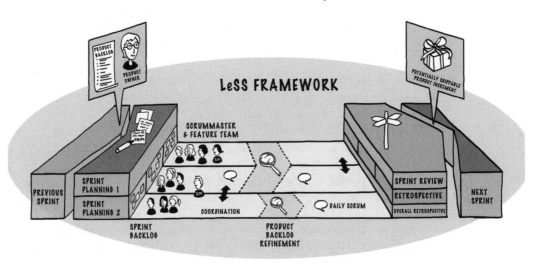

The smaller LeSS framework is for one (and only one) Product Owner who owns the product, and who manages one Product Backlog worked on by teams in one common Sprint, optimizing for the whole product. The LeSS framework elements are about the same as one-team Scrum:

Roles—One *Product Owner*, two to eight *Teams*, a *Scrum Master* for one to three Teams. Crucially, these Teams are **feature teams**—true cross-functional and cross-component full-stack teams that work together in a shared code environment, each doing *everything* to create *done* items.

Artifacts—One potentially shippable product increment, one Product Backlog, and a separate Sprint Backlog for each Team.

Events—One common Sprint for the whole product; it includes all teams and ends in one potentially shippable product increment. Details are explained in the upcoming stories, and in separate chapters.

Rules & Guides—Rules for a barely sufficient scaling framework for empirical process control and whole-product focus. Guides *may* help.

• LeSS Stories •

Learning LeSS—One way to learn is by reading in-depth exposition, and readers preferring that can comfortably skip ahead to the introduction to *LeSS Huge* (p. 33), and then on to following chapters. Others who like stories, keep on reading.

Simple stories—These stories don't explore the complexities of large-scale development—from politics to prioritization—that we experience when consulting. Later chapters unpack those boxes. Here are intentionally plain and simple stories just to introduce the basics of a LeSS Sprint. If you want thrilling dialog and drama, read a *Lean* book.

Rules & guides—In the stories you will notice that the margins refer to related LeSS rules and guides, to clarify and make connections.

Two perspectives—Following are two related stories focusing separately on two key perspectives, to introduce some flows more simply:

1. The flow of *teams* through a LeSS Sprint.
2. The flow of *customer-centric items (features)*.

• LeSS Story: Flow of Teams •

This story focuses on the flow of *teams* through a Sprint, rather than the flow of *items*. In reality the majority of time in the Sprint is working on development tasks, not *meetings*. However, this story emphasizes meetings and interactions, as the goal is an understanding of how multiple teams work together during LeSS events, and how they coordinate day by day.

Mark walks into the room where his team (Trade) works and sees Mira[1], who says, "Good morning! Just a reminder, we're the team representatives for this Sprint, and Sprint Planning One starts in 10 minutes." "Right," says Mark, "Meet you in the big room."

Tip: Rotate representatives each Sprint

Sprint Planning One
(Guide: Sprint Planning One, p. 276)

It's time for a common Sprint Planning One. Around the big room are 10 team representatives from the five teams in this product group. They all work on their flagship product for trading bonds and derivatives. Sam, the Scrum Master of teams Trade and Margin, is also there. He's planning to observe and coach as needed.

RULE: There is one product-level Sprint, not a different Sprint for each Team.

Many Sprints earlier, everyone from all the teams attended Sprint Planning One. That was more useful when the group was not very good at getting items clear and ready, nor at creating broad knowledge across the teams. Back then, Sprint Planning One was used to answer a lot of major questions that everyone needed to hear. But lately that's been much improved, and so now the group is experimenting with using rotating representatives, in what has become a simple and quick meeting with only a few minor questions that tend to pop up. If the new approach doesn't work well, it will probably be raised in an Overall Retrospective, and another experiment for Sprint Planning will be created.

RULE: Sprint Planning consists of two parts: Sprint Planning One is common for all teams while Sprint Planning Two is usually done separately for each team. Do multi-team Sprint Planning Two in a shared space for closely related items.

---

1. To help remember characters and roles, names use an alliteration; e.g. Mira a team Member, Sam a Scrum Master, Paolo a Product Owner.

RULE: Sprint Planning One is attended by the Product Owner and Teams or Team representatives. They together tentatively select the items that each team will work on for the next Sprint

Paolo walks in and says "Hi!" He's the Product Owner and also the lead product manager.[1] Paolo lays out 22 cards on a table and says, "Here's the big themes: German market, order management, and some regulatory reports. I've laid them out in my priority

order. I think everyone here understands why these are the priorities, since we've been discussing this a lot in Product Backlog refinement. But please ask again, if it's not clear."

Tip: Teams choose their items

Mira and Mark walk over to the table (along with the other representatives) and pick two cards for items related to German-market bonds. Over the last two Sprints their team clarified these items in detail, in single-team Product Backlog refinement (PBR) workshops.

Guide: Multi-Team PBR, p. 252

And they pick two more items related to order management that both Team Trade and Team Margin understand quite well. Both teams worked together in multi-team PBR workshops on these items. Why? The teams wanted to decide as late as possible the choice of team-to-item, during some future Sprint Planning. This increases the group's *agility*—easily responding to change—and their broader whole-product knowledge fosters self-organized coordination.

Tip: Don't pre-decide division of items to teams

A minute later, Mary from Team Margin, on scanning another team's cards, asks their representatives, "Do you mind if we do that report? We did something very similar last Sprint and I bet we can get it done quickly. Could you swap for this German-market item?" They agree.

---

1. In product companies, the *product management* or *product marketing* roles—in collaboration with teams—focus on vision and direction, encourage innovation, analyze competitors, and discover customer and market needs and trends. In internal development groups, this role might be filled by a lead user in an operational business group. The Product Owner—the owner of the product—in Scrum and LeSS typically comes from these roles, such as Paolo the lead product manager serving as Product Owner. See the *Product Owner* chapter for more.

LeSS SPRINT PLANNING

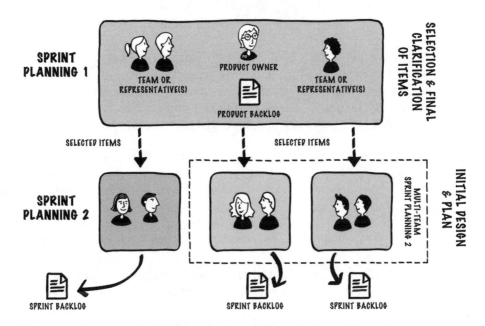

After a few minutes, the teams finish choosing and swapping based on their interests, strengths, and desire to group related items for focus.

Sam (the Scrum Master) says, "I notice that Team Margin has the top four priority items. Could that become a problem?" A quick discussion ensues in which the group realizes there's a chance that one of the highest-priority items for the product could get dropped if things don't go smoothly for Team Margin. They decide to distribute a few of the highest-priority items across more teams (constrained by which teams know which items), making it more likely that top items will get done.

Guide: Five Scrum Master Tools, p. 141

Tip: Spread high-order items

The representatives have chosen a total of 18 cards, leaving four lowest priority items on the table. Paolo looks over the unchosen item cards, picks up two of them, and says, "These two are pretty important to me this Sprint. Maybe I should have given them a higher priority to begin with, but I didn't, and now I'd like to change my mind. Let's find a way to swap them with some items you've already chosen. And of course, if a team gets lucky and finishes early, please pick up the unchosen items."

RULE: Teams identify opportunities to work together and final questions are clarified

After that's resolved, Paolo says, "Okay, let's spend some time wrapping up lingering questions. As you know, I've been focusing more on figuring out prioritization, and most of you know these item details a lot better than me, but let's see what we can do together to clear up minor stuff."

Tip: Diverge to clarify

In parallel, Mira, Mark, and the others think hard about final minor points to clear up for their items, and write some questions on flip-chart papers on the walls around the room. Paolo roams around to different areas, discussing. Everyone mingles and contributes. After about 30 minutes, all the minor questions that could be answered have been.

The group forms a standing circle to wrap up. No one raises any coordination topics, so eventually Sam says, "I notice that Teams Trade and Margin and NotDerivative have picked up strongly related order-management items." Mira says, "Hey, let's get Trade, Margin, and NotDerivative together for a multi-team Sprint Planning Two. We've got opportunities to work together." That's agreed. The meeting ends.

Team and Multi-Team Sprint Planning Two
(Guide: Multi-Team Sprint Planning Two, p. 280)

RULE: Each Team has its own Sprint Backlog

After a break, two of the five teams hold their own single-team Sprint Planning Two meetings to create their own Sprint Backlogs, designing and planning their work for the Sprint.

RULE: Do multi-team SP2 in a shared space for closely related items.

In contrast, Teams Trade, Margin, and NotDerivative hold a multi-team Sprint Planning Two together in a big room, since they are implementing strongly related items—which were also previously clarified together in multi-team PBR—and they foresee value in working closely.

Tip: Whole-group design & shared work session

They talk together in a 10-minute session to set the stage, identifying shared work (common tasks) and design issues. Then they start the clock for a timeboxed 30-minute design session, agreeing to *visualize*: more sketching on the whiteboard, less talking without drawing. During this time, more shared work is also discovered and written on the board.

Guide: No Software Tools for Sprint Backlog, p. 281

Ding! After 30 minutes lots of unexplored details remain, but the teams move on anyway. Each team heads to a different corner of the big room where each starts its own focused Sprint Planning Two, talking more about detailed design issues and creating their own Sprint Backlog with cards. Further coordination is handled by an advanced variation of the *just talk* technique in LeSS: *just scream*.

During the talking, the teams realize the need for an in-depth multi-team Design Workshop. They agree to hold one later that day.

Guide: Just Talk, p. 287

Multi-Team Design Workshop

(Guide: Multi-Team Design Workshop, p. 301)

After Sprint Planning and another break, Mira and Mark from Team Trade, and a few people from Team Margin and Team NotDerivative hold a timeboxed one-hour multi-team Design Workshop for a deeper dive into a common and consistent design for their work. Around a large whiteboard they sketch and talk together towards some clarity and agreement on a design approach and common technical tasks. Fortunately, the conclusions don't seriously impact their existing Sprint plans, but they feel uncomfortable with their process, recognizing they could have predicted the need to resolve these big design questions earlier.

Development Activities Supporting Coordination and Continuous Delivery

After Sprint Planning, the teams dive into developing items, with an emphasis on *communicating in code*. All the teams are *integrating continuously*. The continuous integration of all code across all teams creates the opportunity to cooperate by checking who else made changes in the component being worked on. That's useful, because the group uses *integration as a way to inform and support their coordination*.

Guide: Communicate in Code, p. 292

Guide: Integrate Continuously, p. 293

For example, early during the second day of the Sprint, Mark, a developer on Team Trade, pulls the latest version locally and quickly checks the latest changes related to the component they are working on now. He discovers changes related to code added by Maximilian from Team Margin. He knows that team is working on a strongly related item, so he is not especially surprised. Since the code has communicated that *now* there's a need to coordinate and *who* he needs to talk with, he immediately visits Team Margin down the hall. They *just talk* about how to work together to benefit from one another's work.

RULE: Prefer decentralized and informal coordination over centralized coordination.

Guide: Just Talk, p. 287

For the item that Team Trade is developing, and in fact for every item in every team, they have written the automated acceptance tests *before* starting to develop the solution code. Thus, in addition to integrating the code continuously, they're also integrating the automated tests. These acceptance tests are run frequently by team members, and so when any of them fails, the teams are immediately signaled to coordinate. The code is telling them, "Hey! There's a problem! You need to talk and work it out."

RULE: The perfection goal is to improve the Definition of Done so that it results in a shippable product each Sprint (or even more frequently).

Naturally, another major benefit of the group's practice of integrating continuously, automated testing, and stopping-and-fixing whenever the build breaks, is that their product is more or less continuously ready to deliver into production. There's no separate integration team or testing team that would add delay, handoff, and complexity.

Overall Retrospective
(Guide: Overall Retrospective, p. 317)

RULE: An Overall Retrospective is held after the Team Retrospectives to discuss cross-team and system-wide issues, and to create improvement experiments. This is attended by Product Owner, Scrum Masters, Team Representatives, and managers (if any).

On the second day of the Sprint, Sam and the other Scrum Masters, the Product Owner Paolo, a site manager, and a representative from most of the teams, all get together for a maximum 90-minutes Overall Retrospective related to the *last* Sprint.

Why didn't they hold this Overall Retrospective *before* this new Sprint started? They could have, but they normally end a Sprint on a Friday and start a new one on Monday (in contrast to Sam's suggestion that they try a Wednesday–Thursday boundary). And on the last Friday, they held both the Sprint Review and the team-level Retrospectives. After that they didn't have the energy to hold an engaged Overall Retrospective at the end of the day. So they've opted for an early next Sprint. Sam privately thinks this delay is not a great idea—he'd rather they started Sprint Planning a little later after this meeting—but he wants the group to discover that for themselves.

Guide: Improve the System, p. 320

They focus on a system-wide issue and improvement: how to coordinate, share information, and solve problems across the entire group during the Sprint? Previously they have tried Scrum-of-Scrum meetings and didn't find them very effective. Sam explains the technique of Open Space, and they agree to try it this Sprint.

Activities for Coordination
(Coordination & Integration, p. 285)

The fourth day demonstrates a variety of coordination ideas in LeSS:

In LeSS, each Team holds a Daily Scrum as usual. To support coordination between Teams Trade and Margin, Mira goes as a *scout* to observe Team Margin's Daily Scrum and then returns and updates her team on what she learned. And someone from Team Margin does the opposite.

As agreed in the Overall Retrospective, the group holds a 45-minute *Open Space* meeting for coordination and learning, preceded by drinks and snacks. Sam acts as facilitator to teach the group how to hold an Open Space meeting. Everyone is welcome, but most teams decide to send only a few representatives. Mira and Mark from Team Trade join in. The group plans to try an Open Space once a week.

The Test *community*, with volunteers from most teams, gets together for a half-hour to hear Mary's proposal to try a new automated acceptance-testing tool. They enthusiastically agree, and Mary volunteers her Team Margin to do the actual experimental work next Sprint, since they are really interested in learning this.

Mira is a member of the Design/Architecture *community*. There's no design workshop needed this Sprint related to overall architecture, but she wants to hold a half-day *spike* in the next Sprint for a new technology. She posts her idea on the community collaboration tool, and suggests the community do the spike together with mob programming to increase their shared learning.

The build system seems to have a weird bug. Time to *stop and fix*! This Sprint, Team Trade is responsible for it, and it's one of Mark's secondary specialties, so he volunteers to fix it and asks another team member to pair up with him to help his colleague learn more about it.

Later, Mira and a few other team members visit the customer support and training group, who work closely with hands-on users. Her team has finished their first item and they want to get early feedback from people closer to customers. One of the trainers is free and he plays with the new feature. Team Trade leaves with a few ideas to make it better.

Side notes:

RULE: Cross-team coordination is decided by the teams.

Guide: Scouts, p. 307

Guide: Open Space, p. 305

Guide: Communities, p. 295

Tip: Have an architecture community

Tip: Stop and fix when problems

Tip: Experts teach others

RULE: Clarification ideally between Teams and users and other stakeholders

Tip: Early feedback

Guide: Communi-
cate in Code, p. 292

Guide: Integrate
Continuously, p. 293

Later in the day Mark and the rest of Team Trade are doing tasks for their second item. Mark has just completed a 10-minute TDD cycle and has clean stable code after a micro-change. Once again—about every 10 minutes—he pushes the tiny change to the central shared repository (to "head of trunk"), to *integrate continuously* with his team and all others. He glances over to their big visible red-green screen on the wall and sees that the build system is passing all the tests for the entire group.

Overall Product Backlog Refinement

(Guide: Product Backlog Refinement Types, p. 249)

RULE: Do multi-team and/or overall PBR to increase shared understanding and exploiting coordination opportunities when having closely related items or a need for broader input/learning.

Tip: Rotate repre-
sentatives each
Sprint

Guide: Prioritiza-
tion over Clarifica-
tion, p. 178

On the fifth day, Mark and Mira join an *overall PBR* workshop, with representatives from each team, and Paolo, the Product Owner. Paolo starts by sharing his current thinking on product direction and where to go next in the short term and, most importantly, *why*. To help them understand his reasoning, he reviews his prioritization model with the group, that factors in profit impact, customer impact, business risk, technical risk, cost of delay, and more.

Guide: Five Rela-
tionships, p. 180

Tip: PO engages the
teams in owning the
product

Paolo asks for feedback and ideas from the group for upcoming direction, and the group discusses what items to refine next. Although he knows that he'll make the final priority calls, Paolo works hard to engage the teams in understanding his thinking, and also to learn from their thinking. He wants the teams to also be involved in *owning the product*.

Guide: Splitting,
p. 260

Guide: Scaling Esti-
mation, p. 269

The group then splits a few big new items, doing lightweight clarification (more will follow later), and planning poker estimation as a way to *learn* more about the items—rather than to create estimates.

The representatives from three teams (including Trade and Margin) decide to later do multi-team PBR together for some items to increase their shared understanding and because they are strongly related. And representatives from two other teams choose items to focus on separately in team PBR sessions.

Multi-Team PBR and Team PBR
(Guide: Multi-Team PBR, p. 252)

On the sixth day, everyone in three of the teams gets together for a *multi-team PBR* workshop in the big room.

Although their main business is creating and selling their trading solution, the company has a small group of bond traders that use it, with relatively small positions that keep them engaged but without high risk. This way the company has better insight into market trends as well as some expert users that can easily talk with the development teams.

Tanya and Ted are the traders who told Paolo about a trend that led to the items being refined in the multi-team PBR session. So they both join, as experts to help the teams learn and clarify the new items.

RULE: All prioritization goes through the Product Owner, but clarification is as much as possible directly between the Teams and customer/users and other stakeholders.

The other two teams, in discussion with some other traders, hold separate PBR workshops to complete clarification of some items already under refinement and to start on some new ones. Also, one of the company's three lawyers specializing in financial regulations and compliance joins one of these teams to help them in clarification.

As a last step in the PBR meetings, people take photos of everything on the walls and whiteboards. They add those to the wiki pages that are used to record everything for each item. Plus they update and clean up the text and tables in the wiki pages that were quickly added during discussions.

Guide: Tools for Large Product Backlogs, p. 210

Tip: Use a wiki for item details

A Chat About Team-Level Backlogs and Product Owners

After the multi-team PBR workshop, Mike (who just joined the company) sees Sam by the coffee machine and walks over to talk. Mike says, "Hey Sam. I'm interested in your opinion on something. In the refinement workshop we just finished, of course I noticed that we were working directly with some of the traders to clarify together. But isn't that inefficient? In my last company, every team had its own Product Owner who did the story writing, wireframes, and specifications, and then gave them to us to implement. Then we could just focus on the programming. And each team had its own Product Backlog that the team's Product Owner prioritized. But I don't see that here. Why is it different?"

Sam says, "Interesting questions. Do you mind if I ask you a few questions to explore this?"

"Sure, go ahead."

"Let's first consider one Product Backlog versus many team-level backlogs. Suppose each team had its own backlog. How easy and effective is it for one truly overall Product Owner to have an overview? And how much knowledge will a team have of the requirements and designs of items in a different team's backlog?"

Mike replies, "I can answer that pretty clearly from my last company. Not much."

Sam continues. "Now suppose there are eight teams and eight team backlogs. What if, from the higher company or product perspective, for some reason, the items in *two* of the eight team backlogs are actually by far the most important or highest priority. Maybe there's some change in the market so that this situation comes up. So some questions for you: Can the six teams working in the lower-priority backlogs easily shift to start working on the high-priority items in the other two backlogs? And is it likely that the group will even see this problem, given that they are locked in to each team having their own backlog and local priorities?"

Mike answers, "Our teams at my old place only worked on their own team item backlog. They couldn't shift to others. But why would they want to? Isn't that inefficient?"

Sam responds, "Well, from a company perspective, the teams are only working 'efficiently' on low-priority stuff because of their narrow knowledge created by each focusing in a different team backlog and because the overall priority and overview isn't visible. Let me ask you some questions: Does that seem inflexible or flexible—*agile*? And does that optimize people working on the highest-impact stuff from the company perspective?"

Mike pauses, "Oh! I think I get it. It's actually not *being* agile, even though our group said they were *doing* agile. We weren't responsive to the highest-value changes overall. And my old team Product Owner said she was prioritizing for highest value in our team backlog. But now I see that my team was just busy efficiently working on what could be low-value stuff when you look at it from a higher level."

Sam says, "Exactly. So that's one of several reasons why we have *one* Product Backlog here, and no team backlogs, even though there are many teams. In short, it supports whole-product focus, system optimization, and agility. And of course it's simpler, and it's easy to see what's going across the group."

"Also," Mike comments, "I noticed it was much harder in my prior company for all the teams to really work *together* at the same time, since we were working on very different goals in asynchronous Sprints. Here it feels like all the teams have more of a common focus and direction in one Sprint together."

"Exactly!" Sam replies, then continues.

"Here's another question: If there's only one Product Backlog and one real Product Owner who prioritizes it, but each team still had its own so-called Product Owner who per definition is not prioritizing a team backlog—since there isn't one—then what do they do all day long? "

Mike replies, "Well, in my last company it was the job of the team-level Product Owner to talk to the users and write the stories for the team, so they could focus on efficiently programming while the team Product Owner worked on gathering and writing requirements."

Sam asks, "Mike, before you learned about Scrum terms such as 'Product Owner', what would you have called middlemen in between the developers and real customers—the ones collecting requirements and then giving them to developers?"

"I joined my last company before we adopted Scrum there." Mike answers, "And back in the day, there was a group of business analysts who did that. After we adopted Scrum, we were asked to call them the Product Owners."

RULE: There is one Product Owner and one Product Backlog for the complete shippable product.

RULE: The Product Owner shouldn't work alone on Product Backlog refinement; she is supported by the multiple Teams working directly with customers/ users and other stakeholders.

RULE: All prioritization goes through the Product Owner, but clarification is as much as possible directly between the Teams and customer/users and other stakeholders.

"Today in your PBR workshop," Sam asks, "Did you talk with the traders who were there?"

"Let me think back." Mike replies, "Yeah, I was talking with Tanya about her idea to analyze trading Russian corporate bonds. It seemed a little confusing so I asked her, why? She explained it was because of concerns around money laundering in offshore accounts. Now, she didn't know that we've been recently working on some other features that integrate with new EU and USA regulatory databases to assess this. So I proposed to her a different approach, which I think—and she agrees—will better solve the problem.

"Now that I think about it," he reflects, "that probably wouldn't have happened in my last company, since we rarely talked directly with users."

More Development

Minute by minute and day by day the teams develop code, integrating continuously combined with full test automation. They stop and fix when the build breaks, working towards their perfection goal of having a done shippable product they can continuously deliver to customers. Therefore, when the Sprint is nearly over and the teams are preparing to join the Sprint Review, there's no late mad rush of effort to integrate and test a big batch of code—it's been integrated and tested all along.

Sprint Review
(Review & Retrospective, p. 313)

RULE: There is one product Sprint Review; it is common for all teams.

Finally it's the last day and time for an all-together Sprint Review. Who's there? Paolo (the Product Owner, lead product manager), all the internal bond traders, a few trainers and customer service representatives, a few people from Sales, and four users from external clients who pay lower annual rates in exchange for participating regularly in these reviews. Also, there's all the team members.

SPRINT REVIEW

TEAM   PRODUCT OWNER   TEAM   USERS & STAKEHOLDERS

TEAM RETROSPECTIVE

TEAM

TEAM

OVERALL RETROSPECTIVE

MANAGER   SCRUMMASTER   PRODUCT OWNER   SCRUMMASTER   TEAM REP.

Because there are many items to explore, the group starts with a one-hour *bazaar*—something like a science fair—with many devices set up in the room, each available for exploring different sets of items. Some team members stay at fixed areas to collect feedback while everyone else uses and discusses the new features.

Guide: Review Bazaar, p. 316

Tip: Discuss direction for upcoming Sprints

After an hour, the group comes together to discuss the questions and feedback, in a session led by Paolo. After that, they discuss future direction. Paolo shares what's going on in the market and with competitors, and his thoughts on where to go next, and asks for advice.

Team Retrospectives

RULE: Each Team has its own Sprint Retrospective.

After a break, Team Trade (and all other teams) hold separate team-level Sprint Retrospectives. They decide that holding a multi-team Design Workshop with Team Margin after Sprint Planning (rather than earlier) was far from ideal in this case, because major issues were left unexplored until the last minute—issues which could have seriously blocked or complicated development. So for the next Sprint they decide that during their PBR sessions they will strive to identify items that have major design issues worth discussing with other teams. And if so, hold a multi-team Design Workshop as soon as possible.

The End

Guide: Belgian Tripel Karmeliet

Sprint done! Sam invites Team Trade to join Mira and him at the Belgian-beer pub down the street—Mira's favorite—to celebrate her birthday.

Summary

Some key points from the story:

> it emphasized flow of people and teams through a Sprint in LeSS

> it connected story elements to specific LeSS guides and rules

> for a reader who knows Scrum, the events should be familiar

> the story shows whole-product focus, even with many teams

> the activities emphasized team-based learning and coordination

> develop items by integrating continuously so that communicating in code supports decentralized coordination and just talking, in addition to continuous delivery

> teams clarify directly with users and customers, to reduce handoff and increase understanding, empathy, and ownership

• LeSS Story: Flow of Items •

This story focuses more on the flow of *items (features)* through part of a Sprint, primarily during refinement and development.

Portia wraps up her meeting with the government regulator and heads to the airport, and home. She's another product manager; she helps Paolo, and specializes in regulatory and audit trends.[1]

Later, Portia meets with Paolo. Writing on cards, she summarizes the new rules that are going to impact their product, and what clients she thinks are going to want certain features first. Paolo points to the five cards and asks, "So this covers all the work, as far as you know?" Portia smiles and says, "This is regulatory. It's *never* finished or clear."

Paolo asks, "Can you put these in the Product Backlog for me, unordered at the bottom for now?"

"Sure."

A week later Paolo tells Portia, "Soon, I want to start delivering some parts of the big regulatory requirement for bond derivatives. In the next Sprint's Product Backlog refinement workshops, I'm going to ask for some teams to focus on that. You know the most about it, so please be at the overall PBR and at whatever team refinement workshops where

Guide: Product Owner Helpers, p. 179

Guide: Tools for Large Product Backlogs, p. 210

Tip: Spreadsheet and wiki for large Product Backlog

---

1. In addition to a lead product manager—who often serves as Product Owner—many large groups have a few supporting product managers, each specializing in a major market segment or customer area.

they want you. Also, can you set up a wiki page with links to the new regulatory docs, to share with the teams?"

"Already done," answers Portia.

Overall PBR

Guide: Product Backlog Refinement Types, p. 249

Paolo kicks off a quick overall PBR workshop, "We've got lots of work around new regulations. Soon we need to deliver related items because of a legal deadline end of fiscal year. We'll know better after some splitting and estimation, but I wouldn't be surprised if it ultimately involves three or more of the teams for implementation, and lots of time."

Guide: Splitting, p. 260

The group splits the new giant item into only a few large parts, to learn major elements. More splitting will happen later in a single-team or multi-team PBR session. Portia heads to the whiteboard; on the left side she writes "regulations for bond derivatives." Then in conversation with the group, they sketch a tree diagram with four arms representing a splitting into four major sub-items. But they don't go any deeper—they're avoiding over-analysis.

Guide: Scaling Estimation, p. 269

Next, the group creates four cards for the new items, and everyone together estimates them with planning poker and relative-size points, baselining the points against existing well-known items in the Product Backlog. Their main goal is not to create estimates but to surface questions and drive more discussion, which they do with Portia.

Next, Paolo asks, "So Portia, of these four big ones, which one first?"

She points to the second card. "Over-the-counter exotic bond derivatives."

Paolo says, "We need to start delivering some of that as soon as possible. It's moving way up the Product Backlog. So I'd like one team to take a bite into this, next Sprint. Who's interested?"

Team Trade volunteers.

Finally, team members from three other teams decide to hold a multi-team PBR workshop for related items.

Team PBR: Biting In

The next day Team Trade holds a team PBR workshop with Portia. They have only one of the four giant items to focus on: New regulations for over-the-counter (OTC) exotic bond derivatives. Sam (their Scrum Master) is also there. Portia says, "This is a gigantic complex item, in an area that frankly nobody is really clear about. It's going to take us a long time to split this up, really understand it, and specify it well."

Sam asks, "Do we really need to understand *all* of it? And will all that analysis teach us more, or could it actually *delay* our learning?"

He reviews with them the idea of *Take a Bite*: to just split off one tiny fragment, really understand that, and implement it quickly. Sam concludes, "You know, diagrams don't crash and documents don't run."

Guide: Take a Bite, p. 202

With Portia, the team splits off one tiny bite of a thin customer-centric end-to-end item.

From now on they will focus on that tiny bite, clarifying and implementing it. Only after implementation and feedback will they return much later to more splitting and refinement. Using *specification by example* Portia and Team Trade spend the rest of the day chewing on their bite.

Tip: Specification by example in "Clarifying" on page 254

Multi-Team PBR: Rotation Refinement

One outcome of overall PBR was the decision to take a bite with Team Trade. Another was the decision for three teams to hold a multi-team PBR workshop for related items, to increase learning and the agility of multiple teams knowing and thinking about the same items.

Guide: Multi-Site PBR, p. 254

In addition to everyone from the three teams, the internal traders Tanya, Ted, and Travis join to help the teams start clarifying about a dozen new items.

To start, they form three temporary mixed groups with people from each team. The mixed groups start clarifying different items in separate areas in the room, each with a whiteboard, big wall space, laptop, and projector. Tanya is with one group, Ted another, and Travis, the third.

Then they do *rotation refinement*: After 30 minutes, a timer goes *ding*! One group walks over to the other's area, and vice versa, but Tanya, Ted, and Travis don't move. The timer is restarted, the traders explain the current results to the incoming groups, and they continue clarifying.

Figure 2.1 multi-team PBR

Throughout the day, as different items become relatively clear—or are left with hanging questions that will have to be explored later—new items are introduced at a work area. Some of the bigger items are split into two or three new smaller ones.

Guide: Scaling Estimation, p. 269

A few times during the day, the groups stop their clarification and do some estimation, mostly to learn and to prompt conversation. They're using relative (story) points; to remain synchronized against a common baseline, they calibrate against some already completed and well-known items in the Product Backlog.

Updating the Product Backlog and Product Owner

Guide: Product Owner Helpers, p. 179

The day after the PBR workshops, Portia and a few team members

> update the Product Backlog with the new split items derived from the original ones, and delete the originals

Guide: Dealing with Parents, p. 204

> add links to the new wiki pages of item details, created in the PBR workshops

> record new estimates, and items ready for implementation

Later, Portia and those team members meet with Paolo to review the Product Backlog changes and to answer his questions.

The End

Some key points from the story:

> Take a Bite on a giant item to learn from delivery of something small and to avoid premature and excessive analysis.

> Do multi-team PBR for items, for shared knowledge across teams, which increases organizational agility, broadens whole-product knowledge, and fosters self-organized coordination.

> Strive for whole-product focus, even with many teams.

Next—The next section shifts to the *LeSS Huge* framework, used for large groups of many teams.

LeSS Huge Framework

• Requirement Areas •

With 1000 or even just 100 people on one product, divide-and-conquer seems unavoidable because of the complexity of so many requirements and people. Traditional large-scale development divides these ways:

> single-function groups (analysis group, test group, ...)

> architectural-component groups (UI-layer group, server-side group, data-access component group, ...)

This organizational design yields slow inflexible development with (1) high levels of waste (inventory, work-in-progress, handoff, information scatter, ...), (2) long-delayed ROI, (3) complex planning and coordination,

(4) more overhead management, and (5) weak feedback and learning. And it is organized *inward* around single-skills, architecture, and management, rather than outward around customer value.

The Magic Number Eight, p. 12

But in the **LeSS Huge** framework when above about eight teams, division is around *major areas of customer concerns* called **Requirement Areas**. This reflects the *customer-centric* LeSS principle.

Size—A Requirement Area is *big*, usually with between *four and eight teams*, not one or two. The following *Area Feature Teams* section on p. 35 explains why.

Dynamic—Requirement Areas are *dynamic*. Over time an area will change in importance, and then it grows or shrinks with teams joining or departing—most likely to or from another existing area.

Example—For example, in a *Securities* product (to trade stocks), these could be some major areas of customer interest—Requirement Areas:

> trade processing (from pricing to capture to settlement)

> asset servicing (e.g. handling a stock split, dividends)

> new market onboarding (e.g. Nigeria)

Conceptually in the *one* Product Backlog, a Requirement Area attribute is added, and each item is classified into one and only one area:

Item	Requirement Area
B	market onboarding
C	trade processing
D	asset servicing
F	market onboarding
...	...

Then people can focus on one **Area Product Backlog** (conceptually, a *view* onto one Product Backlog), such as the *market onboarding* area:

Item	Requirement Area
B	market onboarding
F	market onboarding

Common Sprint—Does each Requirement Area work separately in its own Sprint, with delayed integration until a far-future date? No.

In LeSS Huge, Integrate Continuously in One Common Sprint

There is one product-level Sprint, not a different Sprint for each Requirement Area. It ends in one integrated whole product, and all the teams across all the Requirement Areas are striving to integrate continuously across the entire product.

• Area Product Owners •

In LeSS Huge one new role is introduced. Each Requirement Area has an **Area Product Owner** who specializes in that area and focuses on its Area Product Backlog.

Large product groups usually have several supporting product managers specializing in different customer areas, and some of these are likely to serve as the Area Product Owners. Sometimes the Product Owner also serves double duty as an Area Product Owner for one area; that's more likely in small *less huge* LeSS Huge groups!

• Area Feature Teams •

Area feature teams work within one Requirement Area (e.g. asset servicing), with one Area Product Owner focusing on the items in one Area Product Backlog. From a team's perspective, *working in the area is like* *working in the smaller LeSS framework*—they interact with their Area Product Owner as though she were the Product Owner, and so on.

The team members come to know the customer domain of that area well. And fortunately, the items of one Requirement Area tend to cover a semi-predictable subset of the entire code base, thereby reducing the scope of what they have to learn well within a vast product.

Key point about size: *Many* feature teams work in a Requirement Area.

> **A Requirement Area normally has *four to eight* teams.**
> **An implication is that a Requirement Area is big.**

The Magic Number Four

First, why does a Requirement Area have a suggested upper limit of eight teams? See *The Magic Number Eight, p. 12.*

What about the lower limit of *four* teams? Why not one or two teams? Naturally, *four* isn't a magic number, but it strikes a balance so that the product group is not composed of many tiny Requirement Areas.

What's the problem with many tiny areas? They reduce visibility into overall product-level priorities, increase local optimizations, increase coordination complexity, require more positions, and create teams that are too narrowly specialized and lack the flexibility (agility) to take on the emerging highest-value items from a company perspective. Furthermore, in a tiny area the Area Product Owner is increasingly likely to act as a business analyst between the users and one or two teams.

Are there any reasonable *exceptions* to the lower limit of four? Yes:

> An early transitional situation when the group is incrementally growing a new area that is fully expected to ultimately have four or more teams. Then, start small and simple with one team.

> When re-balancing teams from an area with a decreasing demand to one with an increasing demand causes an area to go from four

to three teams. Ultimately, merge two reduced small areas back into a new larger area.

Example Requirement Areas and Teams

In summary, a *Securities* product could have

> one Product Owner and three Area Product Owners, all together forming the Product Owner Team

> six feature teams in the trade processing area

> four feature teams in the market onboarding area

> four feature teams in the asset servicing area

• LeSS Huge Framework Summary •

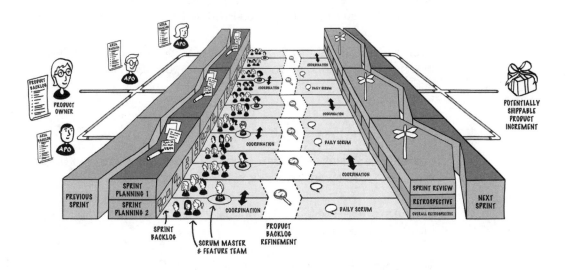

Each Requirement Area works as a (smaller framework) LeSS implementation, each working in parallel in one overall Sprint. We sometimes summarize a Sprint in LeSS Huge as *a stack of LeSS*.

> **From the viewpoint of a team in one area,**
> **LeSS Huge looks like (smaller) LeSS regarding events.**

As with LeSS, there are **rules** and optional **guides** for LeSS Huge; those are introduced in the following stories and fleshed out in later chapters.

Roles—Same as LeSS, plus two or more **Area Product Owners**, and four to eight Teams in each Requirement Area. The *one* **Product Owner** (who focuses on overall product optimization) and the several Area Product Owners form the **Product Owner Team**.

Artifacts—Same as LeSS, plus a *Requirement Area* attribute in the one Product Backlog and thus an **Area Product Backlog** view for each area.

Events—There is still only one common Sprint for the product; it includes all the teams and ends in a common potentially shippable product increment.

• LeSS Huge Stories •

Learning LeSS Huge—Readers who prefer exposition can comfortably skip ahead to following chapters, bypassing these stories.

Simple stories—These are intentionally plain and simple stories just to introduce basics in LeSS Huge.

Two topics—Following are two stories with distinct topics:

1. Creating and growing a new Requirement Area to deal with a new gigantic requirement.
2. Working with multi-site teams. (This happens in the smaller LeSS framework too, but is especially common in LeSS Huge.)

• LeSS Huge Story: A New Requirement Area •

Priti welcomes Portia to her first day in her new job.[1] As a mid-level Operations manager in the Securities division of the large trading company as well as Product Owner for their internal *Securities* system, Priti is also responsible for finding and retaining talent for her Product Owner Team of Area Product Owners. And she thinks Portia is a fantastic find, as her expertise is exactly what is required for dealing with some new huge requirements.

Guide: LeSS Huge Product Owner, p. 193

During the recent job interview—when Portia was still a product manager specializing in regulatory issues at a company that made a system for trading bonds—Priti had laid out the situation. "Portia, after the last crash, the regulators are coming down hard and they require us to be compliant with Dodd-Frank. Right now, we don't know what it exactly means or how it will impact our system. You've got incredible knowledge of this space, and a great professional network with the regulators. I would love it if you would join our group and help us figure out how to deal with this."

A Big Surprise

A few days later… Priti welcomes Portia, Peter, and Susan into her office. Peter is Area Product Owner for market onboarding, and Susan is a Scrum Master from the trade processing area.

Priti says, "As you know, Dodd-Frank is coming, and it's huge. What you don't know is that this morning the regulators called us and they want us to take action *now*. I'd been working under the assumption we could start next year. So we're going to have to adapt, big time.

"I don't think anyone is clear what it means in detail—even the regulators. And we don't know how it will impact our system and how much work this is going to take, other than, a lot! But now Portia's joined us and she has a better understanding of this than anyone, although she's totally new to our systems. So, how can we help her start tackling this mountain of work?"

---

1. Reminder: Naming uses an alliteration for role recall. Priti is a Product Owner, Portia an Area Product Owner, Susan a Scrum Master, Mario a team member.

Susan asks, "You guys understand the Dyslexic Zombies, right?"

Peter and Priti nod. Everyone knows about them—and it isn't just their name. The Dyslexic Zombies[1] have probably the broadest experience of all the teams. They've been around for years and they were a true pain in the ass when they adopted LeSS. The team contained two former members of their now-abandoned architecture group and a couple of people who had been working on the system for over fifteen years. Those people's resistance to the LeSS adoption was legendary as they were afraid they'd lose their "system perspective." To their surprise, the opposite happened! Because of their deep knowledge they continuously get tough items to develop. And they regularly participate as expert-teachers in current-architecture-learning workshops with newcomers, and Mario—one of the former PowerPoint architects—is now coordinator for the architecture community. When fed enough beer, he'll admit that working closer with code and tests has increased his *real* understanding of the system.

Susan continues, "If any team can quickly help Portia get a better understanding of the size and impact of Dodd-Frank, it'll be the Zombies. And they led the work on Sarbanes-Oxley a few years ago. Tomorrow is their PBR session. They are just about wrapped up on a new feature. Why don't we re-direct the meeting to include them in a discussion on Dodd-Frank, and soon after, ask them to focus full-time on it?"

Refining with Zombies

Next day at the refinement meeting with the Zombies, Portia explains the situation, "You've probably all heard about the Dodd-Frank legislation. But here's the surprise: We've just been told by the regulators that they want us to take action 'now' and demonstrate significant compliance by the end of the year. Otherwise they might restrict our trading."

---

1. Yes, that was really their name, in Lisbon!

The Zombies are visibly surprised. They had heard rumors but didn't expect such a rush!

Mario says, "OK Portia, give us a quick summary of what this means. And how is it different from Sarbanes-Oxley?"

Portia picks up a pen and starts sketching on a whiteboard. After about 45 minutes, she is finished with the overview and the Zombies looked a little stunned.

"End of the year, they said?" says Mario. "If the *whole group* started today, it wouldn't get finished. This is huge!"

He takes a pen and at the whiteboard starts a rough sketch of their system, talking with the other Zombies about the impact it might have.

He says, "Portia, let's also use this as a chance to help you understand the system better. Ask away."

Portia says, "Can you hold on for a second? Let me start a video recording to help me remember this."

Michelle, a veteran in the team, says, "We'd better start on some real development soon and learn more as we go because otherwise we'll end up analyzing forever. I've seen this story before."

Susan, their Scrum Master, says, "Reminds me... Tom DeMarco once said that the reason for every failed project is that it started too late." Everyone laughs. She continues, "So here's a suggestion: *take a bite.*"

Guide: Take a Bite, p. 202

Creating a New Requirement Area

The next day, Portia, Priti, and rest of the Product Owner Team meet. Portia shares a summary of the scope as she understands it now.

Priti says, "This is even bigger than I expected, and we need to show some tangible progress to the regulators within a few months, and major progress before fiscal year end—seven months from now. To state the obvious, they're now authorized to require more from us, and with the power to shut us down. As you know, just last month the CEO made it crystal clear that new regulatory requests take priority over any other concern. It's my experience that our goodwill and flexibility with the regulators goes up if we can give them something early, and be transparent and responsive. So that's what we're going to do."

Guide: New Area for Giant Requirement, p. 223

Priti continues, "It seems to me that we'll need a new area for this big surprise. And of course that's probably going to impact some of our existing high-priority goals, since we'll have to shift some teams. Let's prepare for a deeper discussion of overall prioritization impact in a couple of days. But for now, I'd like your input about spinning up a new area."

After a short discussion, it's clear that everyone recognizes the importance of creating a new area.

Priti then says, "Portia, I know you are new to us, but do you think you would be able to handle the Area Product Owner responsibility for this?"

Portia nods.

Guide: Leading Team, p. 308

Priti continues, "Peter, do you think the Zombies could start work on this? And we'll need them to learn more Dodd-Frank and figure out the impact on our system before we can add more teams to this."

Peter says, "I don't think we've got any choice."

Priti says, "OK Portia, so currently we've got a few items in Peter's Area Backlog, the one huge item I think you called "remainder of Dodd-Frank" and the tiny item which the Zombies and you split off of it. Please ask Peter to show you how to set up a new area in the Product Backlog and move the items over to it."

Priti continues addressing the group, "The next Sprint starts in three days. Let's move the Zombies into your area and get started on this monster. Probably in a couple of Sprints we'll be ready to—and need to—grow your area by moving in another team. Folks, please think about two major concerns: First, preparing for a serious prioritization impact meeting in a few days. And second, what other teams will be good candidates for the new area."

Sprint Planning in the New Requirement Area

Each Requirement Area holds its own Sprint Planning meetings, all more or less in parallel. In Portia's new area, she starts her Sprint Planning by introducing two unfamiliar faces to the Zombies.

She says, "Gillian and Zak have been in contact with the regulators regularly and will help us flesh this thing out. They've agreed to help us now in Planning, during our PBR sessions, and as much as they can spare daily during upcoming Sprints."

She continues, "Here's my tentative plan of attack for the next two Sprints. First, together we need to learn more about Dodd-Frank, and also split it into some major and manageable pieces so we can start to clear the fog and get a better sense of priorities.

"Second, we implement the smaller bite we've taken, starting this Sprint. That'll give us better information about the real work and the impact on our product. And we'll have some concrete visible progress.

"Third, we prepare for more teams to join our area. What do you think of this approach? Other suggestions?"

During the short discussion, Mario says to his team, "Let me give a bit more context, because I represented our team in the recent Product Owner Team meeting with all the Area Product Owners and Priti. To start with, it's just us to start. We're going to take the lead on early

Guide: Leading Team, p. 308

implementation, and getting the big picture of the item, and understanding the overall impact on our architecture."

Michelle interrupts, "Like a tiger team working on a new product?"

"Yes, like that," says Mario. "Think of Dodd-Frank support as a new product that needs to be continuously integrated into the rest of the product. But we're in a hurry and it's a ton of work, so in a few Sprints one more team will join us and shortly after, probably two more teams. We keep developing too, but we'll be the *leading team*, which means we'll need to bring the other teams up to speed and make sure we keep the overall product in mind."

Michelle says, "It's starting to sound to me like we're going to become the architecture and project management team!"

Mario laughs, "No. I'm done with that. We're still a normal feature team, but besides development we'll focus on mentoring and bringing the new teams up to speed as fast as possible. But let's be clear: team coordination and management is still the responsibility of each team."

The First Sprint in the New Requirement Area

Guide: Take a Bite, p. 202

Guide: Handling Gigantic Requirements, p. 224

Their first Sprint is an unusual balance of clarification versus development, but nevertheless quite useful in this extreme situation. They spend almost half the Sprint in clarification with Portia, Gillian, and Zak. That's because even for this extremely small bite, trying to understand what is wanted in the obscure realm of new government regulations—with no direct access to the politicians and policy writers—required a lot of investigation, reading, discussion, and communicating with outsiders. They expect that in future Sprints, the amount of time needed for clarification will soon drop down to a more common 10% or 15% of their Sprint.

And so they also only spend about half the Sprint developing *one* small item. But the discussion and the learning from coding pays off. Slowly but surely they start to split Dodd-Frank apart—at least the parts that any of them can understand.

While implementing the small item they had bitten off first, they spend much of the time together at whiteboards to discuss the overall design implications on the system. The team moves frequently back and forth between the code and the wall.

Sprint Review in the New Requirement Area

The overall Securities product group works together in one Sprint, with one final shippable product increment. But each Requirement Area holds its own Sprint Review, all more or less in parallel.

In Portia's area, during their Review, she, Gillian, and Zak explore the one "done" item that the Zombies have managed to complete and integrate into the overall product. They had originally forecast two items, but Portia is impressed that they got even one done, given how fast this new work was thrown at them.

The Second Sprint

In the second Sprint they're able to make slightly better progress on items, though they once again spend a lot of time clarifying together with Portia, Gillian, and Zak.

In the middle of the Sprint they hold a multi-team PBR session with the second team that is planned to soon join the area, teaching them about Dodd-Frank. They hold a current-architecture learning workshop to introduce the team to the major design elements already in place.

Guide: Current-Architecture Workshop, p. 303

The Zombies know how big the work is and look forward to more help.

Product Owner Team Meeting

A few Sprints later... It's time once more for the per-Sprint Product Owner Team meeting. They use it to align and coordinate between the different Area Product Owners, and for Priti to give guidance.

Guide: Product Owner Team Meeting, p. 283

The Area Product Owners each share in turn their situation and upcoming goals. When it's her turn, Portia says, "To none of our surprise, the progress is little and the surprises are big. But the fog is clearing and the teams and I are getting our heads around the work. Gillian and Zak have been tremendous help."

Pablo, the Area Product Owner of asset servicing, comments on some close item relationships he now sees between their areas. Portia agrees to meet with Pablo and some team representatives later.

Priti asks, "Portia, about our upcoming Sprint. What are your goals?"

Adding a Third Team

Two Sprints later… At the Product Owner Team coordination meeting, Priti says, "As you know, Portia's area still has only two teams. I know that Pablo would like to keep his six teams in asset servicing, but Dodd-Frank is just too important to me this year. So we're going to move one team from Pablo's area into Portia's. Pablo, please ask for a volunteer team from your group and let me and Portia know."

The End

Some key points from the story in LeSS Huge:

> The Product Owner is responsible for finding Area Product Owners and developing their talents.

> The Product Owner is responsible for deciding to start, grow, or wind down Requirement Areas.

> Requirement Areas are large, normally requiring four to eight teams, but during initial startup they may be smaller, especially if initiated with one team using a Take a Bite approach.

> A Leading Team works solo to tackle a gigantic item until they understand the domain and development, and then they coach more incoming teams to help with the vast work.

• Multi-Site Teams: Terms & Tips •

Next is a LeSS Huge story involving multi-site teams. But first, some clarifying definitions, because the common term *distributed teams* confusingly means several things. The clarifying terms are as follows:

> **dispersed team**—One team of (e.g. seven) people spread out in different locations; either different rooms, buildings, or cities

> **co-located team**—One team working literally at the same table

> **multi-site teams**—One co-located team working at one site, and another co-located team working at another site

Second, an observation and guidance:

> A dispersed team is rarely a *real team*; it is much more likely a loosely connected groups of individuals. The communication and coordination frictions are higher, and they seldom *jell as a team*.

> When your product group is 50 or 500 people, *dispersed teams aren't necessary.* Each team of seven-ish people can easily be co-located. However, some teams may be in different sites, so that the product group has *multi-site teams.* Dispersed teams are usually the result of bad organizational decisions and ignorance about the cost of not having co-located teams.

Rule: Each team is
(1) self-managing,
(2) cross-functional,
(3) co-located, and
(4) long-lived.

• LeSS Huge Story: Multi-Site Teams •

Portia is the Area Product Owner for a new Requirement Area in a Securities trading system. The new area started with just one team for focus and simplicity. A few Sprints later Portia's area adds a third team. Her first two teams are based in London with her. But her third new team, *HouseDraculesti*, is based in Cluj Romania at a major development site for the company.

Why not add a third team from the London site? That would have avoided the many aggravations and efficiency penalties that can come from multi-site development within one area—costs potentially so high that *adding a team* can effectively result in *deleting a team*.

But on the positive side in this case, Cluj is only two time zones from London, and everyone there speaks English well. And they are all strong developers with Computer Science degrees, in a city that values long-term and hands-on engineering mastery. Also, this is a dedicated internal development site for the company, so these are experienced internal teams that have in-depth knowledge of the product and domain.

And bottom line, Priti (the Product Owner) didn't want any of the other London teams to shift from their current areas.

Priti knows that multi-site teams are a new situation for Portia, and so at their next meeting, she says, "Please ask your Scrum Master to talk with Sita, and also ask Sita to coach some of your events. She's a Scrum Master in asset servicing, and she's observed their multi-site situation for a few years. She knows the importance of Scrum Masters co-located with their teams, and she's helped facilitate many multi-site meetings."

Priti continued, "Also, we've had a super profitable year, so I'm providing funding for you and the Zombies team—at least those that can travel— to spend a Sprint in Cluj as soon as possible. Work closely with them, all in one room. The Cluj team could come here to London, but you want to send a strong signal that *they* are important, at their site. Try to avoid making them feel that London is more important than Cluj. Oh—and you'll want to regularly visit every few months."

Multi-Site Sprint Planning Part One

Guide: Sprint Planning One, p. 276
A few Sprints later, Portia walks into the room. There's a computer projector attached to a laptop, displaying via video a room in Cluj. The whole team in Cluj are sitting and waiting. Sita suggested it would improve learning and engagement if the entire Cluj team participated in multi-site meetings for the first few months of their addition to the area.

All the team representatives have tablets or laptops with them.

Portia begins. "Welcome and let's get started. My offer of items this Sprint are highlighted in the shared spreadsheet. Can you all see it? I think you all understand why these are the themes and priorities, since we've been discussing this in PBR and it reflects your input and mine. But please ask again if you'd like clarification. Other than that, you're invited to enter your team names beside the items you want."

That done, the group enters a Q&A phase to wrap up lingering questions about the items. The London representatives tape up some flip-chart papers and start writing questions. The Cluj team members enter their questions in separate sheets of a shared spreadsheet. Portia spends some time at the different paper flip charts, discussing answers and sketching on the paper. And she spends some time at the spreadsheet, typing in answers for the Cluj team, while also talking with them face-to-face via the video session.

After about 30 minutes the separate questions have been resolved, and Portia asks everyone to come back together. She says, "Any issues or questions that you want to discuss together, before we wrap up?"

Multi-Site Overall PBR

People enter the workshop room in London. Two projectors are set up. One shows a video session of the workshop room in Cluj. The other displays a browser on Portia's computer.

Guide: Product Backlog Refinement Types, p. 249

Guide: Multi-Site PBR, p. 254

Portia says, "Let's get started. I want to focus on splitting some items. I've invited Zak to join us because he knows quite a lot about this."

Using a mind-mapping, browser-based graphics tool, Zak starts to create some branches, while discussing with the group.

Afterwards, they use a shared spreadsheet to discuss and write a single example for each of the new split items, so that the people at both sites gain a lightweight but concrete understanding of the details. Later, the group does estimation of the new items, using especially big planning poker cards that can be easily seen by the cameras and video when held up.

The End

Some key points from the multi-site story in LeSS Huge:

> Multi-site teams frequently create both obvious and subtle fric-tions and costs that are surprisingly large in their negative impact.

> Qualities that reduce the friction of another site include similar time zone, internal dedicated site (not outsourced), developers that are fluent in the same spoken language, a location and culture that highly values long-term hands-on developer excellence.

> A Scrum Master must be co-located with their teams.

> Each site must feel like a peer, not a second-class citizen.

> Sites must be visited regularly and cross-pollinated.

> In meetings, strive for face-to-face with video tools.

> The use of shared-document tools make it easy for everyone to modify artifacts together and at the same time.

ONWARDS

Rather than asking, "How can we *do agile* at scale in our complex and awkward organization?", ask a different and deeper question, *"How can we simplify the organization, and **be agile** rather than do agile?"* And since truly scaling Scrum starts with changing the organization rather than changing Scrum, the next major section focuses on understanding and adopting a simpler customer-focused LeSS *organization*.

This is followed by major sections on a more customer-focused *product* and *Sprint* in a simpler LeSS organization.

LeSS Structure

Contents

managers thinking about improvements to help

3

ADOPTION

If you do not change direction, you may end up where you are heading.
—Lao Tze

ONE-TEAM SCRUM

Scrum is simple. Adopting Scrum isn't. Why not?

Scrum isn't a process. It doesn't magically solve your problems and create "hyperproductive" teams. It's a framework that creates short feedback loops that dramatically increase transparency. This acts as a mirror showing the team how good they are at making a product. It also exposes problems in the team and organization. This visibility underpins empirical process control, which, along with inspect-adapt cycles, puts the team, Product Owner, and organization in a continuous improvement loop.

That's the good news. The bad news is that this sucks. In reality, transparency is discomforting or even *threatening*, which makes adoption hard.

One-team Scrum doesn't say much about Scrum adoption other than to start "by the book." This isn't because the Scrum zealots want to force their favorite rules on the world but is a recognition that improvement starts with following and understanding the standard. Or in lean thinking, "Where there is no standard, there can be no kaizen." Experiencing Scrum by the book creates understanding of how Scrum principles and practices relate—a systems-thinking perspective. That's critical for succeeding with Scrum.

An experienced Scrum Master and a team with a deep understanding of Scrum will dramatically improve the likelihood you will achieve a successful adoption.

LeSS Adoption

LeSS adoption involves big organizations and many minds with deeply rooted assumptions about how organizations *should* work. Successful adoption requires *challenging* these *assumptions* and *simplifying the organizational structure*, with all the explosive politics and "loss of face" that working across a big group entails. Adoption needs everyone to improve towards a shared goal.

When scaling, principles related to adoption include:

Continuous improvement towards perfection—Naturally, a group adopting LeSS brings to the table their assumptions and habits about adoption. Which are those? Create a change vision and kick off many change projects. When the original goal is *apparently* achieved then,

1. "the change is done", and
2. the organization settles into a new status quo, until
3. the next change effort surfaces, and then
4. undoes the previous change.

This classic approach is like the sequential and "big batch" approach of software development, where *change is an exception* strictly managed... by *many* change-control boards.

In LeSS adoptions, there is no change initiative, no change group, no change managers. In LeSS, change is continuous through experimentation and improvement and *change is the status quo*.

• LeSS Rules •

For the product group, establish the complete LeSS structure "at the start"; this is vital for a LeSS adoption.

For the larger organization beyond the product group, adopt LeSS evolutionary using Go and See to create an organization where experimentation and improvement is the norm.

Guide: Three Adoption Principles

These principles are crucial to an organizational LeSS adoption:

> deep and narrow over broad and shallow

> top-down *and* bottom-up

> use volunteering

Deep and Narrow over Broad and Shallow

Prefer adopting LeSS in one product group[1] really well over applying LeSS in many groups poorly.

Poor LeSS adoptions harm. Lack of deep understanding destroys transparency and the feedback cycles that are keys to empirical process control and continuous improvement. We've even seen "LeSS" abused as a marvelous micro-management tool. Then, it's *really* hard to change again after a micro-management LeSS adoption is the established norm. It's tough to re-learn what you already know.

Therefore, focus LeSS adoption effort on one product group, give them all the support they need, and ensure that they work really well. This minimizes risk and if you face big problems, it triggers a *focused* learning opportunity. And when you succeed it creates a positive "word on the floor" that's vital nourishment for further adoption.

---

1. In case of LeSS Huge, one Requirement Area.

Top-down *and* Bottom-up

We are often asked whether adoption is best top-down or bottom-up. That's a false dichotomy. Either one is likely to fail. Do both.

for more on management in LeSS, see the *Management* chapter

Purely top-down—The manager-driven, "thou shalt do LeSS"-adoption causes resistance and sets up the organization for failure. Ordering teams to manage themselves is a contradiction. LeSS adoption requires deep understanding that doesn't come from directive but from discussion. Only by understanding, choice, and a sense of personal safety will people take the additional responsibility to reflect and improve. Lack of these is exacerbated by an us–them relationship between managers and workers. In that setting, forcing LeSS into the organization encourages victimized behavior and further degrades relations. People will claim, "We have no choice, our manager says we must do LeSS!" And secretly and perhaps unconsciously, they rest in that victimization as a comfortable—or at least familiar—position.

Purely bottom-up—These LeSS adoptions aren't sustainable. In the beginning, they create a delightful burst of energy from people who want to do the Right Thing. This leads to an open mind, accelerated learning, and deeper understanding. Really wonderful! Then these energized people energetically hit the organizational walls. Bam! Without top-level support to change structures and policies, the enthusiasts lose energy and become frustrated by obstacles and rigidity. Many eventually quit or become embittered by hopes squashed. It makes us feel sad too.

Top-down and Bottom-up—A successful LeSS adoption needs both the energy of people doing the Right Thing and the support of people with organizational power. The managers' frame of mind must be support, not control. They ensure the proper supporting structure is in place for the grass-roots energy to flourish and expand.

We commonly hear the wish for managers' support. Be careful what you wish for!

> No management support often leads to victimized behavior. "We can't do anything without my manager's support."

> Having management support can lead to an even worse situation. "We must do this LeSS because our manager says so." This mindless obedience undermines any LeSS adoption.

What kind of management support do you need?

Management support from those who have the organizational authority to make structural changes in your group—usually the head of your product group. This support must be... supportive.

Authentic support starts with self-education. All managers in the product group need to take time to educate themselves about LeSS. This includes *several days* in an introductory training and *several books* to read. In addition to education, managers also need to provide clear communication and action about (1) the intention to adopt LeSS, (2) the promise to make the necessary structural changes, and (3) providing education and coaching.

What kind of management support do you *not* need?

The support of high-level managers who oversee multiple products beyond your single product group often backfires. How come? Ignorance of real problems—they aren't involved enough with the actual development. Their support often includes making "optimization" and "harmonization" decisions that seem to make sense from their high-level position but rarely lead to real benefits at *gemba*—the place of real value work. And then what happens? Dealing with these well-intended harmful decisions saps energy from dealing with the real problems.

Neither do you need management support from managers who do not yet have a deep understanding of LeSS and its impact. We are frequently requested to summarize a 3-day in-depth training in a 1-hour presentation because those managers "are too busy" for a 3-day course. So far, we've not been able to squeeze 3-day's worth of understanding into a 1-hour presentation. Our bad.

Use Volunteering

How to form new teams? Who will be in a community? How are you going to answer these questions, and many more?

Use volunteers! True volunteering is a powerful way of engaging people's minds and hearts. It's underused, likely because managers feel they'll lose control. But for the volunteering teams it feels *empowering*.

Volunteering starts with education. Suppose you simply ask for volunteers for a *promiscuous pairing* experiment. You probably won't get many takers, and those that do respond are, at best, confused. But if you first explain that promiscuous pairing is a pair-programming technique that uses frequent pair swapping to *increase learning*, you'll see more and better volunteers and a better outcome. So first, provide enough education and discussion so people understand what they are volunteering for.

Here are some examples of volunteering:

Initial-product volunteering—Which will be the first product group to adopt LeSS, with all the implied organizational design changes? Ask for a volunteer group by canvassing senior R&D and product managers.

Initial-teams volunteering—Suppose the initial product group to adopt LeSS is already well-established and has about 50 people. There may be people outside the group that are really interested in joining. And people inside that want to leave! So before "flipping the entire group," use volunteering once again: Invite the entire company to join (explaining both what and *why*). And invite people inside the group to leave. Thus, the initial people will be open for learning and will take responsibility. They are likely to make the initial teams succeed because they aren't just a *head* being counted anymore, their *heart* is in it.

Teams-formation volunteering—How to form teams in LeSS? Support "self-designing teams." This is done in a facilitated workshop where all the future team members join. The facilitator kicks off the workshop by describing the goal of the product and the workshop. Together they then define the template for a typical team, adhering to any constraints agreed previously. (The facilitator already knows a good template, but it is best if the group owns the idea.) Example template:

> Each team is co-located.

> Each team is cross-functional so they can achieve "done."

> Each team has deep knowledge of several components.

> Each team has around seven people.

The details of "cross-functional" and "cross-component" are discussed and listed during the definition of the template. Next, the space is open for a short (e.g. 15 minutes) timeboxed period for people to form new teams by volunteering, using the template as a guide. Then they review the nascent teams against the template. If it is not good enough, the group continues with more rounds; it usually takes two to four.[2]

Guide: Getting Started

The three adoption principles imply starting adoption in one product group. How can you increase the likelihood of its success?

0. educate everyone
1. define "product"
2. define "done"
3. have appropriately structured teams
4. only the Product Owner provides work for the teams
5. keep project managers away from the teams

0. Educate Everyone

The best LeSS adoptions we have seen had everyone participating in several days of Scrum and LeSS training. This was followed up with team, organizational, and technical coaching.

---

2. See on the web: *How to Form Teams in Large-Scale Scrum? A Story of Self-Designing Teams.* (also at http://bit.ly/1WSJhKo).

This step isn't for us to sell more Certified LeSS Practitioner courses, although we wouldn't mind. Any excellent education will do; the main purpose is that without education you won't get a lot of volunteers when using the adoption principle of *use volunteering*.

Teach *why*—Besides educating on the what's and how's of adopting LeSS, it's even more important to help everyone understand *why*. There is too much blind adherence to processes without understanding why.

A great trainer and a great coach will have this focus on why and will make a world of difference in your LeSS adoption. How to choose them? Use these guidelines:

> **Prefer hands-on experience.**
Ensure that your trainer/coach has hands-on experience in LeSS from both inside (as a team member) and outside (as coach). Avoid training providers who don't care about who teaches, and avoid trainers with only theoretical knowledge. They aren't useful.

> **Evaluate a person, not a company.**
You are looking for a unique person. Great coaching is personal. Find your coach and form a long-term relationship. Avoid giant consulting companies and training companies.

> **Require technical depth and understanding.**
LeSS requires *technical excellence*. Technology, team, and organizational decisions are strongly related and your coach needs to have this broad and deep perspective. Avoid people with no or limited technical expertise. These are often ex-PMI-project managers.

> **Expect long-term engagement.**
LeSS adoptions require patience and take time. Find a coach that is committed to see your adoption through—for *years*. Avoid "drive-by" coaches that come, comment, criticize, and go.

> **Look for quality over cost.**
Hiring a cheap but bad trainer/coach (ignoring the previous fac-

tors) is truly penny-wise and pound-foolish. Flawed and failed LeSS adoptions are certainly possible; a bad coach doesn't help.

> **Don't delegate the selection.**
The decision is too important to leave to people who aren't going to be directly involved themselves. Avoid delegating the selection to a separate department, such as a PMO, Purchasing, or HR group—they aren't involved enough to see the important factors.

> **De-emphasize certification.**
Most certification of people and courses is almost meaningless. It *probably* doesn't hurt, but *certification* is not a reliable guide. The above points are infinitely more important.[3]

> **Evaluate multiple people.**
The best groups evaluated multiple people before making a decision and investment in a long-term relationship.

1. Define "Product"

Your product definition determines the scope of your adoption, the content of the Product Backlog, and who makes a suitable Product Owner. Broader product definitions are advantageous, but your definition has to be practical enough to start.

Creating a product definition involves

> expanding your product definition via *expanding questions* such as, "what does our customer think our product is?"

> restraining your product definition via *restraining questions* such as, "what is practical in our current organizational setup?"

> exploring improvements for expanding the product definition

The *Product* chapter has more details on why broader is better and how to create the product definition.   see *Product* chapter

---

3. This includes the Certified LeSS Practitioner course. We *do* recommend the course, but *not* for the certification but for the course.

2. Define "Done:

A better and stronger Definition of Done (DoD or "done") requires a broader skill set within the teams. For example, if performance testing is included in the DoD, then the teams need to acquire that skill. It can be acquired by learning, but often it is acquired by moving a person with performance-testing skill from his specialized performance testing group into the team. On the other hand, if performance testing is *excluded* from the DoD, then the separate performance-testing group will stay and operate the same way as before, *until* the DoD is expanded. Therefore...

> **A better and stronger Definition of Done results in more organizational change (eliminating groups, roles, positions, ...) than a poorer and weaker one.**

And a weaker DoD causes additional risk and delay! We explore all these topics further in the *Definition of Done* chapter.

see Definition of Done chapter

The effect on the amount of organizational change makes the DoD a critical management tool for LeSS adoption. Managers need to make a trade-off between a strong DoD, leading to more organizational change and less delay and risk, and a weak DoD, leading to less organizational change and increased risk and delay. The key question is, *"How much change can my organization handle at this time?"*

3. Have Appropriately Structured Teams

Each Team has a shared responsibility for achieving their common goal. To support their success, ensure that each Team is appropriately structured. Requirements for the initial teams:

> **dedicated**—each person is a member of one and only one team

> **stable**—the members of the team aren't changed frequently

> **long-lived**—the team isn't a temporary project team but stays together for *years*

> **cross-functional**—the team has the needed functional skills to achieve *done* functionality

> **co-located**—the team is in one location, often literally at the same big table, so that trust grows through face-to-face communication and learning grows through teaching one another

The *Organizing Around Customer Value* chapter has more details on each of these team attributes.

see *Organizing Around Customer Value* chapter

This new structure implies that people leave their functional departments to permanently join new cross-functional teams. The functional departments should be eliminated.

Why not have people maintain a reporting relationship to a functional department manager? Because that causes *conflicting loyalties* that destroy the team's shared responsibility and cohesion. Right now you might be thinking "They're exaggerating. It can work in our company." Not gonna happen. We've seen many try and it doesn't work. Just don't do it. Instead, all team members have the same manager who is explicitly tasked to build the environment for the team to succeed.

4. Only the Product Owner Provides Work

You know this feeling?... A loooong day at work, busy, busy, busy, what the heck got *done*? It's the Context-Switching Vampire, sucking the life out of you. Unproductive, unfocused, and extremely demotivating.

The initial teams have a tough job: focusing on their shared goals for the product *but also* resolving a mountain of obstacles in their development environment. Obstacles (poor test-automation, tools, policies, etc.) are revealed by working in a cross-functional team in a short cycle to get "done".

These trail-blazers are laying the foundation that future teams will build on, so their need to *focus* is doubly important. How do they lose it? *Well-intended, perfectly reasonable* **interruptions** and requests for extra work from their line manager, Sales, the CEO, HR, etc. Don't let that happen!

Prevent this by ensuring that the Product Owner is the only person who provides work for the teams. Not only does this support focus, it

see *Product Owner* chapter

reduces stress caused from trying to manage competing voices all saying "Me first! Me first!" Prioritization is the Product Owner's problem, not the team's.

5. Keep Project Managers Away from the Teams

The role of project manager within the product group ceases to exist in experienced LeSS organizations. The role is not needed anymore as the project management responsibilities are shared between Product Owner and Teams.

Most LeSS adoptions can *immediately* eliminate the project manager role. In some rare adoptions the role is *temporarily* still needed. That's usually when there's a weak, imperfect Definition of Done (hence, Undone work) or cross-product-boundary coordination. In those cases, organizations do not necessarily immediately forgo their project managers.

So sometimes project managers will still be around for a while. What's the problem? It's likely they would regularly interrupt people and introduce conflicting priorities. But it is *not allowed* for project managers to interrupt teams, coordinate between teams, or give them work.

see *Management* chapter

In essence, this recommendation is the same as "only Product Owner provides work" and is also valid for other management roles. We've discovered that it is important to make it explicit.

Larman's Laws p. 64

And... renaming all your project managers to Scrum Masters won't do.

Next steps?

see *Product Backlog Refinement* chapter

This Getting Started guide gets you started by putting the right structure in place. The next step is to get your Product Backlog in shape. Perhaps you'll use an initial Product Backlog Refinement event; see the Product Backlog Refinement chapter for a guide on that.

Guide: Culture Follows Structure

Culture follows structure is actually the fourth of "Larman's Laws of Organizational Behavior." People in organizations are skilled at *showing* support to the flavor-of-the-month-improvement without *doing* anything. We have observed this repeatedly. Why does that happen?

Craig has a long development career, which started with programming in APL in 1979 and evolved to helping large product groups adopt modern management practices. Over beer, he might mention retirement. He was recently disturbed when he discovered no laws were named after him. He decided to create "Larman's Laws of Organizational Behavior" as a reminder for this dysfunctional self-serving behavior that plagues many organizations.

Larman's Laws of Organizational Behavior:

1. Organizations are implicitly optimized to avoid changing the status quo middle- and first-level manager and single-specialist positions & power structures.

2. As a corollary to (1), any change initiative will be reduced to redefining or overloading the new terminology to mean basically the same as status quo.

3. As a corollary to (1), any change initiative will be derided as "purist," "theoretical," "revolutionary," and "needing pragmatic customization for local concerns"—which deflects from addressing weaknesses and manager/specialist status quo.

4. Culture follows structure.

Anticipating your thought, it's also true that *structure follows culture* (especially in startups). But the phrase is meant to be poetically pithy, not literal.

What do we mean? As long as the *structural* elements—groups, roles, hierarchy, and policies, or more broadly the *organizational system/ design*—aren't changed, the behavior and mindset aren't going to change. The systems-thinking thought-leader John Seddon explains "culture follows structure" this way:

> *Attempting to change an organization's culture is a folly, it always fails. People's behavior (the culture) is a product of the system; when you change the system peoples' behavior changes.*

We have observed many organizations that attempt to adopt LeSS but refuse to change the organizational structure, roles, and policies accordingly. All of them have failed in achieving the full benefits of using LeSS.

Part of the problem is *personal safety*. Of course people don't want to lose a job because of a structural change. That's one reason why LeSS adoption emphasizes the lean-thinking principle of job safety but not role safety.

Guide: Job Safety but not Role Safety

It is difficult to get a man to understand something when his job depends on not understanding it. —Upton Sinclair

Who is going to strive for continuous improvement when the likely outcome is losing a job? Nobody. In a LeSS adoption, it is vitally important to establish the policy that nobody is going to lose employment. At least not due to position or role eliminations from the structural changes caused by the LeSS adoption. Communicate this clearly and repeatedly.

see *Management* chapter for more on management changes

Workers from dissolved functional groups join LeSS teams. Ex-managers of functional groups may do likewise, as they are usually skilled at the hands-on value-creating work. The organization must actively help everyone find *their* new role within the new structure.

Guide: Organizational Perfection Vision

Organizations are wonderfully complex systems in which it's impossible to control everything or to *know* everything.

Everyone makes small decisions and the organizational behavior emerges from these. People make decisions based on their experiences, goals, principles, and values. When decisions are misaligned, then well-intended people scurry in different directions, causing an organizational deadlock or gridlock. When these decisions are aligned, energy gets unleashed and things start moving and improving.

This is especially true related to improvements. We've seen a vast amount of well-intended "improvements" that only caused additional bureaucracy and increased suffering. *When is an improvement an improvement?* Obviously, it has to be a global systems improvement rather than a local optimization. But how do you know? Two questions help separate *most* real systems improvements from local optimizations:

> Will the improvement bring us closer to our organizational perfection vision?

> Will the improvement be an improvement at the gemba—the real place of work?

The gemba is covered in the *Go See* guide in the *Management* chapter. This guide focuses on the organizational perfection vision. First, what is a perfection vision?

see *Management* chapter

The classic *lean* perfection vision is Toyota's just-in-time system—*every time a customer buys one car then exactly one car is produced just in time.* This perfection vision lead to the ideal of "one-piece flow" in which the production system is set up to handle small batches of work, ideally batches of size one. This ideal will probably never be achieved, but it has guided Toyota's continuous improvement of their production system for decades.

Here is the perfection vision for LeSS that we use:

> **Create organizations able to deliver or change direction at any time without additional cost.**

A perfection vision is different from a vision. The goal of a vision is to achieve it, whereas the goal of a perfection vision is to channel improvements. When you achieve a vision, you celebrate, but when you achieve a perfection vision, you are sad as it just became useless.

The successful product groups that we've worked with have an *organizational perfection vision*—an unattainable goal about how their product group is and works. How is it used? People discuss and evaluate decisions based on whether it brings them closer to the perfection vision.

Discussing is important work, but words float away. So people also want to write a vision to help get everyone on the same page, literally. For example, here is an early version of principles established by a client adopting LeSS Huge in a product group:

1. The perfection goal is to have a releasable product all the time. Release stabilization periods need to be reduced and eventually eliminated.
2. Co-located, self-managing, cross-functional, Scrum teams are the basic organizational building block. Responsibility and accountability are on team level.
3. The majority of the teams are organized as customer-centric feature teams.
4. Product management steers the development through the Product Owner role. Release commitments are not forced on teams.
5. The line organization is cross-functional. The functional-specialized line organizations are gradually integrated in the cross-functional line organization.
6. Special coordination roles (such as project managers) are avoided and teams are responsible for coordination.
7. The main responsibility of management is improvement—improve team's learning, efficiency, and quality. The content of the work always comes from the Product Owner.
8. There is no branching in development. And product variation is not to be reflected in the version control system.
9. All tests are automated with the exception of (1) exploratory test, (2) usability test, and (3) tests that require physical movement. All people must learn test automation skills.
10. Adoption is gradual and evolutionary. These principles are considered in every decision.

Of course this is just an example, but feel free to use it as a starting point for your discussion about your perfection vision.

Managers—together with the whole product group—have to establish this organizational perfection vision that guide decision making. This is usually done by informal discussions and workshops, leading to some guiding perfection vision and principles. There are two common ways of imagining this perfection vision: (1) imagine you arrive at work, how would a perfect organization be and work, or (2) envision the perfect product and then imagine the organization creating it.

Guide: Continuous Improvement

A LeSS adoption ends only when you've achieved perfection and world domination. Without that, there are always things to improve.

The job of managers is to build an environment in which teams continuously deliver and continuously improve. Preferably the teams themselves do most improvements, but managers and Scrum Masters are often involved for *organizational* and *environmental* improvements.

see Management chapter

Tips:

> **Focus!**
  Not doing any improvements because everyone is too busy thinking up new improvement ideas is the greatest failure to continuous improvement. "Let's do yet another assessment of our current state." "Hey, they are the same, I wonder why?" Or the popular alternative, "Let's adopt NooDLeS because LeSS isn't working here" (without ever truly trying out LeSS).
  The way out of this? Stop assessing, start doing! Always keep in mind the top two improvements and focus your energy on them. When the improvements aren't done, the teams will quickly lose interest and stop thinking about new improvements.

> **Use retrospectives to create improvements.**
  The prime place for discovering new improvements is the team Retrospectives and the Overall Retrospective.

see Review & Retrospective chapter

> **Focus on true improvements.**
  Not all of the improvements are real improvements. Some are local optimizations—improvements that do not improve the whole system but only one perspective. Two common local optimizations are (1) functional local optimizations, and (2) unchallenged-

assumption-based local optimizations. **Functional local optimizations** are improvements from one functional-specialization perspective that are often harmful from the system-output perspective. For example, "It's an impediment to test each Sprint. We should start testing when the system is finished so that the testing can be done more efficiently." **Unchallenged-assumption-based local optimizations** are improvements based on assumptions about "how things work" that are probably false. The big systems improvements often require that assumptions be challenged; otherwise, the local improvements have little impact. Example of such assumptions, "We have to finish programming before we can test" and "It will be more efficient if everyone has only one skill."

Improvement suggestions that might be local optimizations are valuable as opportunities for learning and expanding perspectives. When these are suggested, analyze them with the originating person or team. This discussion broadens the perspectives and establishes a basis for further improvements.

> **Avoid quality, process, transformation, or improvement people.**

Big organizations usually have the quality and process department staffed with Six Sigma black belts who are responsible for running improvement projects. Or even better, some have a transformation department. Avoid that! Continuous improvement must be done everywhere by everyone, all the time. Having one department responsible for improvement is the best way to kill it and kill engagement of teams. Instead, use existing direct organizational structures to support adoption and improvements.

> **Avoid improvement teams; use normal teams.**

Related to the previous tip. Organizations commonly create *improvement teams* and task them with implementing improvement items.[4] We have seen this approach fail repeatedly. A better alternative is to have the normal teams work on improvement items. This can be together with regular items or focused only on improvement items for a few Sprints. A great advantage is that a

---

4. This organizational behavior reflects the Taylorist influences discussed in the *Managers* chapter.

regular team will probably be a future user of their own improvement and so they will implement it to be more usable and useful.

> **Avoid improvement projects; use the Product Backlog.**
Also, organizations often assume that all improvements must be done using "projects." These are separately managed and are either staffed by improvement teams (see previous point) or even worse, by removing people from their normal teams. The latter causes organizational hustling for "resources" and a lack of team focus, and will break the team's shared responsibility. Rather, involve regular teams, and offer improvement items to them via the Product Backlog. This way, all the work is visible on the Product Backlog and continuous improvement becomes the normal system.

see *Product Backlog* chapter

The most frequent cause of the collapse of continuous improvement is failure to actually improve. This causes frustration in the teams and distrust towards managers. When this happens, managers need to stop and reflect and ask themselves, "What kind of service do we provide?"

Guide: Growing Your Adoption

First LeSS product adoption done! What's next? Do we have perfection and world domination yet? If not, do this:

> **Expand to a few more products, with the same support.**
Obviously you'll expand, but to how many products? Maybe two next rather than one, but not many. The key constraint is the people, resources, and focus you can bring to maintain and even improve the support for each product. A common problem we see is that the laser-sharp focus given to the first adoption in terms of support becomes unfocused and lackadaisical when expanding. Don't let it happen. Each new product needs the same supporting environment and focus.

> **Strengthen the Definition of Done.**
The Definition of Done is unlikely to be perfect. Strengthen the Definition of Done by increasing the teams' cross-functionality; uncovering new hurdles to resolve.

see *Definition of Done* chapter

> **Expand product definition.**
The initial product definition is often restrained by organizational

see *Product* chapter

structure. Try to broaden that to gain better prioritization, more customer focus, and a simpler organization.

> **Improve teams' output, and share how.**
The results from the initial teams are unlikely to be fantastic. They discovered limitations in their environment and development practices. They had a lot to learn and to improve, and many limitations still remain. Resolving these should improve their output. Do share these solutions across the teams and with other products.

> **Improve support.**
How effective was the support for the initial teams? Get that feedback from the teams and use it to improve the support (teaching, coaching, organizational changes, etc.), so that it is available for future products adopting LeSS.

> **Channel bottom-up energy.**
Positive results from the initial teams in the first product can cause teams in other groups to adopt LeSS without the approval of high-level managers. Rather than killing this off, let it be and support it to exploit this bottom-up energy.

LeSS Huge

When scaling further, an additional issue is this:

Too big for all-at-once structural changes—in a huge product group it is harder to make huge structural changes. It isn't *just* the number of people and minds that makes it hard. It's because

> there's a horde of customers who all received promises about new features by certain dates and that makes large changes risky;

> organizational politics cause such changes to be *career-limiting*; and

> it's hard to provide enough education and coaching on that scale.

Thus, a LeSS Huge adoption is done in a more evolutionary way.

• LeSS HUGE Rules •

LeSS Huge adoptions, including the structural changes, are done with an evolutionary incremental approach.

Remember each day: LeSS Huge adoptions take many months or years, infinite patience, and a sense of humor.

Guide: Evolutionary Incremental Adoption

LeSS adoptions are best done all-at-once, but LeSS Huge adoptions must be done evolutionary and incrementally. There are two approaches to LeSS Huge adoptions:

> **Gradual incremental adoption over the whole product group.**
  All the teams gradually improve their scope and capability at the same pace. This could be by expanding the product-level Definition of Done and using tools such as feature team adoption maps.

Guide: Feature-Team Adoption Maps, p. 90

> **Focused deeper adoption at a part of the product group.**
  Improvements focus to make a few teams really good, and then spread one team at the time. This might be by expanding a few teams' Definition of Done, letting them work on specific improvement items, and by focused coaching.

Both approaches work. The *impatient* gradual incremental adoption has the advantage of *hopefully* having faster product-wide results, though it often doesn't happen because all teams need to solve the same problems at the same time—causing new problems. The focused deeper adoption seems slower but avoids pain in all teams. The drawback, of course, is that the already existing pain won't be resolved as they aren't (yet) the focus of the adoption.

The LeSS adoption principles suggest a preference to the focused deeper adoption, which is covered here. The gradual incremental adoption is covered in the *Organizing by Customer Value* chapter.

Guide: One Requirement Area at a Time

The easiest incremental step to start a LeSS Huge adoption is to adopt LeSS within one Requirement Area. This focuses the LeSS adoption first in the area where the benefits are high and the risks low—or at least the latter.

This implies *creating* only one new Requirement Area at a time.

Now here's where it gets tricky: This new (and perhaps only) Requirement Area is still part of the product and therefore there will be dependencies between the Requirement Area and the vast "old organization." The hard part is to find the balance between supporting this young Requirement Area by disrupting the "old organization" and still conforming to the organizational interfaces.

Pick your battles. One disruption that *must* happen in the "old organization" is to *abandon individual/team code ownership*; otherwise, the young Requirement Area doesn't stand a chance.

Guide: Parallel Organizations

The previous guide is an instance of the more general technique for creating structural change *without changing anything*: build a parallel organization. This means you keep your existing organization as it is and gradually build the new organization next to it, starting with a few feature teams or one Requirement Area. This works well with feature teams since they have essentially no dependencies. Once the first teams are working well, you gradually shift teams from the traditional organization. When there is enough momentum, you merge the old organization into the new one.

Some caveats:

> A parallel organization is not a pilot, and one consequence is that the line of organizational reporting must be separate from the traditional organization.

> Don't let the parallel organization branch the codebase as that will lead to merge-hell. They are separate organizations but work on the same product and the same codebase.

> Communicate very clearly that eventually everyone will be in the new organization. That's an important message so that people in the old organization do not focus on rivalry.

Contents

Teams organized around customer value

ORGANIZE BY CUSTOMER VALUE

I want it to be transparent, but I don't want the background to show through.
—*Anonymous customer*

ONE-TEAM SCRUM

A central theme in Scrum is a relentless focus on delivering customer value. The order of the work is based on delivering value to customers rather than on the convenience to development. For the developers who want to build the framework first, this focus on validating technical decisions by delivering value early is a difficult change.

The three Scrum roles provide a balance between a relentless focus on customer value and caring about technical excellence.

> The *Product Owner* is responsible for return on investment. She makes difficult business decisions. What is in? What is out? When to release? How much to invest? She has a customer-centric view on what the product is.

> The *Team* is a cross-functional, self-managing team that consists of professional product developers who share the responsibility for delivering working and maintainable *done* functionality every Sprint. They decide *how* to build the product and thus the effort.

> The *Scrum Master* is responsible for getting Scrum to work and be beneficial for the organization. Her focus is on growing a well-functioning productive Team, a responsible Product Owner, and a continuously improving organization.

ORGANIZE BY CUSTOMER VALUE IN LeSS

When scaling, these principles relate to organizing:

Customer-centric—In a small one-team product, organizing by customer value is trivial. The more teams, the more they become like cogs in the large development machine. Like Charlie Chaplin in *Modern Times*, his job is to turn screws but he has no idea how the customer will use the product... or who that customer actually is. How to scale *and* keep a customer focus?

Large-Scale Scrum is Scrum—We once visited a team that wanted to adopt Scrum. We taught them LeSS; and when they exclaimed, "So you want us to do what we used to do when there was only one team?" we replied, "Yeah." When the company grew rapidly, it brought in "professional management" and layers of projects, programs, portfolios, and other governance. That additional structure had damaged the core of the company—building great products. *How can we keep scaled Scrum as simple as Scrum?*

Systems thinking and whole-product focus—Traditional organizations contain a lot of local optimizations such as a relentless pursuit to optimize individual output. How can we structure our organization with more focus on the whole product and relentless delivery of customer value?

• LeSS Rules •

Structure the organization by using real teams as the basic organizational building block.

Each team is (1) self-managing, (2) cross-functional, (3) co-located, and (4) long-lived.

The majority of the teams are customer-focused feature teams.

Guide: Build Team-Based Organizations

Yoshiro Nakamatsu is the inventor of the floppy disk. His other inventions include a pillow that prevents you from falling asleep, a cigarette that activates your brain, and a condom with an embedded magnet. He claims to hold the world record of the number of inventions with over 4000 patents. He is an example of the modern-day "crazy scientist"... but most inventions—and most software development—is done by *teams*, not individuals.

Products are created by teams, yet traditional (Western) organizations are built around individual accountability. You are held accountable by your manager for your individual performance. This gets reflected in practices such as assigning work to *individuals*, *individual* performance reviews, and *individual* rewarding. These practices promote *individual* crazy scientists but not well-functioning teams that take a *shared responsibility* for achieving their goal.

Team-based—LeSS—organization has the following structure:

> **Dedicated teams**
> Each team member is dedicated for 100% of his time to one and only one Team. This might feel inflexible, but team members require dedication if you want them (1) to take a shared responsi-

bility for the Team's goal, and (2) to take ownership of how a team works—own *their* processes.

> **Cross-functional teams**

Each team contains or acquires all functional skills needed to produce a shippable product. Traditional functional specialized teams might feel the most "efficient" from that function's perspective, but most effort spend and problems in product development are *between the functions*, and thus teams must be cross-functional if you want them to focus on the whole working product.

> **Co-located teams**

Each team is co-located in the same room.[1] This might sound unreasonable. Wouldn't you, in today's globalized world, want to use the best skilled individuals in the place where they are? No. We want the best *teams* that take a shared responsibility for the outcome of the team and learn from each other. Shared responsibility requires trust and humans are more likely to build trust by close cooperation and face-to-face communication. Co-location also promotes faster feedback and team learning—the essence of continuous improvement.

> **Long-lived teams**

A Team stays together *forever*. This might feel idealistic, but Teams need to have stability if you want them to care about how they work as a Team. Anyone who has ever been on a real long-lived team knows that teams get better as the team members get to know each other and learn how to do and improve work together.

This advantageous team-based organizational structure causes interesting dynamics. It is important to recognize these, as sometimes they feel counterintuitive and can cause *organizational anxiety*. These are described below.

Learning humans over "one-skill resources"—Organizations frequently look at people as "human resources" which puts people in the same category as money, machines, and memos. Resources have one skill. A machine does what it does and when you need it to do something

---

1. This does not mean all teams must be at the same site, although that is definitively preferred. Multi-site development is unfortunately common in LeSS organizations.

else... then you will need a *new machine*. People are born fairly skill-less. But we have an extraordinary meta-skill: to acquire new skills. This skill is the most essential for organizations that aim to be flexible. Having dedicated, long-lived teams automatically causes people to practice those learning skills.

Teams *over* individuals as unit of "resourcing"—Resourcing, the process for deciding which people ought to work on a product, is usually based on individual people. When following the team-based structure, the question will no longer be "Which *individuals* do we need?" but will become "Which *teams* do we need?"

Give work to creative teams *over* creating teams around work—Traditional organizations form a project group with *exactly* the right set of skills and people for each new feature request. But organizations with long-lived teams don't re-organize but instead split the work and give it to an existing team that can learn and adapt.

Stable organizations *over* dynamic matrixed structures—Constantly changing organizational structure doesn't create flexibility but causes confusion. Instead, true organizational flexibility comes from splitting work in meaningful customer-centric ways and giving that to suitable teams who make up for missing skills by using their learning skill. The effect? LeSS organizations abandon matrix-based structures in favor of stable organizational structures.

Guide: Splitting, p. 260

Guide: Understanding Feature Teams

Most large product groups are organized around technology following a model we call **component teams**. LeSS product groups organize around customer value following a model we'll call **feature teams**.[2] The shift from organizing around technology towards organizing around customer value is profound.

---

2. We've written extensively about these two models. What follows is a summary of earlier work. For a thorough treatment see *Scaling Lean & Agile Development: Thinking and Organizational Tools for Large-Scale Scrum*, or *feature teams at less.works* or *feature-teams.org*.

What are feature teams?

A feature team (see Figure 4.1) is a stable, long-lived team that does end-to-end customer-centric features.[3] The team delivers *done* features every Sprint.

Figure 4.1 feature team

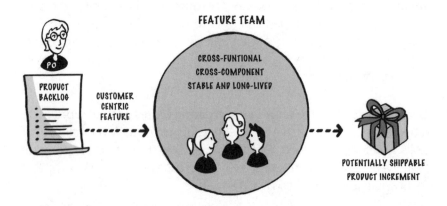

Feature teams have the following advantages, among others.

> > **Crystal-clear responsibilities**—The goal of a feature team is clear. The feature, Product Backlog Item, should be *done* before the Sprint is over. Everything that needs to be done to achieve that goal falls within the responsibility of the team. This simplifies planning and resolves dependencies.

> > **Purpose and customer focus**—Feature teams speak the language of customers. They create features for real people to improve their lives rather than creating technology for technology's sake. This heightened customer focus and purpose enables the team to work directly with customers in their language and to co-create the best product. This is powerful.

---

3. Note, this doesn't mean *any team* can deliver *any feature*. Teams *might* specialize on certain types of features, as long as they still deliver high value.

> **Flexibility and learning**—No more planning hell and enormous dependency matrices. You need a new feature? Find a suitable team.[4] The team won't have *exactly* the skills required, so they get to practice their meta-skill of learning.

A common misunderstanding of feature teams is that a team gets a gigantic feature, covering the whole system, and needs to make changes everywhere. This is not so. Instead, the gigantic feature has to be split before giving smaller end-to-end customer-centric parts of the huge feature to a feature team. A key difference is in splitting work into customer-centric parts instead of into component parts.

Guide: Splitting, p. 260

Guide: Handling Gigantic Requirements, p. 224

Changing to feature teams requires a thorough understanding of how and why they work. We summarize the differences between feature teams and component teams and briefly analyze their benefits and drawbacks. Feature teams have drawbacks too. They are not a quick fix to all your problems. Adopting them requires a long-term perspective.

Component Team Model

Component teams are organized around the architecture, as illustrated in Figure 4.2. Every team is specialized in a part of the system or technology. This could be front-end versus back-end, Java versus C++, or more generally by components (modules, subsystems, frameworks, libraries, etc.)

This is the default for most product groups and has some advantages:

> clear code and design ownership

> clear boundaries (each team in its own sandbox)

> deep specialization

---

4. Important to understanding feature teams is that features aren't randomly distributed over the teams without taking their skill and experience into account.

Figure 4.2 the
component team
model

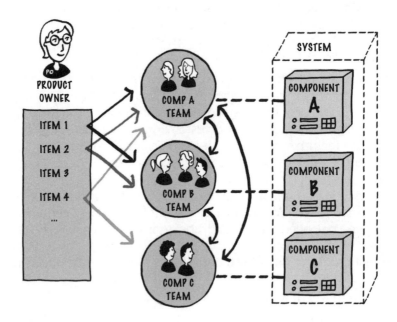

These advantages aren't without significant costs:

Clear code and design ownership—Having ownership of design and code creates identity and clear responsibility. When there is a problem in *our* code, then it is clearly *our* responsibility to fix it.

The flip side is that only one team can change the code, which causes a bottleneck. In addition, the owners also won't receive much feedback on alternative code/design as nobody else really cares about *their* code.

Clear boundaries—We have *our* area in which we can do whatever we want and other teams will not interfere with *our* work.

The flip side is that integration rarely is just pushing everything together. Figuring out who is responsible for what, when the integration failed, is painful and time consuming. LeSS avoids *sandboxing* with a whole-product focus and continuous integration to reduce product risk.

Deep specialization—Our system is complex and nobody can understand everything. Our team has its own area in which we specialized for years and that makes our work better and more efficient.

The flip side is that the specialization is in only one dimension—a technical one. This advantage of specialization (more local efficiency) comes at a price: *not* specializing in other dimensions. More on this in the upcoming guide: *prefer specialization in customer domain.*

The component team model has some serious drawbacks:[5]

> imbalanced and asynchronous dependencies

> focus on amount of output rather than value

> results in sequential life cycle and a long release cycle

Analysis of these drawbacks and typical workarounds show that getting "agile" component teams to work well is perhaps impossible.

Imbalanced and asynchronous dependencies—Customers want features and those tend to involve multiple components. This causes dependencies between the teams. These dependencies are (1) imbalanced, e.g. team Zombies have lots of work but team Draculas have little, and (2) asynchronous, e.g. team Mummies have work that depends on team Werewolfs who won't be working on that as they have more important items. This causes serious coordination and integration challenges.

The typical answer: (1) plan more, (2) create a new role for coordination, and (3) create a "project team" with regular status meetings. All those so-called solutions are futile. The dependencies won't ever be resolved over time, and quick fixes within the existing system causes pain, suffering, and horrible conflict. You may feel we're exaggerating. But if you look closely at what is really going on below the facade of neat status reports, even in groups that have been trying for years, it's a mess.

Focus on amount of output rather than value—Specialization in a technical dimension might increase output as measured in code produced but that does not equal value to customers. Especially when the

---

5. A more complete list can be found in the *Feature Team* chapter of the *Scaling Lean & Agile Development: Thinking and Organizational Tools for Large-Scale Scrum* book or *feature teams at less.works*.

optimization for efficiency influences the prioritization of features. Do your customers prefer lots of code or valuable features?

Results in sequential life cycle and long release cycles—Who does the original customer requirement analysis? Who defines the technical component work for a component team? Who will integrate and test the whole customer centric feature? An analysis team, architecture team, and a system test team? Back to a sequential life cycle with all its handoff problems and additional delay with long release cycles.

These drawbacks are well known and no quick fix in the component-team model can resolve them. Moving to a feature team model avoids them.

Feature Team Model

Feature teams are organized around customer value, as shown in Figure 4.3. Every team might be specialized around one or more types of features in the customer domain. This could be diagnostics, bond trading, or administration.

Figure 4.3 feature team model

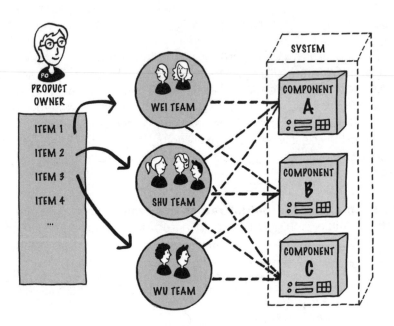

Advantage of feature teams:

> clear feature ownership

> no dependencies that cause delay

> development organization that speaks customer language

As with the component-team model, these do not come without cost.

Clear feature ownership—Who is responsible for ensuring that the whole customer-centric feature works within the existing system? Many organizations love to play the integration ping-pong game of constantly deflecting responsibility to the other team. This dysfunctional behavior evaporates with feature teams as the responsibility is *always* with the feature team.

The flip side is that a feature team works on multiple components. Other teams work on the same components at the same time, and that will impact the design/code of the components. This impact can be positive where the design/code improves. But many people worry that it will get messier. Adoption of modern development practices such as unit testing, merciless refactoring, continuous integration, multi-team design workshops, and evolutionary design can prevent component degradation and grow the product healthily. Furthermore, component mentors and component communities provide learning and support for changing components the team isn't yet familiar with.

see *Coordination and Integration* chapter for component mentors and multi-team design meetings

No dependencies that cause delay—When a feature requires a change to a component, then the feature team makes the change. They do not wait for another team to make the change for them. This reduces synchronization needs for delivering customer features and in turn dramatically reduces the time from feature request to value delivery.

The flip side is that there will be shared components or platforms. If each feature team *just* focuses on implementing *their* functionality then that could lead to the same functionality being implemented many times. They lost the opportunity to cooperate with other teams. This can be resolved by emphasizing cooperation across teams *related to the technical implementation*. Useful techniques for this are multi-team Product Backlog Refinement or multi-team Sprint Planning Two.

see *PBR* and *Coordination & Integration* chapters for related guides

Development organization that speaks *customer language*—Feature teams speak the same language as customers and can directly ask customers for clarification. This makes work more purposeful as the teams know what, why, and who they build it for. It also reduces layers of indirection—analysts, product and project managers—between customers and developers.

The flip side is that some engineers have never considered customer communication to be a required skill. Some might prefer not to talk with customers, some might not be able to. Our experience has been that broadening skills is rewarding but can feel uncomfortable at first.

A feature team model has its own challenges:

> requires developers to learn a larger part of the system

> can lead to messy code/design

> affects the way work is split

These are serious challenges yet not insurmountable ones.

Guide: Current-Architecture Workshop, p. 303

Requires developers to learn a larger part of the system—Developers will need to learn a larger part of the system, yet a common misconception is that developers or teams have to know the *entire* system. This is untrue. People within a team *will* have their primary specialization and teams *will* also have their specialized area. Imagine a system with 50 components. Traditionally a developer knows 1 well. In a feature team, he will need to know a few of them in depth and perhaps a dozen shallowly. He won't *need* to know all 50.

see *Coordination & Integration* chapter on practices that help

Can lead to messier code/design—As mentioned, removing component ownership potentially causes the degradation of the code/design. This stems from the "shared responsibility is no responsibility" thinking. Technical excellence and modern development practices can prevent this degradation. Additionally, sometimes this degradation doesn't happen because developers know others will see their code, so they put in extra effort to maintain their reputation. Stimulate this code pride.

Guide: Splitting, p. 260

Affects the way work is split—With component teams, work is split into technical component tasks. This is usually done by a separate person or group: architects, analysts, or specifiers. This type of splitting is unnecessary with feature teams. Work still needs to be split. This splitting is in the customer domain and is done in Product Backlog Refinement meetings. Customer-centric splitting is not difficult but it is different. Without understanding of customer-centric splitting, feature teams will seem inconceivable.

These challenges are real yet resolvable. A feature team transition is not hard for a 4-team LeSS adoption, but on the other hand for a 100-team LeSS Huge adoption, it takes months or even years. But it is possible and the benefits are substantial.

Dependencies in Component Teams and Feature Teams

Figure 4.4 shows both models; a comparison leads to important insights.

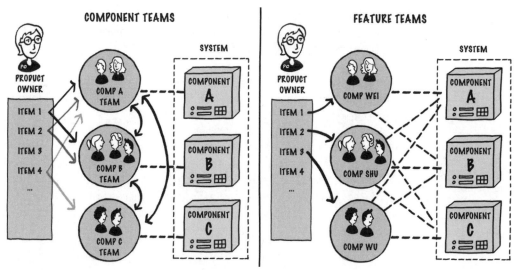

A major problem with component teams is the asynchronous nature of dependencies between teams related to customer-centric features. Feature teams resolve dependencies and create the opportunity for teams to benefit from each other via shared work without being blocked by dependencies. When using development practices rooted in 1980s practices—producing lots of paper before writing code and only integrating all parts when you're done—this shared work causes a major

Figure 4.4 feature and component team models compared

pain as the shared work is just speculation. But with modern agile development practices—focus on clean code, merciless refactoring, and continuous integration—this shared work becomes a true opportunity. The feature dependencies of component teams aren't resolvable as they are structural and systemic in nature.[6]

Thus, LeSS requires the majority of the teams to be feature teams.

Guide: Feature-Team Adoption Maps

What is a component? What is a feature? What is functional specialization? So far, we've looked at them as binary but the answer exists along a continuum. One group's work scope might be limited to an individual class whereas another group could work on an entire subsystem. They are different types of component teams.

A similar scale exists that's related to functional specialization. Some product groups have *five levels* of testing and that gives "include testing in the team" a very ambiguous meaning!

Drawing these scales in a graph, as shown in Figure 4.5, affords some insights in feature-team adoption and the kind of organizational change you can expect.

for product definition see *Product* chapter; for Definition of Done see *Definition of Done*

The Y-axis represents a gradually increasing work scope of the teams expressed as architectural decomposition and the expansion of the product definition. The X-axis represents the degree of cross-functionality of the teams expressed as a gradually increasing Definition of Done.

---

6. And we've seen organizations try over and over again to resolve the drawbacks of component teams. The problem are never resolved. Unfortunately, many organizations have to learn this by themselves.

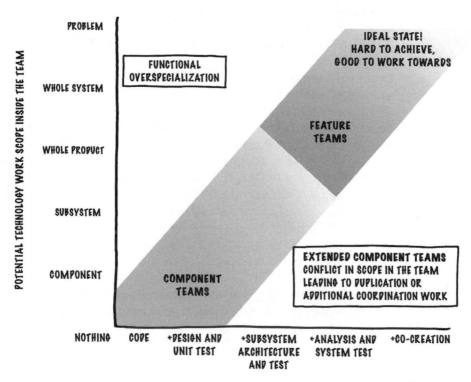

Figure 4.5 feature-team adoption map

Figure 4.5 shows four areas:

Component teams—Any team that (1) focuses on parts of the product rather than end-customer-centric features or (2) focuses on finishing a task rather than delivering a product increment is a component team. The *smaller* the work scope and the stricter the specialization, the *bigger* the component-team problems.

Feature teams—Any team that has a whole-product focus and is involved from clarifying customer-centric features to testing them is a feature team. Feature teams also exist along a scale. They can be limited to just implementing the features stated they need. Or, when the product definition is broad enough, they can be involved with identifying and solving the customers' real problems and thus co-creating the product on the whole system.

see *Product* chapter for broader product definitions

Functional overspecialized team—Any team that performs a limited task on a larger scope is probably functionally overspecialized. This leads to lots of waste due to handoffs. This is to be avoided.

Extended component teams—Any team that has a limited component work scope yet is responsible for checking that their part works within the larger product is an extended component team. The team has an internal conflict as they have both a limited "component scope" and a "whole product scope." This conflict leads to either (1) duplication of work as multiple teams create the same tests or (2) additional coordination effort as the teams have to coordinate their "product focused" testing. The same conflict of scope is true for requirements clarification. The Product Owner will need to remind the team that completely *done* items are expected at the end of the Sprint. These teams are perhaps an improvement over basic component teams but fall far short of delivering the benefits of feature teams.

A perfect feature team is a team that works across the whole system and co-creates the product together with actual users. This is a good yet difficult-to-achieve perfection goal.

Product Owner Guide: Don't Be Nice, p. 189

Examples

With that perfection goal, we can use the earlier chart as a **feature-team adoption map**. Two examples are explored next.

The Figure 4.6 feature-team adoption map is from a huge telecom product adopting LeSS Huge. When they started their adoption they had traditional component teams. They chose the adoption strategy of expanding the teams' functional scope and created *extended component teams*. Their goal for the next few years is to move to full product-wide feature teams. However, there are some shared components created by a peer product group and that makes it hard to include these components as doing so would require a significantly larger organizational change. So, these are excluded from their current goal.

Expanding to the system-scope is difficult because doing so would involve several code bases of millions of lines of code each, an enormous amount of functional specializations, and a full reorganization involving thousands of people. So, cross-product group coordination and integration activities are likely to stay as is for the next decade and will continue to cause a constant headache.

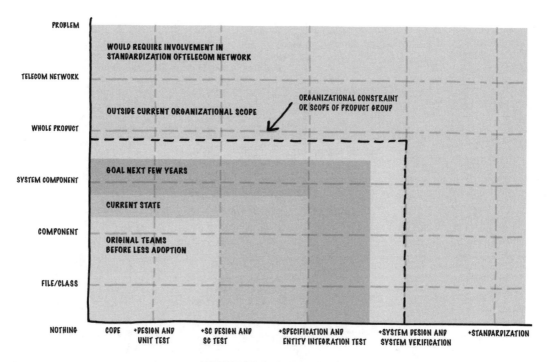

ACTIVITY (FUNCTION) INSIDE THE TEAM. DEGREE OF CROSS-FUNCTIONALITY

Figure 4.6 feature-team adoption map of telecom system

The Figure 4.7 feature-team adoption map is from a trading product and is a much smaller LeSS Huge adoption. They had the same starting point as the telecom product group but decided to go with an all-at-once adoption strategy. Deploying to production is still outside the scope of the feature teams. This is reflected in their imperfect Definition of Done.

The amount of change required in an all-at-once LeSS Huge adoption is often too large for the organization to cope with. That's why we don't recommend all-at-once LeSS Huge adoptions. This case is a great example. The product group adopted whole-product feature teams, with one exception: One rather important component was organizationally in another product group. The changes forced on the organization and especially that product group became one of the reasons the adoption eventually took a few steps backwards. Large-scale organizational change is a breeding ground of nasty politics.

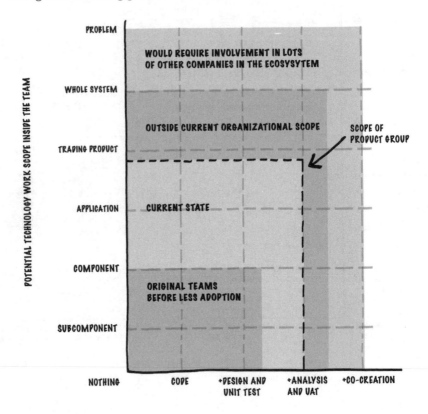

Figure 4.7 feature-team adoption map of financial trading system

Help with Decisions

A feature-team adoption map is an important tool when you are adopting LeSS. It helps with the following decisions:

> **What is "all"?**—A smaller LeSS framework adoption requires an *all-at-once* change to feature teams. Who is included in "all" depends on the scope of the feature teams.

> **Future improvement goals**—The map can be used for setting future goals as the telecom product group had done. These future goals frequently go hand in hand with the expansion of the Defini-

tion of Done. The map also shows the expected changes and their difficulty, as expanding beyond the current organizational boundary involves the hard work of "political" boundaries.

> **LeSS or LeSS Huge?**—The scope of the feature teams influences the size of your adoption and can swing a LeSS group into adopting LeSS Huge instead. For example, a network-performance tool is a customer-centric product and its development-group size leads to the smaller LeSS Framework. However, when realizing it is *always* sold as an integrated part of a network management system changes the product scope and then is likely a LeSS Huge adoption.

Guide: Prefer Specialization in Customer Domain

One essential concept behind feature teams is to organize and specialize in the domain of the customer rather than the domain of technology. The same concept also guides other LeSS structuring decisions.

A common misunderstanding of feature teams is that it leads to abandoning specialization altogether. Part of this misunderstanding comes from the false dichotomy of either specializing in one component or not specializing at all—which we've covered extensively in our writing on feature teams. Part of the misunderstanding comes from the belief that specialization is a one-dimensional thing—specializing in a component. But specialization is multi-dimensional. Exploring these dimensions leads to better decisions on how to balance these.

The conventional way of thinking about specialization is almost exclusively around functional skill or components, as shown in a feature-team adoption map. But other dimensions of specialization exist; they include programming language, hardware, operating system, API, market, type of customer, and type of feature. We can group these as (1) technological (component, OS, etc.), or (2) customer-oriented (market, type of feature, etc.). Looking at the adoption of feature teams from these dimensions leads to the chart in Figure 4.8.

Figure 4.8 two
dimensions of
specialization

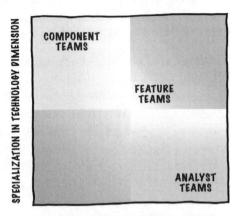

LeSS brings users and developers closer together. The user perspective is almost always lost in traditional large product groups. Feature teams are one way of organizing by customer value, but not the only one. The principle of preferring specialization in customer domain also leads to other structuring decisions.

For example: Banks create mobile apps for banking services on mobile devices. The teams are typically organized by platform such as the iOS teams and the Android teams. These teams are feature teams *and* they are specialized in the technical dimension—namely, the platform. Alternatively, they can be organized in customer domains such as mobile payments, admin, and reporting. This leads to the teams implementing the same type of features on multiple platforms instead of implementing many types of features on the one platform.

Which specialization dimension is better? Traditional organizations tend to specialize in technology dimensions. Why? Perhaps technology is perceived as more difficult and hence specializing in that dimension leads to faster development? LeSS prefers specialization in the customer domain to increase collaboration with real users, remove handoffs, and make work more meaningful. Let's explore another example...

We worked with a company that builds graphics cards. They structured their organization around technology: (1) hardware team, (2) Linuxdriver team, and (3) Windows-driver team. These are component teams, but a move to feature teams requires a cross-functional hardware/software team. That's possible but difficult to achieve in most *hardware* companies—for cultural reasons. The software teams are additionally specialized in driver API. This organization is predicated on the assumption that learning the OS-driver-API is more important and difficult than understanding the hardware—the company's product. LeSS prefers organizing around the customer and thus an alternative team organization is (1) 2D-graphics chip team and (2) 3D graphics chip team.

What is the perfect balance between technology specialization and customer specialization? A hard decision. When adopting LeSS, *prefer specialization in the customer domain.*

Guide: LeSS Organizational Structure

How does this all fit together in an organizational structure? Of course, each organization is different, yet LeSS organizations tend to follow a surprisingly simple structure. The first difference between LeSS organizations and most traditional ones is that the structure is stable as (1) work is organized around teams and (2) mismatch of skills triggers learning and coordination within existing teams.

A typical LeSS organizational chart is shown in Figure 4-9.

Figure 4.9 typical
LeSS organizational
chart

Notice what isn't here:

> **No functional organizations.**
   Having team members with programming skills report to the
   development manager and team members with testing skill report
   to the QA manager won't create great teams. Why? It causes *conflicting loyalty* where a QA person has one loyalty towards the
   team for all the work of the team and one loyalty towards the QA
   manager for his functional specialization. LeSS organizations avoid
   this conflict by abolishing functional organization and instead creating cross-functional line organizations.

> **No project/program organization or project/program manage-
   ment office (PMO).**
   These traditional control organizations cease to exist in a LeSS
   organization as their responsibilities are distributed between the
   feature teams and the Product Owner. Insisting on keeping such
   organizations will cause confusion and conflicts of responsibilities.

> **No support groups such as configuration management, contin-
   uous integration support, or "quality and process".**
   LeSS organizations prefer to expand the existing teams responsibility to include this work over creating more complex organization with specialized groups. Specialized support groups tend to
   own their area which leads to them becoming a bottleneck.

Let's examine a LeSS organization...

Head of Product Group—Most product development LeSS organizations still have managers including a "head of product group." They support the teams by Go See and help them remove obstacles and improve. (We cover manager responsibilities in the *Management* chapter.) LeSS organizations don't have matrix structures and there are no dotted-line managers.

See *Management* chapter for more on the role of management.

The name "Head of Product Group" might be confusing to you. This is probably because different organizations use quite different terms for this. What we mean is the line manager of all the teams, whatever that is called in your organization.

Feature teams—This is where the development work is done. Each team is a cross-functional, self-managing feature team with a Scrum Master. They are permanent units that stay together for the duration of a product (and sometimes longer). Preferably all members have the head of the product group as their direct manager. We've seen 150 people who all had the same direct manager as most management activities were taken over by the teams. But some larger LeSS organizations have some additional team line manager structure. Try to avoid the additional organizational complexity whenever possible.

Product Owner (Team)—This is also commonly called "Product Management." It can be one person but in a larger LeSS organization the Product Owner might be supported by other product managers.

An important point in this organizational structure is that the Teams and the Product Owner are *peers*—they do not have a hierarchical relationship. We have found it important to keep the power balanced between the roles. The Teams and Product Owner should have a *cooperative* peer relationship to together build the best possible product, and a peer structure supports this. This point is further explored in the *Product Owner* chapter.

This organizational structure is especially common for product companies. The frequent alternative, especially for internal development, is for the Product Owner to belong to a different organization—the business side. Thus, he is *not* within the hierarchy of the Head of the Product Group. This is recommended, though it does often require additional

Guide: Who Should be Product Owner?, p. 173

effort to ensure the Product Owner has a close relationship with the Teams.

Undone department—This department, ideally, does not exist.

Unfortunately, sometimes the teams are not yet able to create a true shippable increment every Sprint. This is reflected by their "Definition of Done" not being equal to "Potentially Shippable." The difference between them is called **Undone Work**. *Someone* needs to do this Undone Work, and a common "solution" is to create separate groups that pick up the "undone work"—the *undone department*. More on this in the *Definition of Done* chapter.

Undone departments such as test, QA, architecture, or business analysis groups *should never exist* in the smaller LeSS framework groups; rather they should be integrated into the teams *from the start*. On the other hand, we unfortunately still frequently see an *operations* or *production* undone department in LeSS adoptions, as they often cross organizational boundaries.

A goal in every LeSS adoption is to remove the undone department. How long will this take? The answer is highly dependent on how fast the organization improves its capability.

Guide: Organizing Multi-Site in LeSS

We worked at an online games company when a new Product Owner joined. She asked, "Where are my teams located?" Someone listed the three cities in Eastern Europe. She asked, "How long is the flight to the first city?" Her question triggered laughing. The answer, "There is no flight or airport. You have to fly to Kiev and take a three-hour train ride!" The new Product Owner was astounded. That site was closed down.

Product development is best done with only one site. And yet there are good (and more *not so good*) reasons for having multiple sites. Apply these principles for your site strategy:

Reduce sites—Multi-site might be inevitable due to external factors. Even then, have an explicit policy to co-locate as much as possible. Close down smaller sites and at least reduce time-zone differences.

Reduce time-zone differences—Time is a bigger obstacle than distance. You can mitigate problems caused by physical distance with video and text chat, etc., though all are inferior to being face-to-face at a whiteboard. But the only way to overcome time differences is to shift your work day. Most teams prefer not to do that and thus big time differences guarantee a one-day delay in communication.

Co-locate whole teams—Team members share responsibility for the team's work. Shared responsibility requires a high level of trust. Unfortunately, distance breeds distrust as humans find it difficult to trust people they don't see and directly interact with. Plus the people in one team need to be together to learn from each other.

Do not have sites specializing in functional skill—An unfortunate yet common division of work between sites is based on functional specialization, e.g. one development site and a second (cheaper) testing site. This division of work doesn't work in LeSS as it leads to every cross-functional team having members in multiple sites.

Do not have sites specializing in components—Another common way of deciding "site responsibility" is to take the architecture diagram and assign parts of the architecture to sites. This doesn't work when adopting feature teams.

LeSS Huge

When scaling, context and issues include:

Customer-centric—It is easy to forget the customer in large development efforts when the added structure pushes teams away from customers towards technology single-specialization. How do you prevent that? How do you keep customer closeness with perhaps a thousand developers?

More with LeSS—When scaling to LeSS Huge, it seems inevitable that *some* additional structure is required. Requirement Areas and the Area Product Owner role provide this while keeping the framework small.

• LeSS Huge Rules •

Customer requirements that are strongly related from a customer perspective are grouped in Requirement Areas.

Each Team specializes in one Requirement Area. Teams stay in one area for a long time. When there is more value in other areas, teams might change Requirement Area.

Each Requirement Area has one Area Product Owner.

Each Requirement Area has between "4–8" teams. Avoid violating this range.

Guide: Requirement Areas

A **Requirement Area** is a grouping of Product Backlog items that logically belong together from the customer perspective, such as trade processing or new-market onboarding. Requirement Areas allow us to manage an area as if it is its own product with its own (smaller) LeSS adoption. A Requirement Area consists of:

> **Area Product Backlog**—A subset of the Product Backlog that belongs to one area. This is not a separate backlog but is logically a view on the Product Backlog but *might* be managed as a separate backlog. This is covered in the *Product Backlog* chapter.

> **Area Product Owner**—A separate "Product Owner" who specializes in a logical area of customer requirements. The Area Product Owner acts as the Product Owner towards the teams. She also works with the overall Product Owner and other Area Product

Owners as part of the Product Owner Team to keep the whole-product focus. This is covered in the *Product Owner* chapter.

> **Feature teams**—The Teams that specialize in part of the product while still speaking the language of the customer. Each Team belongs to exactly one Requirement Area.

Requirement Areas are the prime structural addition to LeSS when you are scaling above "8" teams—thus creating LeSS Huge. They were created to resolve the following problems encountered when scaling LeSS:

> **Product Backlog too big**.
> Suppose there are four items per team per Sprint with 3 Sprints' worth of clarified granular ready items, and 20 teams. That implies 240 items in the fine-grained section of the Product Backlog. Having so many items in just the fine-grained section—not to mention the many less-refined items—makes the Product Backlog unmanageable.

> **Product Owner stretched too thin**.
> How many teams can one Product Owner work with? If the Product Owner is not involved in detailed clarification of every item and she focuses instead on prioritization, customers, and team collaboration, then we see there is a tipping point somewhere between 5 and 10 teams (e.g. "8"). Above that, there's too much going on to maintain a balance of outward and inward focus and to be sustainable.

> **Meetings too crowded**.
> Two team representatives from each of 20 teams lead to *big* Sprint Planning meetings It is hard to keep meetings of *that* size productive and focused.

> **Teams lacking focus**.
> Teams get frustrated and go slow when they change focus too frequently or when they cover *too* broad an area. Specializing a team in a customer-centric area creates the focus required to create a productive team.

Figure 4.10 shows an example of a Requirement Area structure:

Figure 4.10
Requirement Areas

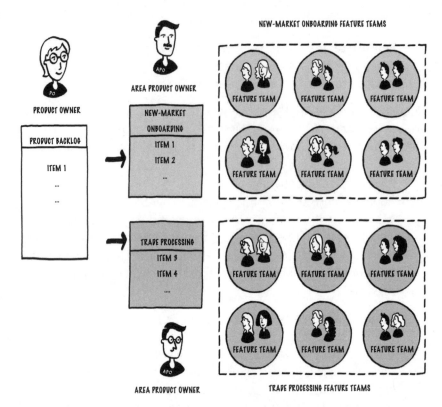

The Product Backlog contains all Product Backlog Items. Each of these items is assigned to one and only one Requirement Area. Each Requirement Area has one Area Product Owner, and all items that belong to that Requirement Area form the Area Product Backlog. Each team belongs to one Requirement Area for a long time.

The overall Product Owner monitors the value of the items across all areas. When the value difference between areas becomes too large, then the Product Owner can move a team to another area. This way the Product Owner focuses on the return on investment of the whole product.

Guide: Dynamics of Requirement Areas

Requirement Areas contain four to eight teams. But why four? Having smaller Requirement Areas inevitably leads to lack of transparency and local optimizations. Why? Let's first explore the evolution of a Requirement Area over time.

LeSS Huge Story: A New Requirement Area •, p. 39

Birth—There are two ways in which new Requirement Areas are born:

> A Requirement Area grows "too big" and is best split into two smaller Requirement Areas by grouping items inside the Area Backlog to discover a natural split. This is the preferred way of creating new areas and is equal to how smaller LeSS adoptions grow to LeSS Huge.

see previous guide *Requirement Areas* for signs of an area becoming too big

> A (probably big) new product opportunity arises[7] that is significantly different from earlier features. When that happens, we can create a totally new Requirement Area, move one team into it and gradually grow into at least four teams.

Guide: Handling Gigantic Requirements, p. 224

Midlife—The relative importance of a Requirement Area *will* change during its lifetime. That's because customers won't neatly divide their needs into Requirement Area, but instead one area will get a higher priority for some time while others fall in priority. It's the responsibility of the overall Product Owner to recognize this and dynamically adjust Requirement Areas by moving teams to where the most value is.

When Requirement Areas are not dynamic, then this hints at deeper systematic problems.

Retirement—It is rare for a Requirement Area to just disappear, as there will always be small changes in the area. But they will shrink to below four. Then what? Merge Requirement Areas. Take two Requirement Areas, expand their scopes to be the same and then merge the Area Backlogs and have one Area Product Owner continue. Having a meaningful combined scope is best, but if that can't happen, then taking the name of the first Requirement Area, appending the word *and*, and taking the name of the second Requirement Area will do to start.

---

7. This could be a whole new market or it could be one insanely huge feature that would require many teams many months.

So, why combine small areas and avoid areas smaller than four? Tiny Requirement Areas at best cause a lot of work for the overall Product Owner in dealing with cross-Requirement-Area prioritization. This should cause the Requirement Areas to be rapidly changing. At worst, it doesn't happen and the cross-Requirement-Area prioritization is lost and with it, the overview on the Product Backlog. Having tiny Requirement Areas is usually a sign of these problems: (1) silo-Requirement Areas with too powerful Area Product Owners, (2) lack of customer focus leading to a lack of prioritization in the overall Product Backlog, or (3) the Area Product Owner's being too involved with the clarification and therefore unable to handle more than two teams.

this often happens when sites and Requirement Areas are aligned

Guide: Organizing Multi-Site in LeSS, p. 100

Guide: Transitioning to Feature Teams

When adopting (smaller framework) LeSS, the transition to feature teams is all-at-once. But when adopting LeSS Huge, you can choose from several transition strategies. Which one is best? These simplistic steps help you determine the best strategy for your organization:

1. Determine your context.
2. Determine your transition strategy.

Let's explore both in more depth.

1. Determine Your Context

The transition to feature teams is influenced by several factors:

Size of the product group—Obviously it is easier for a 10-team product group to transition to feature teams than for a 100-team group.

Lifetime of the product—Products that will probably be around for the next 30 years tend to make slow changes, ostensibly to lower risk. Products that last only a few years must change faster.

Degree of component and functional specialization—More specialization makes feature-team adoption a larger change. Use the feature-team adoption map to draw the current state of component/functional specialization.

Number of development sites—More development sites makes feature-team adoption harder. This is doubly true when sites specialize in certain components or function. This site specialization is an obstacle to cross-component and cross-functional learning.

2. Determine your Transition Strategy

There are three broad transitioning strategies:

All-at-once—As also used in LeSS adoption. In LeSS Huge all-at-once is less common because of the amount of organizational change it requires. Yet when (1) the product group is relatively small, (2) the lifetime of the product is short, (3) the specialization is low, and (4) the development is co-located at one site, then all-at-once is a good strategy. A common mistake in all-at-once LeSS Huge adoption is to underestimate the amount of learning and coaching required.

Gradually expand component team responsibility—You can plot the current state of your organization in a feature-team adoption map and mark future goals for expanding the scope of the teams. The cross-functional expansion is achieved by expanding the Definition of Done. More on this in the *Definition of Done* chapter.

We've encountered this transition strategy repeatedly. It can work but has a couple of big weaknesses: (1) It gives you the drawbacks of both feature and component teams while not giving the best benefits; (2) it is hard to adopt customer-centric Requirement Areas when the teams are still component teams.

Still, this transition strategy is a good idea in a multi-site environment when a lot of multi-site learning must happen.

Parallel organization—In this strategy you keep the existing component team organization in place and gradually build a feature team organization next to it as a parallel organization.

Guide: One Requirement Area at a Time, p. 74

Figure 4.11 grow a
parallel organization

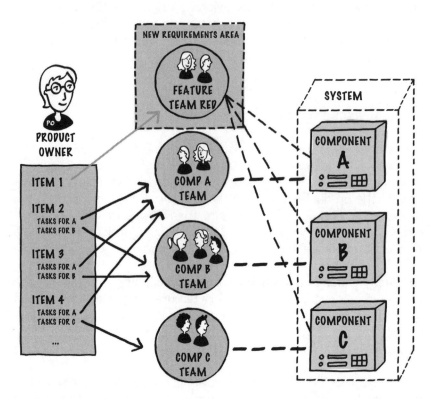

The existing component-team organization keeps functioning the way it did before, except that the new feature team(s) will change *their* code. The new feature team(s) take on valuable but painful features (those with the most dependencies) and work across the components by changing the components directly. Remember: Seek *volunteers* for these nascent feature teams.

This strategy is gradual and low-risk and is well-suited for *huge LeSS Huge* product groups. Its most important drawback? It will take a long time.

When using this strategy, give your young feature teams *a lot of* support and do not expect much output. They have to resolve obstacles such as different practices in different components, different component structures, different tool usage, and different test environments. On top of that, they'll also need to deal with learning new component and new functional skills. Give them lots of support and time, as they are the messengers of all weaknesses and dysfunctions in the organization.

Guide: LeSS Huge Organization

Scale is often accompanied by additional organizational structure. Before we explore the typical additional structure, we need to stress that scale doesn't *have to* mean additional structure. Additional structure usually causes narrower responsibilities, which paves the way for loads of organizational dysfunction and politics. Keep organizational design simple.

With that caveat, a LeSS Huge structure is built on top of the LeSS structure. A typical LeSS Huge organizational chart looks like the one shown in Figure 4.12.

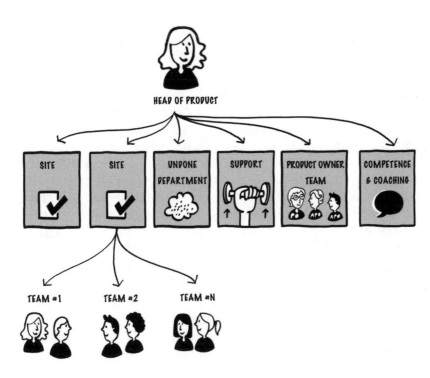

Figure 4.12 typical LeSS Huge organizational structure

Notice that there is still no project/program organization (or PMO). In Scrum and LeSS adoptions, these departments cease to exist.

Let's examine parts that differ from the LeSS organization.

Teams in sites—LeSS Huge adoptions are almost always multi-site, and organizations usually prefer to keep the line organization local. This allows managers to Go See easily and really help the teams to improve. Avoid having the Requirements Areas be equal to the organizational structure as it leads to them being difficult to change.

Product Owner Team—Conceptually the same as in a LeSS structure. The team is larger since it includes all the Area Product Owners. In huge LeSS Huge groups, the Product Owner Team has sub-teams based on the Requirement Areas.

Undone Department—Also conceptually the same as in a LeSS structure. In LeSS Huge groups there tend to be bigger Undone departments, and it takes a longer time to get rid of them. In huge LeSS Huge groups, there will be additional structure in the Undone department, potentially with their own antiquated project management practices.

Support—This department provides development environment support for the teams. In LeSS the teams support each other without the need for a separate group. But a LeSS Huge organization typically does centralize some support because of the massive volume of work. Still, this department should be as small as possible with the attitude "How can we help?" rather than "Take it this way!" Why? Support groups often end up taking over responsibilities from the teams and become huge ever-growing pulsating abominations controlling rather than supporting the teams.

Configuration-management support is a common example of a support group becoming a *control* group. They take ownership of the build and create all the build scripts. The effect? Teams have no idea what happens when "the build is done," are clueless as to why it takes 92 minutes, and don't feel empowered to make the build better. It's all magic to them and out of their control.

Limiting understanding of the build to a support group causes bottle-necks, inefficiency, local optimizations, and dis-empowerment. The con-figuration-management *support* group ought to be the experts who help *teams* improve it and who explain the build and teach better build designs *without* becoming the owners. They might pair up with team members and observe how they work so that they can together devise ways to improve.

Other common support groups include laboratory support, continuous-integration system support, or operations support.

Competence and Coaching—Software is created by people. Improving people improves products. This seems obvious, yet we rarely see orga-nizations that are truly committed to relentlessly training and coaching their people. LeSS Huge organizations have a dedicated training and coaching department which is essential for continuous improvement.

The competence and coaching department focuses on three things:

> observation (Go See)

> training

> coaching

In traditional organizations, the training and coaching requests go from unaware-of-reality managers to a really unaware training group. They then create an alternate-reality training and waste people's time. This is not a good idea. Instead, the competence and coaching group consists of skillful practitioner-experts who actively Go See and observe how people work. They pair up and work with people to discover their train-ing needs. People don't ask for training on subjects they don't know exist or for skills they don't know they are weak at.

Coaching is key! It is the most effective way to help teams improve. Coaches work with or in teams. They observe, pair, shadow, and ques-tion. They give observations, feedback, ideas and examples on how the team can improve. Coaching happens on three levels: (1) organizational, (2) teams and Product Owner, and (3) technical. All these levels are important. We have yet to see a successful LeSS adoption without active coaching.

Contents

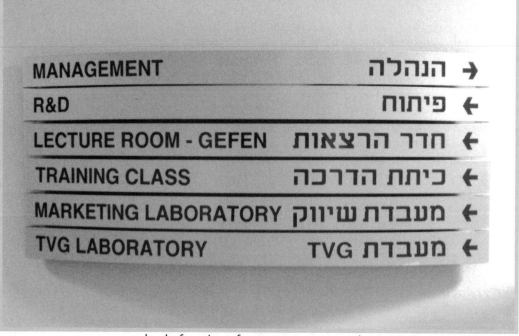

the dysfunction of management separation

MANAGEMENT

The prevailing—and foolish—attitude is that a good manager can be a good manager anywhere, with no special knowledge of the production process he's managing.
—W. Edwards Deming

ONE-TEAM SCRUM

Scrum does not mention managers. But Scrum is a change in management style more than just a development framework. This change is mostly caused by the following three Scrum elements: self-managing teams, Product Owner, and Scrum Master.

With a **self-managing team** the responsibility of the Team is extended to include "managing and monitoring process and progress."[1] These responsibilities are removed from the manager's responsibilities.

All work that the Team does has to come from the **Product Owner**. This removes the responsibility of managers to decide what the Team is working on.

The Scrum Master is responsible for a functioning Team, Product Owner, and organization. She facilitates conflict resolution and improvement by fostering reflection and learning. She is a team coach and an organizational coach.

Traditional manager responsibilities focus on *what*, *how*, and *tracking*. In summary, all these are no longer the responsibility of managers in a

---

1. LeSS uses the term self-managing teams instead of self-organizing teams. In Scrum literature, the terms are often mixed or used interchangeably. Self-managing teams has a clear definition: the team is responsible for the work and monitoring and managing process and progress. This definition was given by the inventor of the term, Harvard professor and team researcher Hackman. In contrast, the term self-organizing teams is frequently used ambiguously or inconsistently.

Scrum organization. With that, the management style changes from command and control to *supporting*.

> **A common problem with Scrum adoption occurs when managers do not give up these responsibilities, thereby causing an organizational conflict between the Team, Product Owner, Scrum Master, and managers.**

What then is the role of managers in a Scrum organization? Scrum is silent and asks organizations to figure that out for themselves. But LeSS is not silent, and opens up the difficult discussion of the change in the manager role in LeSS organizations.

LeSS Management

LeSS follows traditional organizational theory. If you want to increase organizational flexibility (agility), you do so by delegating responsibility so decision making doesn't slow down responses. This leads to flatter organizations and *less* managers.

Most LeSS adoptions are in organizations with no shortage of managers. So, what is their role?

When scaling, principles related to management include:

Empirical Process Control—Ownership of how the work is done ought to be with the people doing the work. They experience feedback and improve. How does shifting process ownership to the teams change management?

Customer-Centric—Teams working directly with customers dramatically increases customer focus and tends to make work more meaningful. Managers are no longer directly involved in this cooperation and neither do they act as intermediaries.

Continuous Improvement towards Perfection—With day-to-day management out of the way of managers, they can change their focus towards improving the system.

Systems Thinking—Pre-LeSS organizational structure often caused a silo mindset behavior. That has to change to a whole-system and whole-product perspective. The change of perspective is often unfamiliar and discomforting and will require significant learning.

• LeSS Rules •

> In LeSS, managers are optional, but if managers do exist, their role is likely to change. Their focus shifts from managing the day-to-day product work to improving the value-delivering capability of the product development system.
>
> Managers' role is to improve the product development system by practicing Go See, encouraging Stop & Fix, and "experiments over conformance."

Guide: Understand Taylor and Fayol

Management is an invented concept. Understanding its origins and context is important in order to adapt and make it relevant for today. Are the problems it solved back then the same problems we need to solve today? Without challenging and deep understanding there is no continuous improvement, but only... continuity from the 19th century.

Two early and key influencers of management are Frederick Taylor and Henri Fayol.

Frederick Taylor, born in 1856, was a mechanical engineer obsessed with worker productivity. As foreman he successfully applied scientific principles to his workers. This led him to open his own consultancy firm and his ideas became known as "scientific management."[2]

Henri Fayol, born in 1841, was a French mining engineer who joined a large French mining group at age 19. His first job was to improve mining safety. He never left the company and eventually became the managing director. Under Fayol, the company flourished and became one of the largest French companies. He formulated his thoughts on management[3] and published them in a landmark book called *General and Industrial Management*.

Frederick Taylor introduced two concepts that unfortunately are still prevalent today.

> > There is one best way of doing a job, which you can prove scientifically. Once discovered, this "best practice" should be pushed throughout the organization.

> > Planning and improvement work should be separated from normal work. The planning and improvement work should be done by special higher-educated people while the normal work can be done by mostly uneducated people. In the words of Taylor, "There is no question that the cost of production is lowered by separating the work of planning and the brain work as much as possible from the manual labor."[4]

Henri Fayol created 14 principles of management, which include division of labor, authority, unity of direction, and chain of command. He also defined the five responsibilities of managers: planning, organizing, coordinating, commanding, and controlling.

Many so-called "modern" management theories can be traced back to the ideas of Taylor and Fayol.[5] They have changed the way companies and the world works.

However, today's world is not the world of Taylor and Fayol. This different context makes some of the best ideas of the past the worst ideas of the present. For example:

---

2. Also known as Taylorism.
3. Also known as Fayolism.
4. From *Shop Management* by Frederick Winslow Taylor published 1903.
5. Other important influencers such as Max Weber and Mary Parker Follett are skipped here but are well worth study.

> Taylor wanted to maximize the productivity of the low-educated workforce. But today's product developers are highly educated and smart people. Separated planning and improvement leads to additional handoff, rigid specialization, and more overhead.

> Fayol wanted to increase unity by improving communication, as it took up to ten days to travel from France to the United States. But today's travel takes less than 7 hours and communication takes seconds. Extensive hierarchies for creating unity and to ease communication are obsolete.

> Scientifically analyzing shoveling to find the best practice and copying it might work when moving pig iron. While using science to analyze work is an excellent idea, copying without context is not. In addition, though sharing good practices in context is a great idea, copying *best* practices contradicts continuous improvement.

> Centralized managers creating *unity* by planning, coordinating, commanding, and controlling might work when optimizing mining. And creating unity or vision in an organization is an excellent idea. But centralizing planning and control is not. The focus on command and control results in less focus on systematic improvements.

Examine your organizational structure, practices, and policies. How many are there because "that's the way it has always been"? Where did these ideas come from? Are they really relevant for your organizational context today?

Guide: Theory Y Management

Consider 1960. This was when the laser and the birth control pill were invented—one year before the Berlin wall was built and two years before the first Bond movie. Over twenty Bond movies later, a lot has changed! Or has it?

In 1960, Douglas McGregor of MIT Sloan School of Management published his landmark management book, *The Human Side of Enterprise*. It examines why the full potential of humans in organizations isn't utilized. And concludes that most "modern day" (1960!) management theories and practices are based on a set of underlying *unexamined assumptions* he called Theory X. These assumptions of human social behavior are limiting management practices, models, and behavior that truly utilize the human potential.

Theory X

Theory X management is based on these assumptions:

> People inherently dislike work and try to avoid it.

> Thus, people need to be coerced, controlled, directed, or even threatened so that maximum effort can be extracted from them.

> People want to be directed as they have little ambition and avoid taking responsibility.

These are rarely stated as simply and directly, yet they form the hidden assumptions under many—if not most—management practices... still today!

Human Resource groups espouse striving for engaged employees. Yet, ironically, most HR practices such as performance reviews, individual targets, and bonus systems have strong Theory X assumptions. But we shouldn't be surprised! What are the assumptions behind the very term *Human Resources* anyway?

Theory Y

To maximize the human potential, we need to replace—in our minds and management practices—Theory X with assumptions based on research conclusions of social sciences. Theory Y assumptions:

> People spend effort to work as *naturally* as they do to play and rest.

> People will use self-direction and self-control for goals that they are committed to.[6] Commitment comes mostly from the intrinsic rewards related to the achievement itself. That is: the challenge, the learning, and the sense of purpose.

---

6. "People commit to" (Theory Y) is not "the commitment was made for them" (Theory X)

> Provided the right environment, people seek responsibility rather than avoid it. Imagination, ingenuity, and creativity are skills all people have.

"Why is it every time I ask for a pair of hands, they come with a brain attached?" is a quote attributed to Henry Ford. Ford was influenced by scientific management and Theory X.

"Good thinking, good products" is a sign on the wall of a Toyota factory where they say TPS doesn't mean Toyota Production System, but it means *Thinking People System*. Toyota formed the base for Lean Manufacturing and was influenced by Theory Y.

LeSS, Scrum, and all Agile development is based on Theory Y.

Why is this relevant? Two reasons:

1. **Theory X *practices* cause problems in LeSS adoption**.
   Most organizations are packed with Theory X practices that focus on individual accountability and manager-control. In a LeSS organization that must change to team accountability and self-control.

2. **Theory X *assumptions* are hard to change**.
   LeSS requires a change in management style—a change in manager behavior and assumptions. Changing these assumptions requires reinterpreting *all* previous experiences—not just work experience. Cultural and family assumptions about how work works are especially deeply rooted and hard to change.

> Many problems in LeSS adoptions can be classified as attempting to apply Theory Y management *practices* with Theory X management *assumptions*.

Oh, today is performance review time! A lot has changed since 1960?

Guide: Managers Are Optional

Guide: Job Safety
but not Role Safety,
p. 66

In LeSS, managers are optional. Organizations that have managers don't have to get rid of them—they can perform a useful role—but you don't *add* managers for your LeSS adoption.

Guide: Manage-
ment Reading List,
p. 131

An important trend in the world is *manager-less companies*. These companies debug the assumptions behind management—what problems does it solve?—and discover different ways of splitting responsibilities[7] and distributing power. Such experiments are great sources of ideas, innovation, and inspiration even when your company still has managers.

Most large organizations have no shortage of manager roles and positions. Challenge these roles when adopting LeSS. In a LeSS organization, the preference is to move responsibility to teams instead of assigning them to manager roles.

Why are many companies stuffed with managers? Because of the default organizational problem-solving technique they adopted:

1. Discover a problem—the blah-blah problem.

2. Create new role—the blah-blah manager.

3. Assign problem to new role.

Blah-blah managers abound in most organizations! Examples: fault managers (we have bugs), release managers (problems releasing), feature managers (problems coordinating), quality managers (problems with quality), etc. The leading organizations have blah-blah departments headed by blah-blah manager managers who guide their blah-blah managers and the blah-blah specialists through their blah-blah career path.

This shouldn't occur in LeSS organizations because of:

> **Systems thinking**—Many blah-blah problems are systemic (e.g. as component team dynamics) and assigning them to a role without changing the system is a simplistic quick-fix. True understanding

---

7. These and related ideas include holacracy, sociocracy, beyond budgeting, #nomanagers and unboss.

of systems dynamics allows for systems changes tackling the causes without additional roles.

> **Team-based organizations**—Some problems can indeed be solved by creating a new role and assigning the problem to them (e.g. coordination with 3rd party). For those problems the preference is to give them to normal feature teams, rather than creating additional roles. Doing this leads to (1) people involved in work making the improvements, (2) improvements based on reality, (3) simpler organizations, no additional roles.

All that said, managers can be of service. But what will their responsibility be in a LeSS organization? The following guides explore this.

Guide: The LeSS Organization

Lean Thinking emphasizes a focus on *gemba*—Japanese term for the real place of work, or the place where customer value is created. We distinguish two gembas:

> the place the product is used—the gemba of value consumption

> the place the product is created—the gemba of value creation

In a LeSS organization, these two gembas should be brought as close together as possible. Needs flow from users to teams and Product Owner. Value flows back from teams to users. Value delivery should flow through the organization without having to be pushed up a hierarchy.

Managers aren't involved with the decisions related to value delivery or product direction. So, what do they do? In a LeSS organization, they focus on the development system—on increasing the organizational-value delivery capability. *Their job is improvement!*

While they might facilitate improvements by coaching the teams and help people grow, they don't *do* the work improvement themselves as this leads straight back to Taylorism. We don't want drones following processes but instead we want to maximize human potential. Thus, managers focus on ensuring that the organization is improving. They do focus on development system improvements which often involves organizational structure, decisions, and policies. Figure 5.1 shows a LeSS organization.

Figure 5.1 a LeSS organization overview

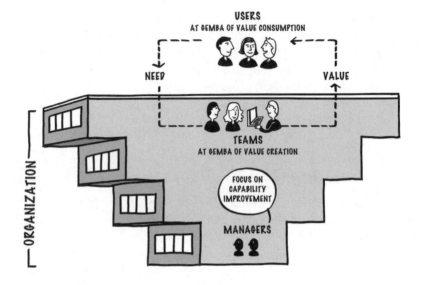

The different roles have a different focus. The three focus areas:

> product creation and delivery

> product vision and direction

> organizational capability improvement

It is a mistake to think that each role fits exactly in one area. There is overlap, indeed there *must* be overlap as the roles work together. Figure 5.2 maps the roles and responsibilities to the focus areas.

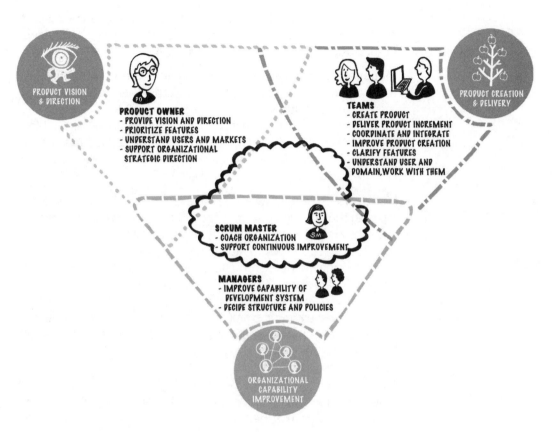

Figure 5.2 roles and responsibilities to three focus areas

Let's elaborate on the overlapping areas.

> **Teams–Product Owner**—The Product Owner determines the direction of the product (the vision) *and* teams need to be involved in that. The teams should *own* the product as much as does the Product Owner. It is *their* product and they work closely with users and must provide input for the Product Owner. Concretely, teams add items to Product Backlog and discuss prioritization with the Product Owner.

> **Teams–Managers**—Teams do improvements while managers focus on *improvement capability* and support with necessary organizational changes. Improvements often require change in organizational structure or policy and often can't be done by the teams themselves. Teams need to work with Scrum Masters and manag-

Guide: Go See, p. 125

ers to achieve these changes. For example, teams improve automated deployment whereas managers change the regulatory and organizational policies related to deployment.

> **Managers–Scrum Masters**—Both managers and Scrum Masters focus on improvement and should work together. Managers focus more on organizational things whereas Scrum Masters focus more on team and cross-team dynamics. For example, Scrum Masters discover and explain the need for expanding the cross-functionality of teams whereas managers do the related organizational change such as eliminating testing groups.

Guide: What Is Your Product?, p. 157

> **Managers–Product Owner**—*First-level* managers have little overlap with the Product Owner as they focus on *improvement*. Perhaps they might encourage the teams to add improvement ideas to the Product Backlog. *Senior* managers have a strategic perspective, covering multiple products. They should work closely with the Product Owners to determine the *right products* and work together with lower-level managers and Scrum Masters on the *right improvements*. For example, work together with all Product Owners on determining new markets to enter and organizational implications.

The preceding section mentions product focus versus organizational focus. Drawing the roles on this scale creates another perspective of the LeSS roles, as shown in Figure 5.3.

Figure 5.3 product and organizational focus of LeSS roles

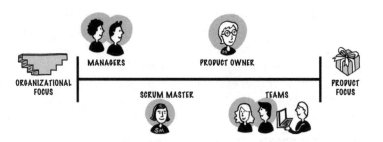

The figure visualizes the slightly different focus of managers and Scrum Masters: managers more organizational, Scrum Master more team and product.

The common question that comes up when observing the similarity between Scrum Master and managers is this: Should we make the managers Scrum Masters? No, not a good idea. Manager/Scrum Master organizational "manager" status impedes team self-management even when she is Scrum Master of a "different team." Why? Team members have deeply rooted assumptions about managers that will implicitly change their behavior. It is best avoided by having less management roles.

Finally, what does *focus on the capability of the development system* concretely mean? The upcoming guides cover these practices:

> Go See

> managers as teachers… and learners

> both domain and technical capabilities

Guide: Go See

Go See is the most important management skill for LeSS managers. The practice seems too simple—you just go to gemba—the real place of work—to see the reality. In practice, it is a difficult practice to understand and master.

Let's first explore what Go See is not. Go See is not micromanagement. Micromanagement can be described as "Go See, Interrupt and Disappear," and it is, at best, a demotivating practice for employees. Approaching Go See with a traditional control-management-mindset is likely to turn it into micromanagement. Be aware of that.

Go See as practiced by managers means they habitually[8] go to gemba to truly understand the real problems and use that understanding for developing the capability of the organization.

What is the gemba? For product development: two places:

> gemba of value creation—teams creating the product

---

8. Most of their time, not an exception.

> gemba of value consumption—users using the product

Both places must be visited regularly to get a sense of reality at gemba.

Go See has at least two important goals:

> better problem-solving capability
> better organizational decisions

Guide: Managers as Teachers and Learners, p. 128

Better problem-solving capability—By exploring gemba and under-standing the day-to-day work reality of the teams, you can truly under-stand the problems they face. Don't "solve" them! No matter how tempting that is. As a LeSS manager, you want *the teams* to solve the problems. If they don't, then your key role is teaching and facilitating the problem-solving with them. In other words, increasing their problem-solving capability.

Improved organizational decision making—Problems at gemba can be categorized as (1) context/team-specific problems, (2) problems caused by decisions outside of the teams. The latter are caused by orga-nizational structure, decisions, and policies; and they tend to be the same across all teams. Thus, a LeSS manager practices Go See to truly understand the work context of a few teams and to get feedback about important management decisions. This real place-of-work feedback causes better organizational decisions that are grounded in reality.

The more senior the manager, the more important this practice because (1) he is further removed from gemba and staying connected requires extra effort, and (2) the decisions he makes tend to have a higher impact. Without Go See, senior managers' decisions are likely to be dis-connected from the reality at the gembas, leading to disastrous deci-sions and the eventual collapse of the organization. Sounds familiar?

Go See is a difficult practice to adopt. Why?

No time—Many managers are apparently not in control of their time but are mostly reactive. Their calendars fill with meetings and they have a hard time finding the *decline* button. They're flooded with action points, since after all saying "yes" to everything got them there. Besides, what is more rewarding than putting out today's fire?

In contrast, practicing Go See would mean a deliberate effort to keep a large part of their time reserved for visiting gemba, ending the meetings and action-points dance.

No understanding—Going to gemba isn't for showing sympathy with the workers. Neither is it for checking up on the progress. No, it is for truly understanding the problems encountered at gemba. It is not just having a chat with a team or inviting them in a meeting—that just leads to superficial understanding. Go See requires observing the teams and asking lots of open-minded questions with a sincere interest in their work and problems. In software products, this is likely to involve watching and discussing code.

No patience—Many managers are excellent problem-solvers, so after they truly understand the problems at gemba, they can solve them. Don't! The teams need to improve by solving their own problems at gemba. They don't need a drive-by, problem-solving manager. What if the team can't solve a problem because the problem is external, organizational, and systemic? Then take action later.

No analysis—Once truly grasping the problems at gemba, ask: do these problems originate from team- and context-specific causes or from organizational and systemic causes? This is not easy to determine. Many managers attribute most problems to context as they don't recognize the patterns and… it is safe as contextual problems require no action from them. Others see everything as having organizational causes and end up making terrible decisions based on the feedback and context of only one team. Finding the true cause is hard.

Go See is a practice that requires practice… lots of it! It also requires an open mind and a natural curiosity for understanding—in detail—the creative work of creating products.

Guide: Managers as Teachers and Learners

There are two common manager styles that we consider a problem and frequently encounter:

> **Dummy manager**—These are managers who stopped learning as soon as they became a manager. They haven't read a single professional book, joined any course, or watched a non-funny movie. They spend all their work-time on administrative tasks such as reporting or performance appraisals. They've become useless automatable administrative drones.

> **Professional manager**—These are managers who didn't stop learning but who read only popular management books[9]. However, they've completely lost touch with the real work of creating products. And why would they keep in touch with the real work, since "as a professional manager you can manage anything, you don't have to understand it." This is such a profound delusion that we prefer dummy managers; at least they tend to be less harmful.

LeSS managers are life-long learners of *everything*. They keep in touch with the latest in domain and technology to ensure they can understand the reality of today and not just the reality of when they became managers. Obviously, this understanding is needed for Go See, but also...

LeSS managers practice the Lean Thinking practice of *managers as teachers*. This practice doesn't mean the managers must be the best technical and domain experts. Instead, they do have a good understanding of both the domain and current technical skills and use that to coach and teach the team in improving their development capability.

How can you, as manager, stay up-to-date? Ideas:

> fix a bug for the team every now and then

> use and test the product

> join code reviews, even when not commenting

> visit or observe users

---

9. We sometimes refer to them as airport books. You can explain so many organizational hypes by seeing which management books are popular at airports.

> refactor some code; perhaps throw it away

> browse latest domain magazine

> pair up with team members doing work

> automate something

> join a community

National culture—In some countries, the practice of managers as teachers is much harder and requires a lot more effort than in other countries. Some national cultures are naturally more engineering focused and have a tradition of knowledgeable managers, whereas others have managers rarely keeping in touch with technology as they've "passed that stage in their career."

Guide: Both Domain and Technical Capability

Teams need the right balance between technical skill and domain understanding. We often experience teams that have excellent technical skills but lack domain knowledge, or vice versa. This is even worse in organizations that have a history of "outsourcing the programming work."[10]

Organize by Customer Value in LeSS, p. 78

LeSS managers should regularly evaluate the skills of the teams in order to determine where to focus their capability-improvement efforts. A common mistake is to overvalue the skills the manager possesses himself and undervalue other skills. Don't fall into that trap.

LeSS Huge adoptions tend to have multiple development sites. In this case, it is common for development sites to have strength in one dimension but not the other. Evaluate sites from this perspective and take action accordingly.

---

10. Having both lived in Asia—Craig in India, Bas in China and Singapore—and based on our in-depth time at gemba and in the code, we consider the idea of "offshoring the programming work" truly misguided and have never seen it work. People we met who claimed it worked spend no time in gemba to *see* that reality.

What action? An imbalance is often caused by a lack of learning invest-ment in one dimension. This is typically due to under-appreciating that dimension. For example, one site we worked with had excellent domain knowledge, yet shockingly poor technical skills, as the culture at the site was that "anyone can program."

So, example actions:

Guide: Communi-ties, p. 295

> increase awareness of this imbalance, discuss with managers, Scrum Masters, and teams

> organize training and coaching

> create sharing between teams, share examples

> promote communities for learning

> encourage teams to select work that reduces the imbalance

> **Great products only get created by teams with balanced technical and domain knowledge working directly with users solving their real problems.**

Guide: LeSS Metrics with Less Targets

A common question from management involved in a LeSS adoption is "What should we measure?" It is a compelling, fascinating, and wrong question. Why? It assumes that metrics are inherently bad or good. Find the right metrics, set the right targets, and good things will happen. Untrue.

The metric itself is not important; much more important are (1) the *purpose* of the metric and (2) *who* sets it.

Our most-liked example is test coverage. Is that a good metric or a bad one? Absurd question. If test coverage is set by managers as an organi-zational target or, even worse, as an individual performance target, it is guaranteed to cause harmful behavior. Sure, we've seen extreme dupli-cation and sabotaged measurements, but our favorite is *tests without checks so they won't fail*. This is smart! It achieves maximum test coverage and lowers maintenance effort. Isn't employees achieving targets while minimizing effort the dream of management?

However, if *the teams* want to improve their test automation and measure test coverage to learn more, then excellent! Likely to result in insights, improvements, more engagement, and ownership. But it wasn't the metric that mattered.

Metrics are useful tools, but please avoid these mistakes:

> having targets without clarifying the purpose

> setting targets for teams

> measuring for control

> measuring something without knowing why

> creating waste for others in order to measure

In general:

Focus on purpose, not on targets.

**Targets without purpose is not
command & control management, it's dictatorship.**

Teach the people who use the metric to set their own metrics. That ensures proper understanding of the metric and its purpose, and eliminates wasteful work to fulfill an arbitrary target.

Guide: Management Reading List

LeSS managers need to continuously learn about their domain and technology. They also need to stay up-to-date on management ideas themselves. There is a lot to learn, and so we suggest books that we consider important:

> *Fifth Discipline*—Peter Senge
This is a true classic on creating learning organizations and on sys-

tems thinking. We consider this an absolute must for LeSS managers.

> *Lean Manager* and *Lead with Respect*—Michael and Freddy Balle
  Both these books are in business novel form and follow a student of lean management (Andy) who needs to make the jump from traditional management to lean management. Especially, *Lean Manager* has perhaps the best description of the practice of Go See.

> *Workplace Management*—Taiichi Ohno
  Taiichi Ohno is the original creator of the Toyota Production System, and his *Workplace Management* a classic in lean thinking and lean management. The way he approaches problems and focuses on Go See is extraordinary.

> *Future of Management*—Gary Hamel
  Do we need managers? Gary Hamel does think so, but the management style of the future is definitively going to change. *How* is explored in this classic.

> *Hard Facts, Dangerous Half-Truths & Total Nonsense: Profiting from Evidence Based Management*—Jeffrey Pfeffer and Robert Sutton
  That context-free best practices is a harmful illusion doesn't mean we can't learn new ideas from one another. Yet, too many ideas are just based on the latest management fad from airport books. Pfeffer and Sutton promote grounding management decisions in solid research-based evidence.

> *Reinventing Organizations*—Frederic Laloux
  Do we really need managers? Frederic Laloux explores current companies that abandoned traditional management. They are completely organized based on self-management principles— often completely removing the manager role. There is no need to take your organization that far, but the book explores possible ideas and structures of the future companies.

Contents

Scrum Master facilitating a large Open Space event in a LeSS adoption

SCRUM MASTERS

A good Scrum Master can handle multiple teams, a great Scrum Master just one.
—Michael James

ONE-TEAM SCRUM

The Scrum Master teaches Scrum to the organization and coaches them in their never-ending adoption. She has mastered Scrum theory and uses this deep Scrum understanding to guide *everybody* to discover how they can best contribute to creating the most valuable product.

The Scrum Master role is often misunderstood and performed poorly because people attempt to map this *new* role to an existing one. It doesn't map. It is not the master of the team, nor is it an "agile" project manager or a team lead.

The Scrum Master role is one of two "meta-feedback loops" to discover whether Scrum itself is working.[1] It is a supporting role helping the organization reflect and improve towards their organizational perfection vision. The Scrum Master creates the environment for people to succeed.

LeSS SCRUM MASTER

The Scrum Master role is a *new* one and often not understood when Scrum is being adopted. A frequent response is to make the "leftover people" the Scrum Masters. They might be nice people but often lack the right skills, motivation, and Scrum knowledge. They morph the role into something else and that becomes accepted within the organization as the role of Scrum Master—after all, the Scrum Master should know,

---

1. The other meta-feedback loop is the Retrospective.

right? Their actions are sometimes then against the Scrum adoption—transforming them into *anti-Scrum Masters*.

The role Scrum Master in LeSS is still called Scrum Master and not LeSS Master, for obvious reasons.

When scaling, principles related to Scrum Master include:

Systems thinking and whole-product focus—The bigger the group, the harder it is to see the whole. A Scrum Master helps people see beyond their perspective to see the system—the product group interactions, delays, causes, and potentials. She also reminds everyone of the whole-product focus—unintegrated individual team output won't create customer value.

Large-Scale Scrum is Scrum—A LeSS Scrum Master will encounter complex large-scale problems, and she'll need to resist resolving them with *complex large-scale* solutions. Instead, she'll need to return to the spirit of Scrum and find simple means that empower people to resolve their impediments. She needs to explore large-scale simple solutions by experimenting.

Transparency—Scrum Masters are guardians of transparency. But most large-scale product development has a persistent haze hovering over it. Clearing the haze—creating transparency—is a hard and thankless job in an organization's political jungle.

• LeSS Rules •

Scrum Masters are responsible for a well-working LeSS adoption. Their focus is on the Teams, Product Owner, organization, and development practices. A Scrum Master doesn't only focus on a team but also on the overall organizational system.

A Scrum Master is a dedicated full-time role.

One Scrum Master can serve 1–3 teams.

Guide: Scrum Master Focus

The *Scrum Master Checklist* by Michael James is an excellent Scrum Master tool. It identifies four areas of focus for a Scrum Master:

> Team

> Product Owner

> Organization

> Development practices

Those focus areas also expose a common Scrum Master problem: too much focus on the Team. An overemphasis on Team leads to shallow LeSS adoptions as the Scrum Master has a key educational and reflective role in LeSS adoption. The cause? One is that the Scrum Master is frequently a part-time role taken by a member of the Team. In LeSS, the Scrum Master is a full-time Scrum Master for 1–3 teams because she is vital for a good LeSS adoption and she needs to focus on *all* areas.

Rule: Scrum Master is a dedicated full-time role.

The four focus areas help us understand the Scrum Master role in LeSS, especially when we plot the typical Scrum Master focus over time, as shown in Figure 6.1.

Figure 6.1 Scrum Master focus over time

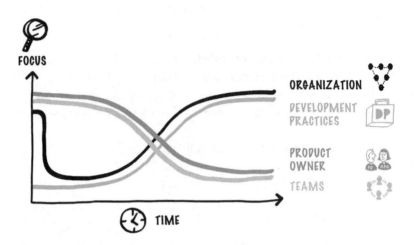

Let's examine this graph and the reasoning behind it.

Focus on the Organization

See *Organizing around Customer Value* chapter for more on structural changes

Adopting LeSS requires an initial structural change, thus initially organizational focus is high. The focus on improving the organization drops once the basic structure is in place. Then it's the teams' turn to produce results. That's the best way to change an organization: produce results. A shippable valuable product. Why would the organization trust you and your teams if you didn't show them results and benefits?

> Producing working shippable software produces credibility.

Here's an important dynamic: *Over time the dominant constraints move from inside the teams towards the organization.* The organizational structure and policies hold the teams back from increasing their performance. Then the Scrum Master's focus towards improving the organization increases.

> Improvement is continuous and the world won't stop changing, so the work of a Scrum Master is never "complete."

Focus on Teams

The initial focus of a Scrum Master towards the team(s) is high, but it should decline over time. When the teams are formed, the Scrum Master spends a lot of effort educating and coaching the team(s) in self-management, inter-team coordination, and increased shared responsibility. Over time, the team(s) rely less on their Scrum Master as they take on all responsibility by themselves.

The maturing of teams is one reason many Scrum adoptions opt for part-time Scrum Masters. But in LeSS, the Scrum Master isn't a part-time role. When the Scrum Master's first Team has matured, then she may take up another team—in fact, up to three. Being a Scrum Master for multiple teams automatically shifts focus to the bigger picture of the organization and the Product Owner.

Focus on the Product Owner

Initially, the Scrum Master focus towards the Product Owner is in coaching her in the role. This includes education on how she can best use the Product Backlog, facilitation of her interaction with the team(s), and being there to help her reflect.

A Product Owner has several relationships, including the ones shown in Figure 6.2.

see *Product Owner* chapter for more on the Product Owner relationships

Figure 6.2 Product
Owner relationships

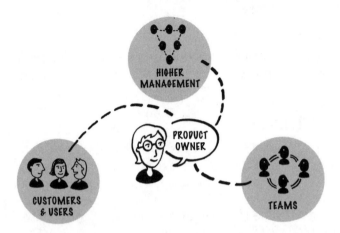

Don't focus only on the *Product Owner-Teams* relationship. The other Product Owner relationships also need the support of a Scrum Master. Let's explore these:

> **Product Owner–Customers**
The Scrum Master helps the Product Owner getting closer to real users and customers. The Product Owner needs feedback from them to validate the direction of the product. It also happens that the Product Owner is not a suitable Product Owner; then the Scrum Master should help the organization to find a better Product Owner who is close to users and customers.

> **Product Owner–Higher management**
The Scrum Master should help the Product Owner to work with the higher management to keep the status of the development visible, to support the Product Owner, and to work towards optimizing the impact of the product.

> **Product Owner–Teams**
The Scrum Master helps build up a relationship of trust, equality, and cooperation. This is hard work as historically this relationship is fraught with opacity, blame, and distrust.

The focus of the Scrum Master towards the Product Owner should decrease over time as the Product Owner becomes more comfortable with her role within the LeSS organization.

Focus on Development Practices

Initially, a Scrum Master is occupied with creating well-working teams that produce *something* together. But as the focus on the team(s) and Product Owner decreases, the Scrum Master increases her focus on helping the teams improve their development practices.

As a Scrum Master, be aware of what the top-notch modern development practices are and promote their introduction to the team. LeSS adoptions usually involve massive codebases with lots of archaic and messy legacy code; applying modern practices—such as test-driven development, continuous deployment, and automated acceptance test—on them is challenging. The focus on development practices stays high as it will only become harder and harder to improve teams further.

Guide: Five Scrum Master Tools

Before diving into more LeSS-specific guides, we included this guide on Scrum Master tools to clarify how Scrum Masters work. We like these five Scrum Master tools:

> **Question**
  As a Scrum Master, you act as a mirror to everyone to help them reflect and improve. One powerful way of achieving this is by asking lots of open-ended questions. But remember, be humble and remember that your job is not to provide the answer but to help people figure out the answer themselves.

Guide: Scrum Master Reading List, p. 149

> **Educate**
  As a master of Scrum, you have a deep understanding of Scrum and need to help the team understand why Scrum is the way it is. Education is one way of doing this. Warning! Avoid being overzealous as that turns people off and no learning will happen. Avoid zealotry, by focusing education on *why*, keeping an open mind, and careful active listening.

Guide: Scrum Master Reading List, p. 149

> ### Facilitate
> Show the teams how to do the LeSS events, and have productive conversations by facilitating them. Create transparency by making conflicts visible, and help the teams resolve them. But remember, you want the team to take most responsibilities themselves. If you still *have to* facilitate the Sprint Planning meeting in Sprint 10 then you are failing.

> ### Actively do nothing
> You need to create the space for people to take responsibility. How? *Don't take it yourself* is a good start. When your team or teams have a problem, first observe and see if they can resolve it themselves without your support. This creates the space to grow.

> ### Interrupt
> Teams need to learn by themselves but when things do get out of hand, then you interrupt to avoid irrevocable damage.

Some commonly practiced and promoted Scrum Master tools are explicitly not on this list. Why? Lets look at why they are best avoided.

Avoid being team representative—In LeSS, several activities require team representation and that is not you—the Scrum Master. Who is then the team representative? That's up to the Team, as long you aren't it. In LeSS, the Scrum Master is a full-time role and thus you aren't a member of the Team. Representing the Team would be strange at best.

Avoid making decisions for teams—The team makes their own decisions. Multiple teams together also make their own decisions. Don't make them for teams but *do* help facilitate their decision making.

Be careful giving suggestions—Your suggestions to the team(s) aren't always interpreted as suggestions. That's especially true for young teams who are looking for an authority to make decisions for them.

Be careful removing impediments—We've seen "removing impediments" used as an excuse for any behavior. Most day-to-day impediments need to be removed by the teams. The Scrum Master focus is on creating the environment for teams to succeed and as such you remove the *organizational cause* of impediments. This is much harder.

Guide: Large-Group Facilitation

Having productive, effective, and fun meetings isn't easy... especially when there are a lot of people. But meetings don't have to be boring. Facilitating large-group meetings is an essential skill that you'll need to acquire. Learn about techniques such as Open Space and World Cafe.

Some techniques we often use in facilitations:

Decentralize—Having all attention focused to one central point slows down meetings. Whenever possible, split into smaller groups and have parallel activities. But include "merging" too, for sharing and alignment.

Arrange for whiteboards and flip charts—Lots! Discussions are so much more productive when people are writing and drawing their thoughts.

Avoid furniture—Had boring meetings around a boardroom table? Just remove the table. This will change the dynamic instantly!

Avoid computers with projectors—Computers are one of the best ways to kill meeting dynamics. They centralize meetings, and the person controlling the computer becomes the bottleneck. If you must use a computer, then use more than one. Don't make them the central point.

Use volunteering—Avoid forcing people in discussion. List topics and decentralize with people volunteering to participate in the topics they are interested in.

> Use volunteering: See *Adoption* chapter

Have clear goals—Start with: Why we are here? What is our goal?

Retrospect—End with retrospection to improve future meetings.

Guide: Promote Learning & Multiple Skills

The essence of continuous improvement is continuous learning—especially for software products where there is no machine but just *people* producing. Unfortunately, many do not seem to consider learning new skills to be part of their job... or lives.

The lack of organizational learning is a major obstacle when adopting LeSS. As Scrum Master, you need to create an environment where people want to learn and move away from being a single-specialist to being a specialist in multiple areas.[2]

Some ideas to promote learning:

> Be the example; learn a new skill.

> Share the things you've learned with your team.

> Ensure that books are lying around.

> Remind your team that they were born skill-less, so they have proven that they *are* able to learn new skills.

> Share articles, not only related to Agile, Scrum, or LeSS.

> Encourage learning sessions, such as mini courses, lightning talks, or "book club" discussions.

> Remind teams they are empowered to plan *learning* in the Sprint.

> Propose to analyze existing skills during their Retrospective.

Guide: Community Work

Guide: Communities, p. 295

A community is a group of volunteers from the teams who share an interest or topic and have the passion to deepen their knowledge or take action through discussion and interaction with peers. Participation in communities is *completely voluntarily*.

Communities create informal networks between teams that are essential for learning, coordination, and continuous improvement. As Scrum Master, you need to perform *community work*—coach communities to be healthy and sustainable. Two communities in particular require active Scrum Master participation: the LeSS community and the Scrum Master community.

---

2. We aren't suggesting that everyone be a generalist and know everything. For more on the subject see the online article: *Specialization and Generalization in Teams*.

LeSS Community

Scrum Masters promote cross-team learning related to any subject including LeSS itself. As teams work within the same context, they are likely to encounter similar obstacles and can learn a lot from each other. The Scrum Masters together can create such a community. Some ideas:

LeSS discussion group—Have a product-group or even company-wide LeSS discussion group for discussion and sharing experiences.

Internal LeSS gatherings—Organize gatherings where people get together to share experiences. Use Open Space for organizing these, as its reliance on self-organization is well aligned to LeSS.

Guide: Open Space, p. 305

LeSS beer—Plan pub meetings with more beer.

Share stories on a blog, wiki, or newsletter—Write stories about your team(s) or convince your team(s) to contribute.

Observe other teams—Invite your team over to observe another team and discuss together how and why they work differently.

Scrum Master Community

Being a LeSS Scrum Master is frequently frustrating. But you are never alone! Reach out to the other Scrum Masters and build a community. Others can coach you in your role as Scrum Master. Some ideas:

Scrum Master-only mailing list—Similar to the LeSS mailing list, but make it elitist invitation-only. Ensure that people thoroughly understand LeSS so that the discussion goes beyond the basics.

Observe other Scrum Masters—Ask other Scrum Masters to observe you and ask to observe them. Follow this up with an open conversation about it, reflect, and come up with improvement ideas.

Pair up with another Scrum Master—Facilitate a meeting together, observe a team together, or pair-coach a team.

Study-group—Ask everyone to read the same chapter of a book and afterwards get together to discuss it. One chapter every week. Perhaps lunch?

Guide: Scrum Master Survival Guide

Organizations are dangerous places full with Dyslectic Zombies, Dummy Managers, Context-Switching Vampires, Undone Developers, and Anti-Scrum Masters. Don't Panic! Some tips to survive:

Convert Blame into Action

Blame is unfortunately a common response when something goes wrong. The more teams and sites, the worse this gets. Blaming is comfortable as it allows you to not take responsibility... after all, it is clearly caused by the other team!

As a Scrum Master, you should never join the blame game. Instead, help your team(s) to convert blame into constructive actions they can do. How do you do this? By asking these two questions:

> **>** What can we do to change X in our environment?

> **>** If nothing, then accept what can't be changed for now. What can we do to avoid or reduce X from impacting us?

For example:

Team: "We can't test as it requires admin access to the environment"
Scrum Master: "OK, so what *can we do* to get that access?"

Team: "We can't get the access due to organizational policy."
Scrum Master: "OK. So, what *can we do* to show the cost of this organization policy so it will be changed, or accepting no admin access; how *can we* best test without it?

Don't Be a Coordinator Between Teams

see Coordination & Integration chapter

Traditional organizations have a coordinator (project manager) who coordinates work between teams. In LeSS, the multi-team coordination is the responsibility of the teams.

Many teams are so used to having a coordinator that they will look for the Scrum Master to take on this role. Don't do it. Help your teams this way:

> Remind them that it is their responsibility, and why.

> Introduce teams to one another.

> Help them agree on a coordination mechanism.

But don't do the coordination yourself.

See Coordination & Integration chapter for more on coordination mechanisms

Team Up to Create Change

The organizational changes required to create the environment for your team(s) to succeed are likely to be hard... and similar for all teams. So work together with other Scrum Masters—together you're stronger.

How? Discuss the currently most impactful change and make a case for it. Gather all relevant information you can and make a proposal to (senior) managers. Don't expect them to accept it immediately but use it as a discussion starter, and remember... patience.

Partner with Managers

The responsibilities of managers and of Scrum Masters are similar. Both create the environment to build the best product. Scrum Masters work closer to the teams while managers are often tasked with additional organizational work. But to bring change they have to work together, as suggested in Figure 6-3.

Responsibility of Managers: See Management chapter

Figure 6.3 Product and organizational focus of different roles

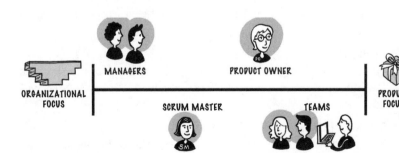

147

Start with regular weekly discussions to create a shared understanding of the current problems. Then pick the most important one, work on it, take the next most important, etc.

Sometimes partnering with managers is easy because the managers became Scrum Masters! But this often causes problems with team's self-management. Some organizations resolve this by making the manager of one team the Scrum Master of another. This works… sometimes. Yet, we don't recommend it. Why? Two reasons: (1) In some hierarchical environments the gap between managers and non-managers is so big that it is nearly impossible for the team to trust a Manager–Scrum Master, and (2) some managers are so occupied with "other organizational work" (the value of which we are never quite sure) that they can't serve as a full-time Scrum Master.

Staying Sane

As a LeSS Scrum Master, you need to change the organization… and you have no *official* authority to do so. This is a good thing. It requires you to convince people to change because they believe it is the right thing to do. But influencing change in organizations is far from trivial and frequently, no matter how hard you have tried, it changes in the opposite direction. The question then becomes, how do you survive? Staying alive and sane in organizations requires these attributes:

> **Patience and low expectations**
  Most organizations change slowly. You'd better set your expectations low (not your goal!) and remind yourself that you will be working on this for years. But *do* celebrate small changes.

> **Persistence**
  Don't expect your change suggestions to be adopted immediately but do expect to explain them a gazillion times (often to the same people).

> **Courage**
  Nothing will change without courage. Don't be afraid to speak up to higher management or make proposals that are way out of your comfort zone.

> **Sense of humor**
  You've worked for a year to convince people to change something.

They did… and they made it worse. What do you do? Take it seriously *and* don't take it seriously. Laugh. It is the only way to survive.

> **Openness and humility**
You must courageously, persistently, and patiently propose change. Laugh it off when stupid decisions ruin your work. And all of this must be done in an open and humble way as otherwise there is no new learning for you. Maybe you are wrong and they were right?

Did we mention *patience*?

Guide: Scrum Master Reading List

We'd expect a Scrum Master to be an expert in Scrum. But did she master Scrum? Mastering suggests that there is not much more to learn. But we have been involved with LeSS adoption for a long time and we still learn more about LeSS. Scrum Masters need to continuously improve themselves. Reading is one way and we recommend reading these books:

> *Leading Teams*—**Richard Hackman**
Hackman's *Leading Teams* summarizes 30+ years of team research and is perhaps the best book on building self-managing teams.

> *The Skilled Facilitator*—**Roger Schwarz**
There is a lot to facilitation and this book is an excellent text on improving your facilitation skills.

> *Co-active Coaching*—**Kimsey-House et al.**
There is a lot to be learned about coaching and this book is one of the better starting points.

> *The Five Dysfunctions of a Team*—**Patrick Lencioni**
Wonderful little fable about how teams work (or don't).

> *Humble Inquiry*—**Edgar Schein**
Schein has 50 years experience in organization development and coaching organizations. One of his conclusion from his experience: We need less telling and more asking.

Guide: Especially Pay Attention To...

Some areas are frequent pain areas that require special attention:

see *Product Owner* chapter.

> ### > Dysfunctional Product Owner—Teams relationship
> There is often a historical distrust between the Product Owner and the teams. The cause is a Product Owner's forcing commitments, a behavior that causes havoc in development.

> ### > Dysfunctional Teams—Product Owner relationship
> Actually producing "done" functionality at every Sprint seems difficult for many teams. One reason is that those teams are accustomed to worrying only about far-away deadlines and don't care about the Sprint. Product Owners make it worse by being "nice" to the team and "accepting" unfinished work, thereby causing even more negligence.

> ### > Us vs. them
> The emergence of opposing groups that point to one another without themselves taking action, makes everyone lose. Example: Teams vs. Product Owner, Teams vs. managers, one site vs. another site.

> ### > Adopting Scrum without change
> "We want to adopt LeSS but we don't want to change anything." As insane as this might sound, it's common. Organizations love playing the big *renaming game*. They attach new labels to old ideas, and tada! They've adopted LeSS. Great, what's next?

> ### > Scrum Master as team assistant or anti-Scrum Master
> Don't be a team-assistant who books meetings and arranges coffee. Neither be the anti-Scrum Master who was assigned this role but doesn't give a damn.

> ### > Remote Scrum Master
> Ensure that the Scrum Master is at the same site as her team(s). The Scrum Master needs to experience the actual work of the team(s) so that she can figure out how to help them and the organization.

> ### > Scrum Master as project manager
> This was already mentioned but seems worth repeating. A Scrum Master is **not** a project manager. Project managers manage the

project by scheduling work, tracking progress, coordinating and taking actions to get the project back on planned schedule. Scrum Masters **do not do any of that** and are **not** responsible for a project. They are **not** the contact point for the project **nor** for the team. Instead their focus is building great teams, creating a healthy organizational environment, and educating.

LeSS Huge

The Scrum Master role in LeSS Huge is essentially the same and so LeSS Huge doesn't add additional rules related to the Scrum Master.

Guide: Avoid Requirement Area Silos

The most common problem in LeSS Huge is this: No cooperation between Requirement Areas. The problem arises most frequently when the organizational structure, site organization, and Requirement Areas are mapped one-to-one. As Scrum Master, you need to help avoid this.

see *Organizing by Customer Value* chapter.

Tips:

> Pick one Scrum Master who helps the Product Owner Team and gives them improvement feedback.

Product Owner Team: See *Product Owner* chapter

> Have a Scrum Master for two teams, each belonging to different Requirement Areas.

> Organize the previously mentioned LeSS community events (such as internal gatherings) across Requirement Areas.

> Organize a multi-area Retrospective and/or Review spanning at least two areas.

LeSS Product

Contents

Two products or one?

PRODUCT

Any product that needs a manual to work is broken.
—Elon Musk

ONE-TEAM SCRUM

Early Scrum was confused.

Most early Scrum descriptions refer to Scrum as a framework for managing complex *projects*. Ken Schwaber, one of the creators of Scrum, wrote *Agile Project Management with Scrum*, which opened with "I offer you Scrum, a most perplexing and paradoxical process for managing complex projects." This feels strange as Scrum has always been about *products*, not projects. There is a Product Backlog and a Product Owner, not a project plan and neither a project manager.

Luckily, this confusion is resolved. The *Scrum Guide* now states, "Scrum is a framework for developing and sustaining complex products" and eliminated projects.[1] Does that matter? Hugely! As we'll touch upon in this chapter:

> **Managing work as products rather than projects changes structures, decisions, and behaviors in product development**

What is your product? The *Scrum Guide* is silent on what *product* means and what the scope of that *product* is. Perhaps because it's obvious? In large-scale development the definition of product is rarely obvious and one of the most important decisions you'll make.

see *Adoption* Guide
Getting Started

---

1. Except noting that each Sprint is like a mini-project.

LeSS Product

Why is the definition of product important? It will define the level and size of the Product Backlog, determine who are your end-customers, and who is a suitable Product Owner.

It also makes LeSS Huge more common than people would expect. A broader product definition often has more teams working on that product which leads to LeSS adoptions becoming LeSS Huge.

When scaling, principles related to product definition include:

Whole-product focus—Obviously, different product definitions lead to different focus. What product definition can lead to a broad perspective while still be meaningful enough to deserve focus?

Systems thinking & Continuous improvement towards perfection— Different product definitions lead to a broader or narrower perspective. Assuming broader product definitions are advantageous, what system dynamics does it cause? If the product definition is flexible, can it aid in continuous improvement?

Customer-centric—Whatever product definition is chosen, it must stay customer-centric. Will broadening the product definition be more or less customer-centric? From this perspective, are there different directions of expanding the product definition that are better or worse?

More with LeSS—Broader product definitions lead to LeSS Huge being more common than initially expected. Does this just add complexity or will it lead to *more with LeSS*?

• LeSS Rules •

The definition of product should be as broad and end-user/customer centric as is practical. Over time, the definition of product might increase. Broader definitions are preferred.

Guide: What Is Your Product?

The *Product* Owner prioritizes the *Product* Backlog, and the Teams incrementally build the *product* while keeping a whole-*product* focus. But what is the product? Is the product the output of the teams? Or whatever your current department happens to build? Or is it a component? A framework? A platform? Does it matter?

It matters. The product definition determines the scope of your Product Backlog and who makes a good Product Owner. When adopting LeSS, it determines the amount of organizational change you can expect and who needs to be involved. The question "What is your product?" might sound simple, but it isn't. It is an essential *choice*.

You can *choose* to define your product *narrowly*. Suppose that a component developed by twenty teams is the "product." That leads to a non-customer-centric technical Product Owner and technical items on the Product Backlog. Is that bad? Yes. It can't be sold, it is not customer-centric, it doesn't deliver customer value, and it often leads to building technical cool stuff that isn't used or usable.

Alternatively, you can *choose* to define your product *broadly*. Broader definitions tend to be more customer-centric. Yet, when your product definition is too broad, it becomes impractical, as it may cover less friendly departments or even different companies. Also, it becomes increasingly hard to express a clear and compelling product vision.

So, what product definition to *choose*?

In LeSS, broader product definitions are preferred because they lead to:

> enabling more customer-centric and finer-grained prioritization—all in all, a better overview of the development and the product

> resolving dependencies using feature teams

> thinking together with the customer—more focusing on the real problem and impact than on the requested "requirements"

> avoiding duplicate functionality

> creating simpler organizations

Enabling customer-centric and better prioritization—Narrow product definitions lead to many separate small Product Backlogs. How can you prioritize across them? How do you know there is a mismatch in priority, as there is no overview? The result? At best, big-batch coarse-grained prioritization between backlogs rather than item level. But more commonly, political games to promote one's favorite team that is *hyper-productively continuously delivering low-value items.* In contrast, with a broad product definition all items are in the same backlog, thereby enabling fine-grained prioritization and increasing the overview in development and product.

Resolving dependencies—Narrow product definitions cause dependencies between *separate* products. Consider a *platform* product with a few "application products" built on top of it. The dependencies between them are managed by creating coordination roles who do lots of additional planning. These so-called products are, in fact, just components of a larger product, and the techniques to deal with dependencies are the same as used in component-team organizations. But we can resolve these dependencies differently. With a broader product definition those "dependencies" are within the same product. They can be resolved by giving a feature team the end-customer-centric feature that spans platform and application. This avoids additional roles and complexity.

Thinking with customers—A narrow product definition limits the possible solutions to real customer problems to the current product scope. For example, a customer requests the ability to export data in XML so that another "application product" can import that data. If the product definition were one of those applications—narrow—then it would be implemented as requested since the requirements (solutions) are limited to the product scope. But if the product definition were broader, it would increase the creative scope of the teams, who could explore better solutions to what the user is trying to achieve. In the case of data export, the teams might figure out a way to link the applications, thus eliminating the manual exporting and importing by the user.

Avoiding duplicate product functionality—A narrow product definition can lead to some similar products or product variants. These end up as separate departments who have or will have separate code repositories. When similar or the same product functionality is needed in multiple products, they end up with either (1) porting the functionality from the first product to the others, which tends to involve additional coordination and code clarification and rarely works well (2) re-implementing the same functionality for the different products, or (3) creating a new internal "component product" and moving the functionality there, with all the associated organizational complexity.

With a broader product definition, though, the product variants are managed as one, through one Product Backlog. This leads to one shared code repository and avoids the need to re-implement the same functionality multiple times. It also leads to simpler organizations.

Creating simpler organizations—A narrow product definition leads to additional organizational structures for the work and decisions *between* "products." For example, the *resolving dependencies* section mentioned *coordinator roles*. Another example of this additional structure is *project (or program) portfolio management*, which boils down to big-batch requirements prioritization. The work from the narrowly defined products must be somehow prioritized and funded. Traditionally, the solution is project portfolio management whereby big batches of requirements—projects or programs—are periodically prioritized and funded together. Notice that *the apparent need for this portfolio management is a consequence of complexity created by the narrow product definitions*!

In contrast, a broad product definition would cause all work to be in the same Product Backlog: leading to all prioritization going through the one Product Backlog. This eliminates the need for the now *obsolete* project portfolio management, leading to a simpler organization.[2]

> LeSS **de-scales** organizational complexity by broader product definitions, dissolving unnecessary complex organizational solutions and solving them in simpler ways.

Restraining Forces that Narrow a Product Definition

So broader product definitions are preferred. However, taking this to the extreme would lead to one Product Backlog for *The World*. What restrains the product definition? In short, commonality and structures.

Commonality—The items in the backlog must have some common reason for belonging to the same product. Three key commonalities restrain the product definition:

> **Vision**
> A common product vision motivates people and facilitates bounded creativity. A too-broad product definition would generalize the vision to "Do Stuff" and people would stop caring. So prefer all items to be towards a common meaningful vision.

> **Customers or markets**
> Multiple related smallish products might serve the same customers or markets. Having the product definition include all these smallish products eases prioritization and encourages teams to explore unserved customer problems. But a too-broad product definition containing all possible customers makes it impossible to figure out whose problems to focus on. So prefer all items to be for a clear and usually related set of customers.

> **Domain**
> Multiple products in the same domain often share a significant amount of similar functionality (or implementation) and require the same domain knowledge. Thus, broadening the product defini-

---

2. Company-level *product* portfolio management makes decisions about which markets the company wants to be in. That will probably remain in *very large* companies.

tion avoids duplicating functionality and allows for finer-grained prioritization. But, when the product definition was expanded to multiple domains—too broad—then no domain specialization would be allowed, causing the teams to forever learn new things without ever building anything. So all items should be in one or a few clear customer domains.

The questions about commonalities lead to both narrowing and broadening the product definition.

Existing structures—These also restrain how broad the product definition can be. The teams working from the backlog work within the same Sprint, coordinate and integrate their work together, and deliver one integrated product increment.[3] Organizational structures need to change when adopting LeSS, but sometimes existing structures prevent a broad product definition... for now. Two existing structures that might prevent a broad product definition are **companies** and **departments**:

> **Companies**

A part of the product might be built by another company. That can limit the product definition. Below are three common types of limiting multi-company structures:

> **Hired teams or outsourced development**—The teams in the other company work only on this product. Thus they should work from the same Product Backlog and in the same Sprint. Avoid letting this constrain your product definition for long. Also avoid giving the other company one component, as that leads to component-team structures with all its associated problems.

> **Customized components**—The other company customizes their generic product, which is a component in yours. They probably can't work from the same Product Backlog as they have multiple customers. At least try to have them continuously integrate their product and customizations to our codebase.

> **Generic components**—Either your company is creating a generic component that is part of a larger product, or your com-

---

3. The one integrated product increment can consist of multiple deliverables or even multiple sellable products. That's a big idea we don't expand on in this introduction.

pany is using a generic component made by another company. Either way, the teams building the component will never work from the same Product Backlog and in the same Sprint.

> **Departments**
LeSS adoption usually involves structural change. However, the existing departmental structures can influence the amount of change and restrain the product definition. For example, application A runs on platform X. Platform X is also built internally and has only a few applications built on top of it. If product A and platform X are organizationally close, they *should* merge when adopting LeSS. Neither A nor X is an individual product but both are part of a broader product definition. However, if the only common manager is the CEO five levels up the hierarchy, then merging them would require a CEO-level decision. That would be impractical and would prevent the LeSS adoption from starting. So, temporarily create or continue with narrow product definitions for A and X but try to expand those over time.

Guide: Expanding Product Definition, p. 168

The previous section mentions a key point: Product definitions can change over time. This is explored later in a separate guide.

Guide: Define Your Product

Deciding on your current product definition and the potential future expansion is an important adoption step. It is usually done with early continuous discussions or sometimes in a more focused workshop.

We approach it by first exploring the *expanding* forces and then the *restraining* ones. We take the following steps:

Step 1: Expand Product Definition as Broad as Possible

Take whatever you consider your current product and ask the following product definition-expanding questions:

> **What would the end customers answer if we ask them, "What is our product?"**
This question eliminates technical internal products and increases the customer focus.

> **Do we have components that are shared or functionality that is the same across our current products?**
> This question looks for product families that might be treated as one.

> **Our product is part of? What problem does the product solve for end-customers?**
> These questions explore larger products or systems that your product belongs to.

Step 2: Restrain the Product Definition as Practical

Explore the restraining forces by asking these questions:

> **What is the product vision? Who are the customers? What is the product's customer domain?**
> These questions explore the commonality that must exist within the product.

> **What development is within our company? How much structural change is practical?**
> These questions explore the structural boundaries of the product definition.

Step 3: Decide Initial Product Definition

Compare the broad product definition (outcome of step #1) with the practical product definition (outcome of step #2) and explore what is a good future product definition. What changes are needed to achieve that?

The output of these steps is the initial product definition and ideas for how to expand it in the future.

Examples of Product Definitions

Following are three examples of product definitions. NB! They are simplified as each could be a book in themselves.

Financial Trading

A financial trading group is often organized by financial product type (e.g. securities, derivatives) and further subdivided into a front office (deal making) and back office (processing). Each has its own business plus support development department.

A simplified trade-life cycle: pricing, capture, validation and enrichment, and settlement. For each step there is a component (or "application") such as the *Derivatives Pricing* component or the *Securities Settlement* component. There is arguably 50% or higher duplication of functionality between components across the product types.

The traditional structure is component teams, with the view that the *Securities Settlement* component is a *product*, and so forth. Is it? Let's apply the *expanding* and *restraining* questions:

> **What would end-customers say if we ask, "What is our product?"**
> Probably "complete trading solution" or "complete securities trading solution".

> **Do we have shared components or functionality that is the same across our current products?**
> Yes, such as *Reference Data* and *Market Data*, and some are potentially shared but currently separated with high (but hidden) levels of duplication, such as *Settlement*, *Trade Capture*, etc.

> **Our product is part of?**
> If it's claimed that *Securities Settlement* is the product, it's part of Securities Back Office, which is part of Securities Trading, which may be part of a larger Financial Trading. Taking that further, the Financial Trading product is part of the Financial Trading system that includes several such products and exchanges.

These expanding answers point to defining the product as one *that allows customers to trade*. It would span securities and derivatives, front to back, and potentially even more. What restrains this?—only focusing on the key questions:

> ### What development is within our company?
Our trading system development is all within our company, but the systems of the securities exchanges are outside. This definitively restrains the definition.

> ### How much structural change is practical?
Securities and *Derivatives* are in different profit and loss centers, and the front-end traders specialize in one financial product. The managing directors of these groups aren't very concerned about company-wide technology efficiency—unless pushed by the CEO. Thus, it isn't yet practical to broaden across the financial product types.

The front/back office technology subdivision encompasses components that no doubt should be within one broader product such as a broader front-to-back *Securities Trading* product. But the separate directors will fight hard to keep their fiefdoms, and no one higher in the organization is yet focused on or especially concerned about merging them. Merging the front and back office is currently politically impractical.

In conclusion, most of the restraining answers support one overall *Trading* product that does not include the external securities exchanges. But the last question—*How much structural change is practical?*—points to political restraints that narrow the products further. Therefore the realistic starting point of defining products might be *four products: (1) Securities Trading front office, (2) Securities Trading back office, (3) Derivatives Trading front office*, and *(4) Derivatives Trading back office*.

In the future, the likely next step is to merge Securities front and back office products into one *Securities Trading* product, and likewise for one *Derivatives Trading* product.

Telecom: Base Stations

A **base station** is the part of a telecom network that talks to your phone and connects it to the Internet. Usually, thousands of people are involved in developing a base station. Each generation of telecom network (2G-GSM, 3G-WCDMA, 4G-LTE, 5G) has a different variant of base station. These variants have different functionality running on different hardware. And within each generation, there might be sub-variants with different technology for different markets. For example, for LTE there are a TDD-LTE and a FDD-LTE sub-variant. A telecom group is often organized around these sub-variants.

One base station variant consists of some major components: *Platform, Application*, and several others. The Platform is shared across several variants and is traditionally a separate department from the Application.

At first, the definition of product seems trivial. But when it is explored with the expanding and restraining questions, it turns out to be far from trivial. We explore only some of the most important questions.

> **What would end-customers say if we ask "What is our product?"**
In that case, if we decide an end-customer is a telecom operator, such as AT&T, then they would say: one specific base-station variant such as a TD-LTE base station.

> **Do we have components shared or functionality that is the same across our current products?**
Yes. The functionality of the variants are similar and they share a common Platform component, suggesting that they are just one product.

> **What problem does the product solve for end-customers?**
A single base station by itself does not deliver any value or useful functionality without the support of the phone and other components in a telecom network. In fact, a base station is just a component in a larger network, which suggests the expanded product ought to be the entire telecom network.

The expanding questions lead to the entire telecom network as the product. That would be pretty funny to everyone in telecom, so let's use the restraining questions to explore *why*:

> **What development is within our company?**
A telecom network potentially involves elements from many vendors and thus would be impossible to treat as one product. But all variants of base stations are within one company, so it would make sense to define the product as *base station* (covering all variants).

> How much structural change is practical?

Different base station variants have their own departments and separate code repositories... that have a common origin but got split off along the way. Merging the departments would be, in the short run, politically hard to achieve, and merging the code repositories would be an enormous amount of work.

The Platform component that is shared between variants also has its own department and thus the organization will initially resist the inclusion of Platform within one variant. All this seriously restrains the product definition.

Conclusion? Unfortunately, the *initial* product definition must be one variant of the base station, albeit with an annoying external dependency on the Platform component, leading to internal component team dynamics. Over time, the product definition should include Platform and expand to cover more variants.

Online Banking

We keep this example short, but include it because of its important conclusion.

A banking group initially viewed online banking as their product. However, when exploring the expanding questions, they quickly realized that online banking by itself was not a product at all. Instead, it was one channel towards their real product—*core banking services*. After they exposed online banking for the component it really was, they realized it was the root cause of a lot of unnecessary complexity, such as synchronization between "products," program management, and project portfolio management.

Unfortunately, the restraining forces exposed the political difficulty of merging their group within the real product, and hence their initial product definition is still just *online banking*. In this case, however, it wasn't their product definition that should expand. Instead the *core banking services* product needs to extend to include online banking.

Guide: Expanding Product Definition

The previous guides determined that the product definition is a choice and explored how the restraining forces can cause the initial product definition to be less than perfect. This opens the door for using the product definition as a tool for continuous improvement.

See *Definition of Done* chapter

During the life of the product, the organization must constantly ask themselves, "What prevents us from expanding the product definition?" The answers provide actions for future organizational improvement. In this sense, the product definition plays a role similar to that of the Definition of Done, except that the product definition tends to be harder to expand, as the organizational impact tends to be bigger, involving, as it does, different departments with their own goals, P&L, and politics.

Guide: Product over Project or Program

With the popularity of project management, most companies seem to assume that all work must be organized around projects or programs. But what defines projects? A project has a clear start-date, a clear end-date that will be missed, and sort-of a fixed scope. Decisions, status tracking, and budgeting are based on the short-term project goal. The project ends with a release, and when a project is done, it's done.

Products are not like that!

Instead, products have a clear-ish start-date, an unclear end-date, and a clear purpose with an unclear and evolving scope. They will be around longer than you expect! One product has multiple releases that are just points in time in which the product is shipped to the customer. Examples of products include nearly all software development. Not only obvious products such as mass-market software or online service products, but also less obvious *internal* products such as trading systems. *Products outlive projects.*

People are so accustomed to projects that they forget to notice that the usage of many projects in companies is to build and extend products. But that's a mistake! Managing products as projects has severe disadvantages. These include: (1) decisions of long-term versus short-term trade-offs will be made based on the short-term, (2) frequent fantastical budget processes, (3) overhead of starting and stopping projects, and (4) temporary teams or even temporary employees.

Don't manage products using projects or programs!

LeSS prefers managing products *as products*. That means one Product Owner with one Product Backlog for the lifetime of the product. Advantages include (1) proper perspective on short-/long-term trade-offs, (2) financing based on the future value of the product rather than on specific features, (3) elimination of project and program structures and the associated overhead, and (4) stable long-term teams.

Much more can be said about the project/product distinction and its organizational impact. It probably deserves a book by itself.

LeSS Huge

The preference for broader product definitions leads to more LeSS Huge cases than most people would expect. In the cases where the earlier narrower product definitions were at least customer-centric, these smaller products might become Requirement Areas of a single larger product definition. For example, in the Financial Trading product mentioned earlier, the Requirements Areas would probably be Securities and Derivatives.

Contents

Product Owner Team prioritizing in LeSS Huge group

PRODUCT OWNER

Personally, I'm always ready to learn, although I do not always like being taught.
— Winston Churchill

ONE-TEAM SCRUM

One Product Owner is responsible for the vision of a great product for customers, and optimizing its impacts (ROI, ...). As Product Owner, you continuously evolve the Product Backlog, adding, removing, and re-prioritizing (re-ordering) items based on learning and adapting to changes. And you maintain transparency by keeping it visible to higher management, the Team, and customers. You work with the Team and customers to ensure that items are clear. You adaptively decide what items to offer each new Sprint, though only the Team decides how much to select. Only the Product Owner can give work to the Team. The Scrum Master coaches the Product Owner in her role and responsibilities.

PRODUCT OWNER IN LeSS

When scaling, these principles relate to the Product Owner:

Whole-product focus—It's easy in large-scale product development for sandboxes to be created where people play with *their part*. *One* Product Owner with one Product Backlog underpins whole-product focus.

Lean Thinking: Avoiding overburden—How to have one Product Owner with many teams while keeping the Product Owner's workload manageable? Many of the guides in this chapter address this, such as delegating most clarification work to the teams, and connecting teams directly with customers/users.

Large-Scale Scrum is Scrum; Systems Thinking—Real Scrum implies the end of the *contract game*, the traditional model where a fixed scope and date internal "contract" is first negotiated between business and development, and then development executes a project to deliver the contract. To be clear: Scrum is not a more efficient mechanism for delivering the internal contract; it is a paradigm shift to customer collaboration and adaption, shipping every Sprint, with someone from the business side with decision-making authority acting as Product Owner. In large-scale traditional development this contract game is *baked into* the organizational design, with a program-management office responsible for the internal contract and myriad related positions, policies, and processes. When LeSS is introduced into this environment, it is incorrectly viewed as something that fits into the current model rather than *replacing it*. And consequently the Product Owner role is incorrectly believed to be held by a program or project manager.

More with less—It's possible in LeSS to effectively scale the Product Owner role with just one person. Less roles, positions, and complexity.

• LeSS Rules •

> There is one Product Owner and one Product Backlog for the complete shippable product.
>
> The Product Owner shouldn't work alone on Product Backlog refinement; it is mostly done by the multiple Teams working directly with customers, users, and other stakeholders.
>
> All prioritization (ordering) goes through the Product Owner, but clarification is as much as possible directly between the Teams and customer, users, and other stakeholders.

Guide: Who Should be Product Owner?

In a group adopting LeSS, where to find a Product Owner?

Step 1: Know Your Development Type

Where to find a Product Owner depends on the type of development. Figure 8.1 summarizes the major cases.

Product development—For external customers or a market.

Internal (product) development—For one or more groups within the company. The development group is called *IT*, *Technology*, or *Systems Development*.

Project development—Usually for one external customer. The work is organized and contracted as a project of some kind, though that does not necessarily mean a fixed scope/date/cost project contract. The development company is usually an outsourcer or systems integrator. Within the client company are both the paying customer and the users, who are not always in the same department.

see also
agilecontracts.com

Step 2: Find a Product Owner

Product development—The company will have either (1) a business unit driving the product initiative (e.g. *Retail Banking*) or (2) a *Product Management* department. Traditional Product Management is responsible for customer and competitor analysis, product vision, coarse-grained feature selection and prioritization, product roadmap, and more. They don't manage the work of a traditional development group, which is instead handled by the Development management who (apparently) take responsibility for meeting the internal big-batch scope-and-date "commitment", coordinating between teams, and more.

Where to find a Product Owner for a group adopting LeSS? If there's a Product Management department, then a *Product Manager* is a good choice. Otherwise, *a person in the business unit that's driving the initiative.*

Figure 8.1 types of
development & PO
location

PRODUCT DEVELOPMENT

INTERNAL (PRODUCT) DEVELOPMENT

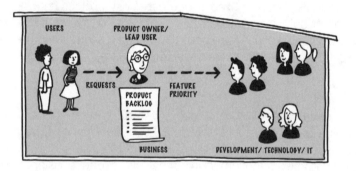

PROJECT DEVELOPMENT

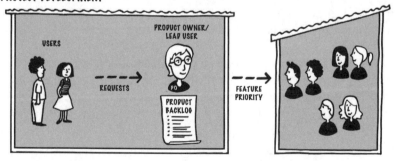

Internal (product) development—A good Product Owner in LeSS (1) is from within the group that will use the system, and (2) is closely involved in and deeply experienced in doing the real work that the system will support. They are very close to the real users. And once they become Product Owner, they need to have serious and independent decision-making authority about the product.

(Outsourced) project development—The key point is that a Product Owner is from the company receiving the system and, as with internal development, is involved in and deeply experienced in the hands-on work, close to users.

A common variant for both internal and project development is the case when the system will be used by *many* departments. Then, a good choice for Product Owner is an experienced hands-on candidate from one of the *major* user departments who is interested in taking on the role and is politically savvy.

Finally, in all cases, a great Product Owner *has a passion for the product,* political savvy, and charisma. No problem!

Step 3: Give Authority and Responsibility to the Product Owner

A Product Owner is not a new name for a traditional project or program manager who delivers a scope and date contract of work, or for a subject-matter expert. Rather, as Product Owner, you have the independent authority to make serious business decisions, to choose and change content, release dates, priorities, vision, etc. Of course you collaborate with stakeholders, but a real Product Owner has the final decision-making authority.

Multi-Site Tip: Close to Customers over Teams

It's more important—leaving aside the global mass-market case—for the Product Owner to be physically close to customers and users, rather than with teams. As a Product Owner, don't co-locate with the teams rather than with customers; you will become too inward focused and lose sight of paying customers and users.

An implication is that there will be *multi-site* meetings (Sprint Planning One, …) with remote teams. Such meetings *can* work relatively effectively with great video collaboration tools; we've seen it many times.

Guide: Start Early or Messy with a Temporary Fake Product Owner

Usually a LeSS adoption is driven from within the development group. Suppose the group decides, "Let's *first* find a great business-side Product Owner and then start the adoption." Potential problems:

> **A later start**—Business-side people who didn't initiate the change are busy, being asked to get involved in something *big*, don't comprehend any benefits, and don't know how to act as a Product Owner. So it will take time to find and prepare someone.

> **A messy start**—When the group starts their first (or second) Sprint, the results can range from a little messy all the way up to a train wreck. A mountain of problems may have been exposed. In the best case, a novice business-side Product Owner will understand what's going on, and have patience. But in the worst case she just sees a mess. Their conclusion? "LeSS is making everything worse, and I don't know why I should be involved at this early phase when nothing is done."

Therefore, an option in this context is to *quickly start a LeSS adoption with a temporary fake Product Owner* who understands what's going on, can perform the mechanics of the role but is not from the business side, doesn't have the specialized business knowledge, and doesn't have ROI responsibility. Complete a few Sprints until the major kinks are worked out, and—important!—the group can deliver a truly "done" shippable increment (or something close) every Sprint. Why? When development people go to the business group and invite them to participate with a real Product Owner, they can *show* a compelling new capability that offers very tangible business benefit. That's attractive!

It's terribly important that everyone understand that the temporary fake Product Owner is… a fake. And is replaced as soon as possible. It helps to literally use the name **Fake Product Owner**.

Guide: Who Are Those Users/Customers?

By *customers* we mean people who buy, acquire, or choose stuff or are deeply involved in the commercial decisions.

Users are a bit more complicated, especially in large-scale development where organizational silos have made it difficult for developers to know who the users are. By *users* we usually mean—though not always—the hands-on people using the product. These are not always the same as the paying customer or senior decision makers. Who and where are they? Or more specifically, who is the source of needs and requirements, and who should validate features and provide feedback?

Type	Sub-type	Who is the source of requirements?[a]	Who validates & gives feedback?
Product development	Innovation-centric, and/or strongly influenced by new technologies and/or standards-driven.	No real users or even proxies provide requirements. Rather, requirements come internally from product managers (including the Product Owner), team members, etc.	*Pseudo-users*: candidate users, internal volunteers, and users of prior related products.
Product development	Driven by customer requirements, and it's a mass market.	User proxies such as product managers, marketers, team members, and other customer- or market-facing experts. Use focus groups of candidate or existing users.	source
Product development	Driven by customer requirements, and there are only, say, 50 customers.	Hands-on users at multiple customers.	source
Internal development	Regular.	Internal hands-on users.	source
Internal development	Special change initiative, e.g. regulatory.	The source of the special change, such as a policy maker or regulator.	source
Project development		Hands-on users at the one paying customer.	source

a. This is an illustrative *introduction*; not meant to be thorough or in-depth.

In most of these cases, the LeSS goal is to dramatically increase direct collaboration between developers and the people who are the *true source* of requirements for clarifying requirements.[1] But it's a big shift in mindset and behavior that challenges status quo positions and processes. So the Product Owner needs to proactively ensure that the old structures are replaced and to act as a *connector* of developers and users.

Guide: Prioritization over Clarification

There are two key *information flows* in Scrum related to the Product Owner: (1) Adaptively deciding the **direction** to evolve the product and reflecting that decision in Product Backlog prioritization, and (2) Discovering and clarifying the **details** of user needs and items. In the first flow (direction and prioritization), information is sought and analyzed related to profit drivers, strategic customers, business risks, etc. In the second flow (details and clarification), the objective is to discover the fine-grained behavior and qualities of items, the user experience, etc.

Guide: Prioritization over Clarification, p. 178

As Product Owner, you focus on thinking hard about direction and prioritization, but delegate to the teams as much of the detailed discovery as possible. You encourage and help teams enter in a direct conversation with users, acting as a *connector*, not an intermediary. In short, you are mostly focusing on prioritization rather than detailed clarification, which is delegated to the teams.

Guide: Don't Do It

You might be wondering, "Wow, can *one* person acting as Product Owner effectively do the work for a product with six teams, lots of requirements, and a gazillion stakeholders?"

As a LeSS Product Owner, it's easy to get overloaded. You are the one steering the development to achieve the product vision and are involved with so much, including all of these:

> direction & prioritization—deciding where to evolve to next

---

1. Throughout, *user* preferably means truly hands-on people or variants.

> vision, evolution, and adopting technologies—taking a long-term view

> relationships and politics—keeping everyone happy (enough)

> judging & predicting—evaluating markets and competitors

Those are core responsibilities; the Product Owner should focus on them. But there are other time vampires that suck up time:

> clarification—discovering the details of what items mean

> administrative work—reporting and tracking metrics

> cross-department coordination—correlating manufacturing, sales, etc.

> learning about markets, technologies, and competitors

That stuff should be delegated, preferably to the teams. And the Product Owner should not be doing these tasks:

> managing dependencies or coordinating between teams

> predicting and planning the work of the teams

> challenging estimates

> more generally, carrying information between people

Guide: Product Owner Helpers

Building on the last guide: Share the Product Owner work. With whom?

Teams—First and foremost, use the teams. Erode the walls between development and product management work, and engage teams increasingly in the *business*. Not only does this share the work, it can increase engagement and seeing the whole. Did anyone consider asking a *team* to learn how to do a market study? Try it! Plan this simply by adding items ("market study", etc.) to the Product Backlog. And, as mentioned, delegate item clarification and meeting with users to the teams.

Product managers—If the Product Owner is part of a Product Management group, she can ask other product managers for help.

Step 2. Discover
Which Activities
Can Be Done Each
Sprint, p. 232

Release manager/coordinator—Large products can have myriad other-department tasks to actually ship, such as preparation for customer support, sales support, and manufacturing. In traditional big groups the coordination is handled by someone often called a release manager. If the LeSS adoption still has Undone Work that includes cross-department coordination tasks, don't have the Product Owner do it. *If it's small work, a regular team member should do it.* But if it's big work, such as shipping telecom equipment, it's probably a full-time role still for the existing release manager. At least, until there is a perfect Definition of Done. And, *a release manager serves and supports the Product Owner and the teams; not vice versa.*

The Product Owner
Team, p. 193

If a helper is so busy that it's a full-time job (such as a cross-department coordinator for telecom equipment release), then she is part of the "Product Owner Team." That said, the core meaning of "Product Owner Team" is a *LeSS Huge* framework term, meaning the Product Owner plus all Area Product Owners.

Caution! No analysts, specification writers, UI/UX designers, or architects in a "Product Owner Team." That would maintain the status quo problems and structures under a new label. Specialists join normal feature teams.

Guide: Five Relationships

A Product Owner needs to understand the five key relationships shown in Figure 8.2 that exist in large-scale development groups.

Many groups that adopt LeSS quickly grasp the Product Owner–Teams relationship, but don't appreciate the others as much, even though they are important for being a successful Product Owner. So the upcoming sections expand on them all.

Product Owner–Teams

Traditional groups: strong silos. We've worked with groups where the product or business managers (one of whom will be Product Owner) have never worked with (or even *seen*) developers. Then there's a lack of trust or understanding on both sides when both parties come together. Know that developers take pride and pleasure in creating features. They will go the extra mile when they have a sense of purpose, and they are directly connected with hands-on users.

From the Product Owner, the teams need to know the product and market vision, and what to create next. *To the Product Owner*, information needs to flow about what the teams require and how she can help them.

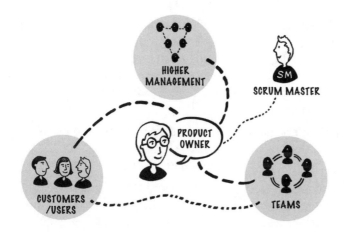

Figure 8.2 five relationships with the Product Owner

Tips:

> **Own it together**—Although one person has the title of *Product Owner*, in a great business the structures and culture encourage everyone to have an intrinsic sense of ownership and feel it's their product too. The Product Owner fosters that by seeking input from Teams during overall Product Backlog Refinement and Sprint Review and asking for help with more business-oriented tasks.

Guide: Overall PBR, p. 251

> **Peers, not peons**—If teams report to the Product Owner directly or indirectly in a hierarchical power relationship, that structure needs to change so that the teams and the Product Owner are peers collaborating. The Product Owner doesn't treat teams like peons for tasks, but fosters a collaborative relationship.

Guide: LeSS Organizational Structure, p. 97

> **Ask Teams for help**—Maybe the Product Owner is feeling over-burdened with tough product management tasks. There is a legion of smart people—the teams—and they will help if asked.

Guide: Theory Y Management, p. 117

> **Build trust**—A foundation of trust is transparency; demonstrate that in the Product Owner's behavior and Product Backlog. Explain the purpose of the work and the motivation behind priorities. And allow those to be challenged. Explain the pressures faced—without shifting those to the teams. Ask teams what help they need; that will create far more trust and goodwill than trying to push work onto teams.

LeSS Coordination & Integration, p. 285

> **Help, except when...**—Helping teams when asked solves problems and builds trust. But what if they are asking the Product Owner to do the *coordination* that is *their* responsibility in LeSS? (By the way, that's common with new teams). Then, with the help of the Scrum Masters, the Product Owner needs to decline and explain why.

> **Don't micromanage**—During the Sprint, the teams are self-managing towards their goals. The Product Owner doesn't track progress, assign tasks to people, and so on. But she may offer help.

> **Retrospect**—Don't treat the Overall Retrospective as an optional event for the Product Owner. Participate and learn from others how the relationship can improve.

> **Visit team sites**—Occasionally the Product Owner visits a site and participates in Sprint events with teams there. In addition to the effectiveness of in-person meetings, there are more chances to talk and increase knowledge and alignment. It can increase goodwill and trust—if the Product Owner doesn't micromanage. She'll have better insight into the situation of her teams, and vice versa. When she leaves and later does video meetings or messaging with remote teams, there'll be a better connection.

Product Owner–Customers/Users

Old groups: strong silos, weak feedback. We've worked with large groups where the new Product Owner had never previously met directly with users. Or if she had, rarely and not in repeating cycles seeking in-depth feedback. As the Product Owner in LeSS, encourage users to participate with the teams in learning cycles based on frequent shipping, transparency, and inspection.

From the Product Owner, customers and users need to know when and how they will be impacted (in a good way), and perhaps the reasoning behind priorities. Involve them, hide nothing, be transparent. *To the Product Owner*, learn with the customers/users what their real goals or problems are (or envision beyond their horizon), and information that will help the Product Owner to prioritize.

Tips:

> **Educate**—As Product Owner, you need to explain how and why the change to LeSS will benefit customers/users, and the changes they can participate in. This includes all new requests ultimately going to you rather than directly into development groups via their old requester networks. Ask the Scrum Masters for help in learning how to communicate this.

> **Participate, with *users* too**—Include paying customers and *hands-on users* in Sprint Reviews, in face-to-face Product Backlog Refinement sessions with teams and you, the Product Owner.

> **Ship at least every Sprint**—Deliver features of value every Sprint or even sooner (unless that's currently impossible or inappropriate). With teams, remove impediments that make it bothersome for customers to use a new product increment every Sprint.

> **Increase transparency**—For example, explain the Product Backlog and the prioritization reasoning. Notify customers quickly when a change will impact them.

Teams—Customers/Users

Traditional development teams in large groups rarely interact with paying customers and users. As a great Product Owner you want the teams to *care about* creating a great product for the customer. That requires empathy—and that requires direct connection. *From customers/users*, teams need the context and detailed knowledge related to features, without indirection and information scatter. Ideally, teams co-create solutions directly with customers by grasping their essential (rather than superficial) goals and problems.

To customers, teams need to confirm that they fully understand the problem or goal and the requirements they are clarifying together.

Even when coaching LeSS groups, we unfortunately notice the continuation of the old avoidance of teams and users directly interacting. Sometimes there's a fake "Product Owner Team" of analysts and UI/UX designers clarifying with the users, creating more handoff problems. Why is that? In addition to turf protection and fear by single-specialists to join real feature teams, sometimes the teams are uncomfortable doing clarification with customers because of prior silo mentality and lack of skill. Another reason is the belief "it is more efficient if one person writes the specification"—the local optimization perspective. And there can be fear of scope creep by open discussion between teams and users. Sometimes it's because the Product Owner has a background in writing specifications and is unused to delegating this work.

To maximize the benefits of LeSS, it's important to see through these avoidance behaviors and actively connect teams and users.

Tips:[2]

> **Be a connector**—As Product Owner, you encourage and arrange for customers/users to interact directly with teams in Product Backlog refinement, during Sprint Review (using/teaching features), usability studies, at-work "field studies"[3], installation visits, trainings, etc.

> **Share business activities**—You invite developers to participate in business-development visits, business analytics, marketing, etc.

> **Teach how to talk with customers**—Someone will say, "We can't let developers talk to customers; they'll say stupid things." It's a valid but fixable concern. You need to give, or ask for the creation and delivery of, a mini-course for developers: "Customer Communications 101."

> **Partner with the customer-relationship group**—Sometimes there's a group that believe it's their remit to "manage the cus-

---

2. These tips focus on how *the Product Owner* can foster a better Teams–customers relationship. For independent teams-with-customers tips, see the *Product Backlog Refinement* and *Coordination* chapters.

3. In Craig's first job, developing software in an insurance company in the 1970s, developers were required to spend time with hands-on users at their place of work, helping them with the work, to better understand their context and needs.

tomer relationship." Education and partnering with these to connect teams and customers is a good Plan A. If that's too slow, don't "wait for the org-chart to catch up." Ignore traditional boundaries, and as Product Owner, connect teams and customers.

> **Integrate the intermediaries**—Traditional business departments used intermediate business-analysis, UX, or change-management sub-groups that gathered and wrote requirements. These people *do* have a useful role: As full-time members within feature teams rather than intermediaries. Along with Scrum Masters and supporting managers, as Product Owner your job is to ensure that the organizational design for LeSS is changed to real feature teams, eliminating those departments and separate functions and creating a simpler organization.

Product Owner–Higher Management

We notice that in traditional groups it's common that no one person has real accountability and responsibility for product success or failure. Product Management handed over *The List* to Development one year ago. Development didn't make the too-big List, and Sales has made unrealistic promises, and... That kinda drives higher management nuts.

In LeSS, higher management beyond the product group (portfolio managers, C-level executives, ...) should clearly and unequivocally view the Product Owner as having the final accountability and responsibility. When the relationship with higher management is working, the Product Owner gets the support needed to focus on delivering a great product.

The Product Owner is responsible for making product development status visible to higher management and realizing their (perhaps implicit) mandate, to optimize desired impacts (ROI, market share, ...). The Product Owner, with support from the Scrum Masters, engages their help to improve the organizational design so the product group has a competitive advantage through business agility.

When higher management doesn't view the Product Owner as being accountable or responsible for product success, the Product Owner will have the following problems:

> Not given the organizational authority to make and execute hard product decisions

> Won't have much influence regarding resources: money, more or fewer teams, sites, etc.

Although these problems can exist in a *single-product* company, they're most common in a *multiple*-products company. Why? Suppose the enterprise has five product groups and *only one has adopted LeSS*. Then the products-portfolio group (executive management, etc.) has interacted with the four traditional groups since *forever*. They expect certain traditional metrics, milestones, and reports. But they're asked to interact differently—via the Product Owner, communicating *outcomes* and *adaptation*—for the LeSS group. Plus, the adoption was probably driven from within the LeSS group, rather than from higher management. *In essence, higher management are being asked to shift between two profoundly different sets of organizational principles... and they might not even realize that yet*! It's important for the Product Owner to grasp this dynamic if it applies and to actively mitigate against the wrong expectations and confusion it can and will cause.

Tips:

> **Self-evaluate**— People considering the role of Product Owner will be better candidates if they evaluate themselves. They (1) have a strong, established, and respected relationship with higher management, (2) are a keen and persistent advocate for the change, (3) are passionate about the product and customers, (4) have or will have serious decision-making authority, and (5) are eager to *take* ownership.

> **Educate others and market the role**—Product Owner is probably a new role in the company. Others won't understand it, and they never will unless the Product Owner markets herself and the benefits of this role. Teach higher managers; it's ideal if the Product Owner does this (to emphasize engagement), but help may be needed from Scrum Masters.

> **Communicate, "to the Product Owner"**—The Product Owner should be the default go-to person for product or status requests from higher management. She should communicate and reinforce that.

Product Owner–Scrum Masters

The other relationships are directly related to "product ownership" of the product. This one is different; it relates to Product Owner knowledge and behavior. If there's a skillful Product Owner who—along with the teams—is continually improving, the group stands a better chance to optimize the benefits from using LeSS. And it should be more enjoyable!

From the Product Owner, the Scrum Masters need to know concerns, questions, and obstacles, so they can help. And a good Scrum Master can be a friendly ear—or a shoulder to cry on. *To the Product Owner*, Scrum Masters educate and provide feedback, for learning. And they make requests, such as coaching for teams.

Tips:

> **Just a few**—A Product Owner works closely with only one or two Scrum Masters.

> **Be a student**—Product Owner learns concepts by participating in courses with the Scrum Masters, by reading what they advise, by doing pair work with them (e.g. to learn about and set up Product Backlog prioritization), by observing them act as facilitators at LeSS events, etc.

> **Reflect**—A Product Owner asks for feedback about behavior with the teams and others and asks them to reflect on situations.

Guide: Customer Collaborations over...

Continuous prioritization means updating "all the time" the priorities of existing and new items in the Product Backlog in order to optimize impacts resulting from learning. Ideally, ship at least every Sprint to deliver early value, to increase transparency, and to get feedback. The feedback will influence new priorities.

Continuous prioritization is often a dramatic change in mindset and behavior for people coming from a large traditional group to LeSS, because they previously played in the *Contract Game*, where it doesn't fit. And sometimes *it's still being played*.

The Contract Game

In a traditional (especially big) development group, one party—often a business unit or product management group—negotiates with the development group to deliver an internal fixed scope "contract"[4] by a particular date (and often for a particular cost). The contract is then handed over to the development group, who are told to "commit to it" and become responsible for delivering it.

In product development, the inherent complexity and variability make it a fantasy that the scope, details, or effort commitments estimates are certain. Thus, meeting the forced commitment becomes like a blame game played between the business or product management group and the development group. The game leads to a slow but inexorable degradation of product quality and organization capability. How come?

Briefly,[5] in order to meet the forced commitment—the internal contract—the game is played for an apparent short-term win. There are quick-fix reactions and shortcuts, which have relatively long-delayed and indirect impacts and debts. The people forcing the commitments rarely stay around for the second game, so will never experience the far-future consequences of these debts. Consequently, when the next Contract Game is played, things are even a little worse, and then starts the downward spiral. Eventually, the product joins the worst league and is retired to "legacy development in Yemen."

Adopting LeSS means giving up the illusion of a fixed scope, giving up the contract game, and using Sprint-by-Sprint information to direct the product development to deliver the most amount of value. That doesn't mean no long-term planning, but it means not confusing plans with reality. It means learning and responding to change, not just following a plan.

---

4. This contract is an *internal* agreement, not a commercial external contract.
5. It's a fascinating set of system dynamics, which we dissected in the "Product Management" and "Legacy Code" chapters in *Practices for Scaling Lean & Agile Development*, and "Systems Thinking" and "Organization" in *Scaling Lean & Agile Development: Thinking and Organizational Tools for Large-Scale Scrum*.

Guide: Ship at Least Every Sprint

Truly shipping to the market (or to internal users) every Sprint is a big mindset and behavior change for big groups. We understand there are cases where it's currently impossible to ship every Sprint, such as with complex hardware development. But, by and large, with pure software products it *is* possible. We also appreciate there are cases where it's not appropriate or possible to truly ship every Sprint, such as when waiting to make a big splash aligned with a marketing event.

But as far as possible, as Product Owner you should decide to ship every Sprint or even more frequently. Why? The reasons include (1) early delivery of value, (2) feedback about the effectiveness of the new features, to adapt better in future Sprints, (3) increased responsiveness to changing business needs, (4) deep improvements in the development group, because the frictions preventing frequent shipping become painfully obvious and require fixing, (5) improved internal motivation among the teams from the feeling of achievement and progress, and (6) increased trust among stakeholders, because of tangible results.

Another benefit, proportional to the organizational resistance to change (which is heightened in large groups), is that...

> **Shipping speaks louder than words.**

The powerful tangible impact of *shipping every Sprint* cuts through much of the argumentation about change in big groups, and quickly becomes the compelling case for delivering more with LeSS.

And once you can ship every Sprint, you can explore even more frequent or continuous delivery of features, towards a flow of value to customers.

Guide: Don't Be Nice

Suppose there's a newly formed LeSS group. It's not all new! People come trained with mediocre habits. Those were tolerated and not even visible in the old system because of long release cycles and silos.

So a new LeSS product group is rarely able to have "done" items at the end of the Sprint. It's understandable as it takes time for the teams to be teams and *to learn to learn*. It is even to be expected... yet it isn't OK.

As Product Owner you play a key role in setting expectations for teams. It will happen that the teams come to you and mention that a *set of items are only half done*. A skillful Product Owner might empathize... but doesn't "accept" it. Don't be nice. Instead make *very* clear that the items are **not done** and that you expect the teams to improve how they work so they deliver done items.

This does **not** mean to demand that all the originally planned items get done each Sprint. That demand just leads back to the dysfunctions of the Contract Game—reduced transparency, more padding to avoid punishment, and reduction in quality and learning. To manage the variability of development, it *is acceptable* for a team to de-scope an item from the Sprint and not even start it. Rather, this guide is about sloppy incomplete work on items that the team is capable of doing but that they leave half-done because of years of not being responsible for creating end-to-end features that are truly "done."

We frequently see "nice" Product Owners who accept not-done items that are due to mediocre practices and silo mindset. That acquiescence leads to teams that endlessly under-perform. As Product Owner you need to ensure the team knows they need to improve and expand the Definition of Done—not weaken it.

Guide: The LeSS
Organization, p. 121

Once that message is clear, it's critical for the organization to quickly and effectively provide the concrete help to improve. To do otherwise would really damage the motivation and trust of the teams.

Guide: Let Go

"Don't be nice" doesn't mean micromanaging. In an effective LeSS adoption there are self-managing, co-located feature teams that do all the work and coordinate with other teams. There is high transparency that comes from delivering (or failing to deliver) a complete product in a short cycle. So the habits of trying to control development during the Sprint can be let go.

Many teams aren't skilled at self-managing, but that weakness isn't solved by telling them what to do! They need *space* and time, and a skilled Scrum Master to help them grow.

Product Owner control in a LeSS group is lightweight and simple. For example, as Product Owner, act like this:

1. During the Sprint, don't inspect the teams or ask for status reports. Nor should any other managers. Let the teams be. Focus on your customers and preparing for future Sprints. Of course, if teams ask for help, then help.

2. At the Sprint Review, use the product and learn what happened. *Adaptively* decide a goal for the next Sprint.

3. At the Overall Retrospective, inspect and learn about the processes, environment, and behaviors that hindered or helped. With your group adaptively decide an improvement experiment.

If the control seems weak or ineffective, the usual countermeasures are shorter Sprints, increased transparency by a better Definition of Done, and more frequent shipments.

Guide: Don't Let Undone Work Be Your Undoing

In brief, the difference between the Definition of Done and Potentially Shippable is the **Undone Work**. It's especially common when LeSS is first adopted within a big traditional group. The quick version of this guide: Read the "Definition of Done" chapter, which explains Undone Work and its implications.

Step 2. Discover Which Activities Can Be Done Each Sprint, p. 232

As Product Owner you need to ensure that any Undone Work is clearly identified, to know how it's going to be handled, and with the teams, to strive to eliminate it. Why? Because Undone Work represents delay and risk.

The best way to cope with Undone Work is to *not have any* and to ship every Sprint.

Guide: LeSS Meetings

see the major *Sprint* section of the book for meeting details

When we introduce LeSS, a frequent question is, "How is one Product Owner going to manage all those meetings with all those teams?" Fortunately, that question is based on a misunderstanding. The one Product Owner in LeSS does not attend a different meeting with each team. For example, there is only one common Sprint Planning One meeting, with people from all the teams together.

What LeSS meetings does the Product Owner attend, and what is their *average actual* duration in a typical two-week Sprint?

1. Sprint Planning Part One: 1 hour
2. If doing overall Product Backlog refinement: 1 hour[6]
3. Sprint Review: 2 hours
4. Overall Retrospective: 1.5 hours

So the total time together in meetings is less than a new Product Owner might imagine: realistically, perhaps *six hours in a two-week Sprint*.

Guide: Just Talk, p. 287

Of course, when the Product Owner needs to talk with teams, don't wait for these meetings. Just walk and talk!

LeSS Huge

When huge scaling, principles related to Product Owner include these two:

Whole-product focus—There's a deluge of details across the Area Backlogs that can drown the Product Owner's ability to see an overview. And because Area Product Owners have a lot of freedom within their area—introducing new directions and details—it's hard to maintain an overview.

---

6. An optional though common meeting in LeSS. See "Guide: Product Backlog Refinement Types" on p. 249.

Customer-centric—Achieving a consistent user experience or complete end-to-end solution when a large requirement spans multiple areas requires more coordination.

The Product Owner Team

The overall Product Owner and Area Product Owners form the **Product Owner Team** in LeSS.

LeSS Huge, p. 101

> No analysts, specification writers, UI/UX designers, or architects in a "Product Owner Team." That would maintain the status quo problems and structures under a new label. Specialists join normal feature teams.

• LeSS Huge Rules •

> Each Requirement Area has one Area Product Owner.
>
> One (overall) Product Owner is responsible for product-wide direction and deciding which teams work in which Area. She works closely with Area Product Owners.
>
> Area Product Owners act as Product Owners towards their teams.

Guide: LeSS Huge Product Owner

The roles of Product Owner in LeSS Huge and in the smaller LeSS framework share some overlap, such as defining a vision and understanding competitors. But they are also quite different.

In the smaller LeSS framework, the Product Owner spends time selecting items for the upcoming Sprint, meeting with the teams in Sprint Planning One, and so on. But the LeSS Huge Product Owner doesn't do that—excluding special cases such as healthy Go See behavior. Her focus includes more coarse-grained and organizational tasks:

> identifying and prioritizing coarse-grained themes and gigantic requirements that span the product, such as "health" or "LTE with FDD support", but not necessarily diving into details[7]

> identifying business and technology trends that should lead to changes in Requirement Areas

> adding/removing and growing/shrinking Requirement Areas

> allocating teams to Requirement Areas

> finding, growing, and supporting Area Product Owners

> inspecting and adapting coarse-grained priority themes within each Requirement Area

> deciding site strategy with higher management

Guide: Five Relationships, p. 180

Besides the five major relationships in the smaller LeSS framework, a sixth is added in LeSS Huge: Product Owner and Area Product Owners.

Guide: Area Product Owners

see p. 173

Find Area Product Owners by the same criteria as in the prior guide for finding a Product Owner in the smaller LeSS framework. For example, in product development a *product manager* who is an expert on the Requirement Area is a good choice.

An Area Product Owner doesn't have identical authority as the overall Product Owner. The latter has the independent authority for product-wide direction, the decision when to ship, and the winding down and up of Requirement Areas.

But as far as possible the Product Owner should devolve responsibility and authority for the vision and prioritization within an area to its Area Product Owner.

---

7. We aren't recommending a disengaged Product Owner who isn't interested in or capable of details, but in huge products she can't get into minutiae.

Tiny areas leading to "wrong" Area Product Owners—A normal Requirement Area has 4+ teams, not less.[8] What happens to the APO role in a tiny area of one or two teams? It mutates into an item-clarification role, a kind of analyst or specification writer, rather than someone with a strategic and profit focus towards a major market area. And then the Product Owner is not collaborating with a few strategy-focused entrepreneurial APOs, but with a large number of business analysts or project managers re-badged as "Area Product Owners."

Agility and job safety—Requirement Areas should slowly, though perhaps more quickly than in a traditional group, come and go over time, reflecting changing large-scale opportunities. If the people (including the Area Product Owner) in a declining area fear for their jobs, there could be resistance and reduced transparency, impacting organizational agility. Naturally, that calls for a policy of job safety.

Temporary Fake Area Product Owner—Same advice as the LeSS see p. 176 framework guide for a *Temporary Fake Product Owner*: Finding a great *real* Area Product Owner (such as an expert Product Manager) may take time. So to avoid a delay for a new Requirement Area, start quickly with a pretender who can perform the motions but doesn't have the specialized business insight or responsibility. Replace that person as fast as possible.

Guide: PO Team Helped by Scrum Master

The Product Owner Team need to learn how to work together in the LeSS Huge framework. In commercial product development, they may already be Product Managers working in the same group and having norms for interacting, but LeSS is a new context for them. In internal development, it's less likely they've worked together. And they need to develop the habit of retrospectives and improving for themselves. Find a volunteer Scrum Master to help them. He or she should attend their Product Owner Team meetings, arrange and facilitate regular retrospectives, and give the PO Team feedback on how they are working.

---

8. A special case is when first growing what is strongly predicted to become an area of many teams. Adoption may start with one *leading team* that first clears the fog and then later coaches other incoming teams about the new area. See "Guide: Dynamics of Requirement Areas" on p. 105.

Contents

Product Backlog in LeSS 197

LeSS Huge 215

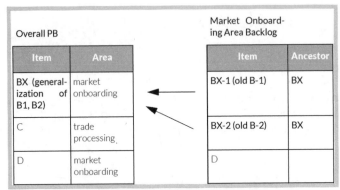

Overall PB			Market Onboard-ing Area Backlog	
Item	**Area**		**Item**	**Ancestor**
BX (general-ization of B1, B2)	market onboarding		BX-1 (old B-1)	BX
C	trade processing		BX-2 (old B-2)	BX
D	market onboarding		D	

unsplitting into the Product Backlog

PRODUCT BACKLOG

> How can you govern a country which has 246 varieties of cheese?
> —Charles de Gaulle

ONE-TEAM SCRUM

A single Product Backlog of ordered (prioritized) *items* is the repository of product requirements. The Product Owner is responsible for its content and order, and for making it visible to the Team and stakeholders. It's ever-changing; items are regularly added, removed, and reordered (to maximize ROI), based on learning each Sprint. Items near the top of the backlog are more refined and ready for implementation. Lower-order items are more coarse-grained and fuzzy. Through Product Backlog refinement each Sprint, items are split, clarified, and estimated.

The *Scrum Guide* includes a key scaling rule: there's only *one* shared Product Backlog when multiple teams are working on one product:

> *[They] often work together on the same product. One Product Backlog is used to describe the upcoming work on the product.*

When scaling Scrum there's no separate per-team backlog of items. Why? That would reduce overall transparency, reduce whole-product focus, increase complexity, and inhibit the agility of teams to shift focus.

PRODUCT BACKLOG IN LeSS

For guidance on first creating a new Product Backlog when adopting LeSS, see the *Adoption* chapter.

When scaling, these principles relate to the Product Backlog:

Large-Scale Scrum is Scrum—So there's only *one* Product Backlog, even when many teams working on one product.

Whole-product focus—A single common backlog increases focus and visibility on the overall product, and seeing and optimizing the whole.

Customer-centric—Traditional large-scale development decomposes work (and related teams) by technical, component, and single-function tasks. In LeSS, backlog items are focused on end-to-end customer goals.

• LeSS Rules •

> There is one Product Backlog (and one Product Owner) for the whole shippable product.

Guide: Don't "Manage Dependencies" but Minimize Constraints

the product defini-tion affects what is internal and what is external, see Prod-uct chapter

A good Product Backlog is simple and provides a great overview of the product development work. But Product Backlogs are often compli-cated because they are used as a tool for managing dependencies. That doesn't have to be.

In product development we distinguish between internal dependencies and external dependencies. Internal dependencies are between the teams within a product group, whereas external dependencies are either outside the product group or to nonfeature teams within the product group, such as in the undone department.

Eliminate internal dependencies

In LeSS, there is no need to manage internal dependencies. There's more on this subject in the *Organizing by Customer Value* and the *Coordination and Integration* chapters.

> There are no *internal* dependencies and no dependency management with feature teams that use shared code.
>
> Teams can benefit by working together on shared work but wouldn't depend on the output of the other team.

Why? Any feature team can work across the code base for their items. And teams manage their coordination between themselves, applying ideas such as continuous integration, communities, multi-team workshops, and sharing and swapping work.

LeSS Coordination & Integration, p. 285

It's not complicated, but it's a huge mindset shift for a group that previously had component teams with private code, and traditional dependency management, such as via an integration team or big planning events.

Don't manage external dependencies but minimize constraints

Suppose completing item-A is (apparently) dependent on a delivery *external* to the product group, typically for a data feed, service, interface change, hardware component, or library. That's common in large-scale development. A traditional way that a Product Owner handles this:

1. adds an external dependency to item-A in the backlog,
2. predictively plans some Sprint in the future when item-A can be done, synchronized with the delivery of the external thing, and
3. adds the planned Sprint in the Product Backlog.

Now, in big products this won't just apply to item-A, it'll apply to many items. Then there's predictive planning with synchronization points across a range of future Sprints. The planning is messy and time consuming. Plus the predictions fail, so you'll have wasted time planning and have to repeat, wasting even more time.

Don't do that! Rather than seeing dependencies as immutable milestones you must plan around, *re-frame them as constraints* that can be broken. Principles:

1. Don't let dependencies trick you into predictive planning. Don't try to "manage dependencies" with future synchronization points, which just leads to painful predictive planning.
2. View *dependencies as constraints* causing inflexibility and delay.
3. *Challenge, minimize, and remove constraints*, as much as possible.

Consider the word *dependency*: It suggests you are *powerless* as you depend on others. But "minimize or remove constraints" says action, options, empowerment as the constraint is within your control. This affects the contents and priorities of the Product Backlog.

Ideas to Remove Constraints

How to remove or minimize constraints? For example, suppose to do item-A our group is ostensibly dependent on external group-X to make an interface change in their product-X. First, re-frame that: *There's a constraint on getting item-A done*: the interface change. How can that be minimized or removed? A few ideas:

> **Do "their part"**—Maybe get an agreement with group-X to change the code in product-X, combined with some quality-assurance techniques such as a design workshop with them and/or daily code reviews. Or just write the code (without asking group-X) and then show them it's working and ask permission for them to include it, combined with some quality checks.

> **Pair-work "their part"**—Your people offer to join their people and help do it together.

> **Simplify or split item-A so that the other group's change is small**—Split item-A into smaller variants, such that only small easier interface changes in product-X are needed incrementally. This can also be viewed as *reducing the batch size* of external changes.

And combining *small batches* with *continuous integration across products* reduces constraints and increases feedback.

> **Split item-A into (1) item with a stub, and (2) fully integrate item**—Implement item with a stub (simplified simulation) of product-X. Once the interface is done in product-X, remove the stub.

> **Split item-A into (1) item using an alternative interface, and (2) item using the final interface**—Implement the item with an alternative (e.g. a manual) interface. Once the final interface is available, remove the alternative interface.

> **Explain the constraint**—Share with group-X the consequences, costs, and benefits, to influence their prioritization.

> **Bypass the constraint**—Perhaps redefine item-A to work with other existing interfaces, at least for now.

> **Achieve the outcome a different way**—Perhaps there's a different solution for realizing the goal.

Example Changes in the Product Backlog

The chosen idea will usually be reflected in the backlog. Two examples:

Splitting an item into simpler variants—For example, suppose a Financial Risk Management product uses data from a Trade Processing product. Suppose item-A in the Risk Management product requires 30 new data elements from Trade Processing and retrieving all those is a lot of work. Perhaps Item-A can be split into the following items, each still meaningful to users:

> item-A1 with 10 elements that are most important in risk analysis

> item-A2 with remaining data elements

Splitting item-A into (1) item with a stub, (2) item fully integrated—For example, Item-A splits into two new items in the backlog:

> item-A with stub

> item-A complete (or just "item-A")

"Item-A with stub" means that your group will use a (usually simple) software simulation or stub for the unfinished part of product-X, as though it were complete. "Item-A complete" implies the work in product-X is also done, the stub has been removed, and there's full integration across the two products, with still-valid tests that were written when the item with the stub was done.

Prioritization When Waiting on Another Group

In the undesirable case that "item-A complete" *must* wait for group-X to do work, predictive planning with synchronization points still isn't necessary. Rather:

1. Raise the priority of "item-A with stub" so that it gets done very soon and keep the priority of "item-A complete" lower. There's no need to predict in what Sprint this item must be done, though it's important that "item-A complete" be as small as possible so that it's easily achievable within a Sprint.

2. Add a "constraint info" column to the Product Backlog. For items that have a temporary constraint on another group, record noteworthy details such as *speculated* delivery date.

3. Educate group-X in the consequences, costs, and benefits, to influence their prioritization.

4. Later, when group-X signals that their part is done, simply adapt by raising the priority of "item-A complete" so that it's done in the next Sprint. That's what agility is for!

Guide: Take a Bite

Guide: Handling Gigantic Requirements, p. 224

In the large-scale world of giant requirements, even in many so-called scaled agile adoptions, it might take *months* before a requirement actually gets into the Product Backlog. Why? Well, *"the development teams won't be able to handle such a rough, big requirement."* Therefore multiple analysis, architecture, or system design groups consume months analyzing the giant and taking it apart, writing specifications, or doing feasibility studies.

The traditional mindset and behavior is to eagerly decompose and analyze much of the giant item before starting implementation. *"We can't start the implementation before we fully understand the requirement and its impact... what if we only discover something important later?"* But, unless you can time travel, you *will* discover things later!

And the cost of this early over-processing? Ironically, one cost is *delayed learning* precisely because of lots of early analysis and speculative design.

> **Why? Because diagrams don't crash and documents don't run.**

On top of that, the group now lives on work-in-progress mountain, piled high with hidden risks and defects, handoff wastes, and delayed delivery of benefits. Occasionally a boulder rolls off and kills someone.

Don't live like that. Don't have separate analysis, system design, and specification groups, and don't start analysis so early—but do start development so early.

How? In short, have one Team split the giant into a few chunks and then *take a bite* from one and chew it down to implementation. Split off a tiny item from a big item, clarify all its details in refinement and start!

Team PBR: Biting In, p. 31

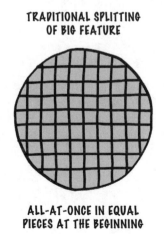 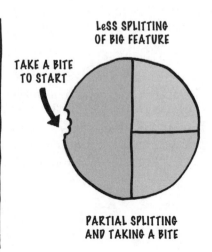

TRADITIONAL SPLITTING
OF BIG FEATURE

LeSS SPLITTING
OF BIG FEATURE

TAKE A BITE
TO START

ALL-AT-ONCE IN EQUAL
PIECES AT THE BEGINNING

PARTIAL SPLITTING
AND TAKING A BITE

Figure 9.1 take a bite, with a leading team

Why do this?

> Start early! The best way to finish implementing early is to start implementing early—take a small bite, learn, and adapt. The road to agility and flexibility is limiting WIP and increasing learning with stronger feedback loops.

> Involve the teams into the splitting and analysis of the big item since they will implement the bite; that increases learning and reduces handoff.

> The starting team carries through from beginning to end, reducing handoff and knowledge loss.

> Increase feedback and learning to discover how many bites and chews are optimally nutritious—maybe you don't need all bites to feel satisfied. And by fully implementing a small bite-sized piece discover what's the next-most tasty bite to take.

> Have you ever thought really hard about an idea, then you start doing it and you go "Oops, I hadn't thought about..." That moment needs to be earlier rather than later.

The habitual mindset is to "fully understand" a requirement before implementation. The irony is that *avoiding* early implementation *prevents* understanding. But it's a strong institutionalized habit—reinforced by having separate analysis groups that don't also implement. Break the habit with smaller and more frequent meals. "No analysis group" doesn't mean no analysis, it's just done by the same teams that implements items.

Guide: Dealing with Parents

Big items that have to be split smaller are common in large-scale development. When an item is split, what happens to the original—the parent or ancestor? For example, when *settle a trade* is split into *settle a buy* and *settle a sell*, what to do with *settle a trade*? There are two alternatives: remove or keep the ancestor. Let's look at the trade offs and applicability.

Remove the Ancestor

Removing the ancestor from the Product Backlog is like cell division (cytokinesis); the ancestor is replaced by the new items. Advantages? The first is simplicity: The backlog structure remains simple and no extra effort is required to link a parent with children. A second and subtler advantage:

> **The new items are naturally or obviously prioritized independently from each other and from their ancestor.**

What do we mean? In traditional large-scale development, *all* the sub-requirements of a big requirement have the same priority as the parent, and they travel as a single batch through the development processes. Problems? This leads to spending time and money on items of lower value along with higher-valued ones, delayed delivery of the smaller high-value items, delayed feedback, and delayed risk mitigation.

But for agility, *item independence* is important. Each new item should be independent from others and from its ancestor. Although the simple choice of removing the ancestor doesn't guarantee a shift to that mindset and behavior, it creates a backlog in which it is natural and obvious to order items independently. For example, suppose that before splitting "settle a trade," the Product Backlog order was

1. X
2. settle a trade
3. Y

After splitting and removing the ancestor, the order is defined by the Product Owner as

1. settle a buy
2. X
3. Y
4. settle a sell

Settle a buy and *settle a sell* can obviously be ordered independently. That supports early delivery of only the most valuable parts, and flexibility, and agility. This is great, but it's a big mindset change.

Any disadvantages with this approach? A loss of context and associations that might have been useful when refining items or when wanting to define a theme of related items for delivery.

In a small backlog or in a domain where people are intimately familiar with all the requirements, removing the ancestor is unlikely to cause a problem. Since it's a simple solution, prefer it for simple cases.

Keep Your Ancestor

When to keep ancestor information? When there's a big Product Backlog with a vast number of items, or lots of complexity, that makes it hard to remember (or discover) relationships between new sub-items and their ancestors. How might ancestor information be useful?

> for big-picture context, aiding comprehension or decisions

> as a source of inspiration for new sub-items

> to identify release themes

Guide: Area Back-
logs, p. 215

> in LeSS Huge, to help manage the Area Backlog as separate artifacts

Where to keep ancestor information? Add an "ancestor" column to the Product Backlog and put the information there. For example:

Order	Item	noteworthy direct/indirect ancestor?
1	settle a buy	settle a trade
2	X	
3	Y	
4	settle a sell	settle a trade

A few pointers:

> Avoid a deep hierarchy of many ancestor levels. See "Guide: Three Levels Max" on p. 222.

> Ancestor information is optional; use it when *noteworthy*.

> The recorded ancestor doesn't have to be the direct parent of a new sub-item, it can be a *distant* ancestor when an original gigantic item spawns a world of offspring. That's usually preferable because it's simpler and makes it easier to see the connection between distant descendants.

> Notice something subtle yet key in the example table: the left-to-right order is *item->ancestor*, not ancestor->item. That reflects the mindset and prioritization change of sub-item independence.

Guide: Handling Special Items

Besides customer features, other items can go in the Product Backlog, including defects, improvements, innovation, and special study.

Defect Items

The standard advice in Scrum is to record customer-reported defects as Product Backlog items. Excellent advice when there are 10 or fewer defects—as should be the case—and do that when applicable.

Big bug list—But when there are 714 defects, forget it, because all those defects will already be in a defect-tracking tool; if they were moved (itself a big and error-prone task) into the Product Backlog, they would swamp it with noise. This is typical in big products that have years of accumulated defects, and only then adopt LeSS. Therefore, when first creating a proper Product Backlog, if there are a gazillion bugs, keep using the defect-tracking tool *until the defect count is small enough to use just the Product Backlog*. And in that case, temporarily put a "defect count = N" item at the top of the Product Backlog to keep the problem visible, and *drive it down to zero quickly*. As soon as possible, record all specific defects in the Product Backlog, because *out of sight, out of mind*. Make defects visible so people see and respond.

Getting to zero—During the initial step, how to go from 714 to zero defects? Broadly, apply the lean thinking "stop and fix" principle and focus on the defects. Scrub the bug list and discard the noise. Dedicate one or more feature teams to killing them off, perhaps in rotating tours of duty. Perhaps hold a problem-solving workshop with the group and ask the developers to generate and try bug-killing experiments.

Urgent new defects—If defects are known at Sprint Planning, get them planned and fixed. What about urgent defects that come up during the Sprint and need fast response? One approach is to identify a regular feature team as the *fast-response team*, rotating this responsibility each Sprint. They absorb the interruption and variability so that the other teams remain focused. Another advantage—contrasted with interrupting whatever team "can solve it fastest"—is that they may learn about less-familiar areas.

Improvement Items for Teams

Many improvement items can and should be done by *teams*. These may be organizational improvements, but are often technical or environmental improvements. Improvement items that teams should do usually come from retrospectives (team or system level) or meetings of communities (Architecture, Test, ...).

Where to record improvement items that *teams* will do?

Big improvements in the Product Backlog—Especially if they're big investments, put them in the Product Backlog. This has several advantages: (1) the work for teams is visible and in one place, (2) the Product Owner can decide what big improvements to prioritize investing in, and (3) continuous improvement is handled in the normal work flow. Here's an important tip when recording them:

> Express big improvement items in terms of
> benefit to the business and Product Owner.

The teams want to rewrite a major component? What's the benefit?

Small improvements *not* there—Why? Because in a large group there will be so many from all the teams that adding them to the Product Backlog will *swamp it with noise*, making it harder to focus on its main purpose: customer features. And myriad tiny improvement items increase the effort of backlog management and prioritization. And that leads to *micromanagement of micro-improvements*, killing the spirit of self-management, trust, and continuous improvement.

Guide: Theory Y Management, p. 117

What to do instead? For example, agree on a policy that (1) only improvement items bigger than "X" are added to the Product Backlog, and (2) that each team can use "20%" of their time for small improvements (that are not in the Product Backlog) each Sprint. This simplifies things and fosters self-managing and trust.

Items for Innovation or Unusual Study

Consider these common cases in big product development:

> alternative chips or third-party software components

> innovation

> competitor analysis

> future technology analysis

These are typically big tasks with lots of variability. And the Product Owner and Teams need more information to make a decision or prioritize. How to handle this in LeSS?

> Add an innovation or study item to the Product Backlog.

> Bound the effort within the Sprint to prevent these open-ended activities from using up all the time (e.g. "max 50 person hours").

> Use a regular feature team, not a "research group."

> Use *Take a Bite* whenever possible, rather than long study.

> Focus study on information or recommendations for the Product Owner and Teams to help them make decisions.

> Share at Sprint Review, with next-step advice.

> When it's innovation, strive to quickly create some experimental product features and get feedback from *reality*.

This kind of unusual study or research is not regular analysis or design or architecture work. In contrast, beware *fake study*:

> Do NOT create fake "study" items for regular and
> repeating analysis or design activities such as business
> or UX analysis, UI design, or architecture analysis or design.

Beware!—Don't create a "special people" group given the charter to *go off and figure out that big problem. You'd be better off taking a big pile of money and lighting it on fire. At least you'd get some heat.*

Guide: Tools for Large Product Backlogs

"We're not agile. Analysts write use cases and scenarios in Word, record them in SharePoint, and tell teams where the information is, via an email."

"We're now agile! Product Owners write epics and stories, record them in the Rally backlog, and tell teams where the information is, via a notification."

Of course, it's a delusion that using new words and tools with new labels means that anything meaningful has changed.

> Tools aren't agile. Agility is an organizational behavior.

We've seen plenty of big and multi-site groups successfully manage simply with a (e.g. Google) spreadsheet for their Product Backlog, linked to a wiki for details. In fact, *groups are better off doing that.*

> What Product Backlog tool at scale?
> Use nothing more complicated than a spreadsheet and wiki.

Why? Because of the problems with using so-called "agile" tools:

> The focus is on tools rather than the deep systemic problems, and that diverts or avoids focusing on what's important: changing behavior and the system. These tools don't solve the real problems.

> These tools contain and promote *reporting* features, reinforcing traditional management-reporting and control behaviors.

> They convey a facade of improvement or agile adoption, when nothing meaningful has changed; "agile" tools have *nothing* to do with *being agile*.

> They often impose inflexible terminology and workflows to the teams, taking away process ownership and restricting improvement.

> The backlog is often hidden for most people as access requires an expensive account.

> These tools enable complexifying rather than simplifying.

It is, of course, possible to gain all these problems also with spreadsheets by *maximizing their complexity*. Try to avoid that.

Tracking Progress

Tracking *Within* a Sprint

Here are some prominent front-page marketing quotes copied verbatim from well-known "agile" management tools:

"Track team progress at a glance", "Get progress reports", "Report on your [projects]", "50+ prepackaged agile metrics and reports", ... ad nauseam

So-called agile-management tools focus on tracking and reporting functions that display individual and team tasks and Sprint Backlogs and "progress" *to managers*—the antithesis of the agile principles of *trusting people* and *self-managing teams*. As the team researcher, Richard Hackman, explains, "In self-managing teams, the responsibility of tracking the progress is delegated towards the team."

So management has no responsibility or reason for tracking team progress inside the Sprint. These tools are optimized for reporting—not for success, improvement, a better flow of value, or teams owning and improving their processes.

In Scrum the Product and Sprint Backlogs are *separate*, and they have different purposes. Whereas the Product Backlog is for managing customer-centric items, the Sprint Backlog is for a Team to manage themselves and their tasks during the Sprint. It's not for the Product Owner or for external tracking. The *Scrum Guide* puts it simply: *[The Sprint Backlog] belongs solely to the Development Team*. So each Team needs to choose their own Sprint Backlog tool and be able to change their choice. And different Teams may use different tools. Therefore:

> ### Don't use same tool for Product Backlog and Sprint Backlogs

Tip: Although any tool for the Sprint Backlog is possible, we consistently notice that teams that just use "cards on a wall" are *much* more likely *real* teams, working together and actively improving.

Tracking *Across* Sprints

Guide: Don't Be Nice, p. 189

Understanding overall progress of customer-centric items across the Sprints is useful. Do groups need a special "agile tool" for that? No.

Transparency and ease of tracking dramatically increases when the focus is on *done* items. At the end of every Sprint, mark items as done or not done. Don't track "almost done" or "90% done." Just track progress of done items in the Product Backlog. Simple tools will suffice.

If a *progress chart* is requested, first explore and challenge *why* it's being requested. Why aren't the interested parties at the Sprint Review? Is the so-called Product Owner just a program or project manager under a new label? If a chart is *really* desired, use the charting feature in the simple spreadsheet-like tool that records the Product Backlog.

Guide: More Outcome, less Output

We once worked with a large product group where a senior manager made an announcement: "In the last 12 months we've *spent* 1.3 million person hours on the product. Great job everyone!"

Ouch! "Progress" is being measured by the amount of activity and how many deliverables (e.g. done items) are pumped out. Even the popular *velocity* measure is for *effort of output* of features—and that's a problem. What problem? *All that activity and deliverables can have little or nothing to do with outcomes.* When someone asks for a "new workflow management tool with features A to Z", what are the *goals*? Will those features reduce median cycle time by 25%?

So what? Especially in large groups the focus is on *outputs rather than outcomes* because

> there's a seductive attraction to managing outputs since they're easier to measure;

> the traditional annual budget process demands a list of cost-estimated features (outputs, not outcomes); and

> the big Product Backlog becomes a dumping ground for hundreds of feature requests with no clear connection to outcomes.

One of the LeSS principles is *More with LeSS*. In this context, that means:

> **More outcome, less output.**

What are some techniques to shift the focus to outcomes?

Technique: Write Items as Outcomes or Goals, not Solutions

A large package-shipping service in Norway had complaints about usability at their website, and considered writing a new item like this:

Show all the shipping option details on one webpage.

This is a *solution-oriented* item that presumes a solution to the problem. It might not be a great solution, and the purpose isn't clear. Prefer outcome- or goal-oriented items, such as this:

Shippers can find all top-quartile shipping options in less than 1 second.

This outcome-oriented item invites more options and ideas, and enhances motivation because of the creative challenge for the team.

Technique: Do Impact Mapping

Impact mapping[1] is a collaborative, fast, and visual technique for a group to (1) identify an outcome (e.g. *reduce trade errors*), (2) define a measure of success, and (3) generate alternate ideas to impact the outcome.

Figure 9.2 impact mapping encourages a focus on an *outcome* rather than outputs, and alternate impacts that could achieve it

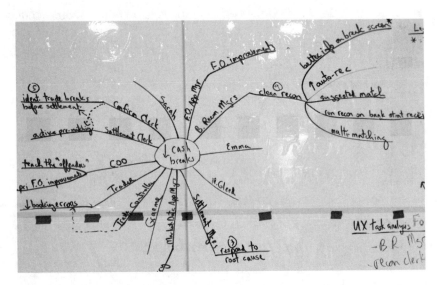

How does impact mapping help? (1) It fosters collaboration with a focus on *outcomes*, (2) it focuses on *multiple and alternate* impact ideas, and (3) it links impacts to outcome.

---

1. See *impactmapping.org* and the book *Impact Mapping*.

LeSS Huge

When huge, principles related to the Product Backlog include this one:

Whole-product focus; Transparency—When the Product Backlog is decomposed into Area Backlogs, how to keep a view on and focus on overall goals and priorities without drowning in details?

• LeSS Huge Rules •

There is one Product Backlog; every item in it belongs to exactly one Requirement Area.

There is one Area Product Backlog ("Area Backlog") per Requirement Area. This backlog is conceptually a more granular view into the one Product Backlog.

Guide: Area Backlogs

First, to review, a **Requirement Area** is a big grouping of items that logically belong together from the *customer perspective*.

Some key points:

Each Requirement Area is a grouping from customer perspective, not a grouping from technical perspective.

Requirement Areas are a scaling technique for huge groups. A Requirement Area is expected to be for 4+ teams.

Conceptually in the *one* Product Backlog, a "requirement area" attribute is added, and each item is classified into one and only one area:

Item	Requirement Area
B	market onboarding
C	trade processing
D	asset servicing
F	market onboarding
...	

An **Area Backlog** is conceptually a *view* into the one Product Backlog, for one Requirement Area, such as the *market onboarding* area:

Item	Requirement Area
B	market onboarding
F	market onboarding

see *Product Owner* chapter for more on the Product Owner and Area Product Owner role

For the Area Product Owner (APO) and teams dedicated to this area, their Area Backlog looks and functions like a regular Product Backlog. The highest priority in an Area Backlog might not be the highest priority in the Product Backlog. When this happens the Product Owner will determine whether the priority difference is large enough to warrant moving teams to other areas.

> **An Area Backlog is NOT for 1 or 2 teams;**
> **it is for a Requirement Area, which usually has 4+ teams.**

There are two ways to realize Area Backlogs: *views* or *separate artifacts*.

Area Backlogs via Filtered Views

The simplest way to realize Area Backlogs is with a filter on one Product Backlog, to create a view. With a spreadsheet it's easy as pie. When to use a view approach? When there are only a few (e.g. three) Requirement Areas[2] and not too much depth in split items. We know those are vague guidelines; the tipping point to moving to separate artifacts is situational, but you'll probably know it when you see it.

Start with this simple approach: filtered views.

Area-specific prioritization—Area Product Owners prioritize their Area Backlog more or less independently. So each area has a different first item, second item, and so forth. For example:

Item	Requirement Area
B	market onboarding
F	market onboarding
C	trade processing
M	trade processing
...	

first in area

Area Backlogs via Separate Artifacts

When there are lots of Requirement Areas[3] and myriad split items, the simple view approach will start to hurt. The one Product Backlog will feel overwhelmingly large and detailed, filled with myriad fine-grained items from all the areas as splitting happens.

Then an alternative is to have separate artifacts (e.g. separate spreadsheets) for the Area Backlogs and for the overall Product Backlog. As will be explained, this approach has some drawbacks different from those of the simple filtered-view approach.

---

2. Also called a **less huge LeSS Huge** product group;)
3. Also called **huge LeSS Huge**!

Area-Specific Splitting

Suppose backlogs start out as shown in Table 9.1. Now suppose that in Market Onboarding, B is split into B-1 and B-2, as shown in Table 9.2. In the *separate-artifact* approach the *overall Product Backlog* remains unchanged. But the *Market Onboarding Area Backlog* does change.

Table 9.1 Area Backlog before split

Overall PB

Item	Area
B	market onboarding
C	trade processing
F	market onboarding

Market Onboarding Area Backlog

Item	Ancestor
B	
F	

Table 9.2 Area Backlog after B is split; Product Backlog unchanged

Overall PB

Item	Area
B	market onboarding
C	trade processing
F	market onboarding

Market Onboarding Area Backlog

Item	Ancestor
B-1	B
B-2	B
F	

Area-Specific Prioritization

Having separate artifacts allows the Product Owner to work on a higher level of granularity than do the Area Product Owners but also causes less transparency for the Product Owner. That's because the priority in the Area Backlog is the decision of the APO, and the priority of the split items need not follow priorities in the overall Product Backlog. In this next example, parts of B are a higher priority than D and parts of B are a lower priority than D:

Overall PB

Item	Area
B	market onboarding
C	trade processing
D	market onboarding

Market Onboarding Area Backlog

Item	Ancestor
B-1	B
D	
B-2	B

Usually the priority difference isn't big and then this is not really a problem... but sometimes it is. For example, this is a problem:

Overall PB

Item	Area
B	market onboarding
C	trade processing
D	market onboarding

Market Onboarding Area Backlog

Item	Ancestor
B-1	B
B-2	B
D	

**Overall
PB**

Item	Area
E	market onboarding
F	market onboarding
...	

**Market Onboard-
ing Area Backlog**

Item	Ancestor
E	
F	
B-3	B
B-4	B

In this scenario parts of B are high priority (B-1 and B-2), whereas other parts of B aren't (B-3 and B-4). That case is reflected in the Area Backlog but is invisible to the Product Owner. And *that* causes misunderstanding and subsequent problems; for example the Product Owner might conclude that B isn't done until all items of B are done, though that doesn't reflect the priorities of the Area Product Owner.

To correctly reflect a *big* difference in priority—small ones can be ignored as they won't create meaningful problems—the APO needs to *unsplit* items back into the overall Product Backlog. *Unsplit* means to create a new generalized bigger item from a set of smaller ones. For example, see Table 9.3.

In that way a major priority difference is correctly reflected in the overall Product Backlog. And because items B1 and B2 were generalized as one item BX, the overall Product Owner doesn't drown in detail.

Overall PB	
Item	**Area**
BX (general-ization of B1, B2)	market onboarding
C	trade processing
D	market onboarding
E	market onboarding
F	market onboarding
BY (general-ization of B3, B4)	market onboarding

Market Onboard-ing Area Backlog	
Item	**Ancestor**
BX-1 (old B-1)	**BX**
BX-2 (old B-2)	**BX**
D	
E	
F	
BY-1 (old B-3)	**BY**
BY-1 (old B4)	**BY**

Table 9.3 *unsplit* (generalization) of several items

Pros and Cons of Filtered Views versus Separate Artifacts

Filtered Views—Advantages: (1) simple, (2) no synchronization issues, (3) easy to keep overview. **Drawbacks:** (1) filters make prioritization harder, (2) Product Owner sees all details of all areas, which at first might seem an advantage but drowns her in details and can lead to the temptation of "micromanaging" priorities in an area, creating conflict in responsibility between the PO and APOs.

Separate Artifacts—Advantages: (1) Overall Backlog stays at higher level and then the PO doesn't drown in details, (2) APO can easily prior-itize his backlog, (3) Supports clear separation of responsibilities between PO and APOs. **Drawbacks:** (1) Synchronization between dif-ferent backlogs, (2) Priority differences not visible in overall Product

Backlog, (3) Increased chance of silo mentality in each area rather than APOs caring about whole-product focus.

Guide: Three Levels Max

Guide: Splitting, p. 260

The *Splitting* guide advised the use of an *Ancestor* column. Naturally, this also applies to the overall Product Backlog in LeSS Huge when the separate-artifact approach is used. For example:

Item	Ancestor	Area
XA	X	trade processing
XB	X	trade processing
…		

Key point: Creates *two* levels.

And consistently, the Trade Processing Area Backlog will also have an Ancestor column:

Item	Ancestor
XA-1	XA
XA-2	XA
…	

Notice that the ancestor XA not only conveys ancestor information, it also *provides a link between the overall Product Backlog and Area Backlogs.*

Key point: Creates *three* levels total across the backlogs. For example, XA-1 to XA to X.

One can introduce more levels. But don't. *Stop at three levels maximum.*

Why? We've noticed that groups that record many nested levels of split items fall into the trap of *not* defining *customer-centric* requirements. Instead they start defining fake requirements that are actually *technical activities* or *tasks*. And/or they keep information that they are not using, which increases complexity with no benefit.

Keeping a maximum of three levels of split items helps keep the Product Backlog simple and customer focused.

Guide: New Area for Giant Requirement

A common problem in *huge LeSS Huge* product groups is dealing with gigantic multi-person-year requirements. The normal LeSS Huge way to deal with these is to just add them to a Requirement Area and let them be split by the teams. When the requirement is really big, new teams will be needed, so the area grows. Eventually, the Requirement Area is too big and it needs to be split.

An alternative to this is to speculatively create a new area when the gigantic requirement arrives. We never put it in an existing area, but instead we immediately identify that more than four teams are going to work on it. So, we create a new Requirement Area and a new Area Backlog with only one item in it. We then move only one team to this area, temporarily breaking the rules related to the size of areas but knowing that the area will grow.

Why do this? Having a gigantic requirement in another area and gradually splitting it will make the Area Backlog messy—it will contain many split items of the gigantic one mixed up with the other ones. Creating the area early, on the other hand, creates an early focus on this gigantic requirement from the Area Product Owner and the initial Team.

Sometimes your speculation was wrong and the area never grows beyond a couple of teams as the requirement turned out to be less impressive than initially speculated. In that case, merge the area with another one so that you don't keep small areas around.

Guide: Handling Gigantic Requirements

In this chapter and the *Product Backlog Refinement* chapter we've introduced several techniques for dealing with gigantic requirements. In the early *LeSS* chapter we told the story of a group dealing with gigantic regulatory requirements. In this guide we share a scenario to illustrate *several techniques working together to deal with giants.*

Traditional Handling

Before the new story, for compare and contrast context, we share our experience on how these are traditionally dealt with in giant groups.

Giant requirement *BigReq* enters the giant enterprise somewhere and someone (a senior analyst, product manager, systems architect, systems engineer) analyzes the requirements for months and writes a hundred-page specification. He hands it over to more analysts and architects, who each pick a part of the specification and work it out in more detail, and each writes a hundred-page specification for their area. Eventually, the downstream development group gets these specifications as input and extracts backlog items out of them and creates a Product Backlog. The items arrive at the backlog about six months to *two years* (yes, we have seen this) after they entered the enterprise, with myriad handoffs and lots of information scatter and loss.

LeSS Handling

BigReq arrives at the door of the enterprise and the Product Owner immediately puts it in the Product Backlog. She figures out it's a multiyear requirement. She decides this is or will be important, and creates a new *Requirement Area for the giant requirement,* and looks for a suitable Area Product Owner who is familiar with this particular requirement. The Area Product Owner creates an Area Backlog with exactly one item in it. See Figure 9.3.

Guide: Dynamics of Requirement Areas, p. 105

Guide: Splitting, p. 260

Guide: Take a Bite, p. 202

The Product Owner Team looks for an *existing Team that has the most experience and knowledge* related to BigReq and moves the team to the new area. Before their first Sprint in the new area, the team has a Product Backlog Refinement session where they *partially split* the item and *Take a Bite* out of it. See Figure 9.4.

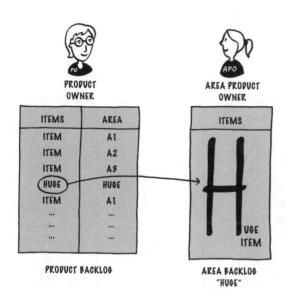

Figure 9.3 new area with only one item

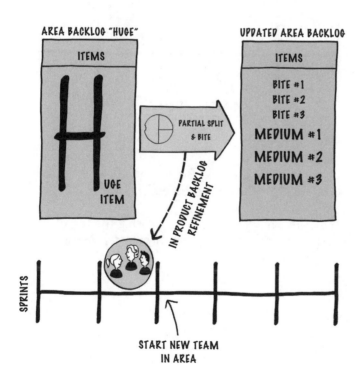

Figure 9.4 before first Sprint, partial splitting and taking a bite during Product Backlog Refinement

The first Sprint, the team implements the small bite. And they also *spend up to 50% of their time in Product Backlog Refinement* for upcoming Sprints, where they gradually split the item further. See Figure 9.5.

Figure 9.5 build the bite, while spending perhaps 50% in Product Backlog Refinement

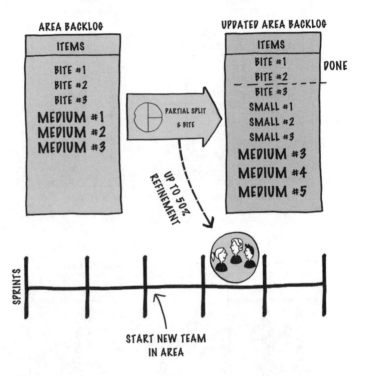

Notice that they have delivered the first bite as working software, so within one month of the arrival of BigReq into the enterprise something got delivered—some meaningful progress was made.

The Team carries on in more Sprints, clearing the fog of analysis and implementation by a focus on learning through delivering and feedback.

Once the fog is sufficiently cleared and there's a strong need to start sharing the gigantic work, the Product Owner Team decides to *gradually move more teams into the area*. The new teams join the initial Team in *multi-team Product Backlog Refinement* where they refine together and learn more about the BigReq. When the new teams join, the initial Team takes on the special role of *leading team*, to teach and mentor new teams and to keep an overview of BigReq, especially related to the consistent integration of all its parts. The initial Team stays in the area until BigReq is done, so there is no handoff of information, and the same Team sees BigReq from the beginning until the end. See Figure 9.6.

Guide: Multi-Team PBR, p. 252

Guide: Leading Team, p. 308

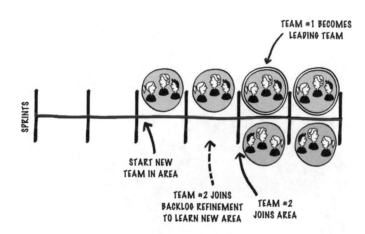

Figure 9.6 new team joined Product Backlog Refinement before joining area; original team becomes leading team

A summary of the techniques used in this scenario:

> Create new Requirement Area for gigantic requirement.

> Not all teams are equal, so start with more experienced team.

> Partial splitting; Take a Bite.

> Spend up to 50% of Sprint on refinement, while building the bite.

> Gradually grow a new Requirement Area.

> Use multi-team PBR for learning.

> Initial team becomes leading team with additional mentoring and overview responsibilities.

Contents

Done!

DEFINITION OF DONE

People who say it cannot be done should not interrupt those who are doing it.
—George Bernard Shaw

ONE-TEAM SCRUM

A developer we met defined "done" as *finished typing*. He caused considerable confusion. Most developers suffer from the "I'm almost done" disorder. "Almost" means you have no idea about your progress towards "done"—itself an undefined end state.

Scrum requires and creates transparency. One technique for increasing transparency is formally defining the meaning of "done"—the Definition of Done. Product progress is measured binary—an item is "done" or not "done."

A perfect Definition of Done includes everything a team has to do inside the Sprint for an item so that the product is still shippable to end-users and with the new "done" item in it. Shipping your product every Sprint or more frequently is relatively easy for one-team Scrum. When teams aren't yet able to achieve this perfect Definition of Done, they define "done" as a subset of the perfect set. The goal then becomes: Improve the Definition of Done until it is perfect and they can ship each Sprint... or more often.

The Definition of Done[1] is an agreed list of activities the Team performs for each and every Product Backlog Item. When all relevant activities are completed, the item is done.

---

1. Alternative ways of expressing the Definition of Done is (1) the state of the Product Backlog Item, or (2) the state of the Product Increment with the Items in it. A Definition of Done expressed per Item promotes Continuous Delivery.

Don't confuse the Definition of Done with acceptance criteria; the latter are conditions a specific item has to fulfill to be shipped. "Fulfilling all acceptance criteria" is usually included in the Definition of Done.

LeSS Done

These days, a one-team product group should be able to have a perfect Definition of Done and might even be able to continuously deliver during the Sprint. But for many large product groups, a perfect Definition of Done feels *impossible* while they still measure *stabilization* periods in months. Bas remembers being surprised when he received a bonus for some code he had written *two years* earlier. The product had finally shipped.

When scaling, these principles are related to Definition of Done:

Transparency—In traditional large groups, visibility is often attempted by installing additional management control and reporting. LeSS groups have a clear, shared Definition of Done and an integrated product at least at the end of each Sprint. This creates real, painfully clear transparency.

Continuous Improvement towards Perfection—What to improve? The gradual expansion of the Definition of Done gives direction to improvements and their measures.

• LeSS Rules •

> One Definition of Done for the whole product common for all teams
>
> Each team can have its own stronger Definition of Done by expanding the common one.
>
> The perfection goal is to improve the Definition of Done so that it results in a shippable product each Sprint (or even more frequently).

Guide: Creating the Definition of Done

The initial Definition of Done must be agreed on before the first Sprint starts, usually in the initial Product Backlog Refinement workshop.

Initial Product Backlog Refinement: See Product Backlog Refinement chapter.

Try this to create the Definition of Done:

1. Define the activities needed to ship to end customers.
2. Discover which activities can *now* be done each Sprint.
3. Explore what to do with the Undone work.
4. Create first improvements for expanding Done.

Let's explore these steps in more detail.

1. Define the Activities Needed to Ship to End-Customers

The key question is "What activities are currently required to ship our product?" Remind everyone...

> Shipping means "delivering to *end*-customers" and not "send out of the development department." Everybody must understand the whole picture of what is required to ship products.

> Challenge the need for intermediate artifacts or auxiliary tasks. Do we *really* need that specification document? Do we *really* need to

update *all* technical documentation? How is the technical documentation used? Such artifacts and tasks are a legacy from traditional ways of working where they were handed over between specialized groups.

See *Evolve the Definition of Done* guide.

This step requires diverse roles so people see the *whole* picture—more roles than just the Teams and the Product Owner. Managers involved with the LeSS adoption are required to participate as the Definition of Done is an important tool for driving organizational improvements.

The Teams, Product Owner, and other stakeholders brainstorm the required activities and write them on sticky notes, a mindmap, or list them on a flip chart. The activities typically include coding, testing, and customer documentation but may also include setting up customer support, building the hardware, or even legal work. The testing activity is usually divided into different levels such as unit test, system test, or system verification. We refer to this list of activities as **Potentially Shippable**, and it's the *perfect* Definition of Done.

In our experience, although the list can be long, participants are often surprised that the list is shorter than they expected. That's because few of them had an overview of what had to be done to deliver the product.

See guide "Organizational Perfection Vision" in *Adoption* chapter

The result is often included in an organizational perfection vision for the product group. In huge product groups with hardware and software, making a *perfect* Definition of Done a reality could take years or even decades of improvements; in small, co-located pure software groups, maybe just a few Sprints.

2. Discover Which Activities Can Be Done Each Sprint

The key question is, "Considering our current context and capability, what activities can be completed each Sprint." That subset is the initial **Definition of Done**. We call a Definition of Done *weak* when it is only a small subset, and we consider it a *strong* Definition of Done when it is almost equal to Potentially Shippable.

The Definition of Done is created either by grouping the sticky notes or by underlining the activities that are part of it (as shown in Figure 10.1).

Figure 10.1
Potentially
Shippable and Initial
Definition of Done

POTENTIALLY SHIPPABLE

+ TEST
+ <u>STATIC ANALYSIS</u>
+ <u>INTEGRATION</u>
+ <u>PACKAGING</u>
+ <u>STAGING</u>
+ CUSTOMER DOCUMENTATION
+ RISK EVALUATION
+ <u>CODE</u>
+ APPROVAL
+ UPDATE MARKETING MATERIAL
+ REGULATION
+ PREPARE FOR CUSTOMER FEEDBACK

UNIT
INTEGRATION
USER ACCEPTANCE
ACCEPTANCE
SYSTEM
PERFORMANCE
STABILITY
USABILITY
STRESS
MONKEY
SMOKE

<u>UNDERLINED ONES ARE THE DEFINITION OF DONE</u>

The difference between the Definition of Done and Potentially Shippable is referred to as **Undone Work**. The Sprint is planned according to the Definition of Done and thus the Undone Work is excluded—it is *planned to be left undone*. These terms can cause confusion. To clarify:

Mathematics of Done

Potentially Shippable = Definition of Done + Undone Work

Work in Sprint = Product Backlog Items × Definition of Done

Potentially Shippable—All activities that must be performed before the product can be shipped to end-customers. This list does *not* depend on the skills of the teams or the organizational structure, but depends *only* on the product.

Definition of Done—An agreement between the teams, the Product Owner, and managers on which activities are performed during the Sprint. A Definition of Done is said to be perfect when it is equal to Potentially Shippable.

Undone Work—The difference between the Definition of Done and Potentially Shippable. When the Definition of Done is perfect, then there is no Undone Work. When this isn't the case, then the organization has to decide (1) How do we deal with the Undone Work? and (2) How do we improve so that there is less Undone Work in the future?

Items not done yet or not finished—A Product Backlog Item that was started during a Sprint but wasn't completed. This is often confused with Undone Work. "Not done yet" is a Product Backlog Item that was started but not "done" before the end of the Sprint, whereas Undone Work was never even planned for. When a team has an item that was not finished—partially done—then they ought to feel concerned and discuss improvement actions during their Retrospective.

Not started—A Product Backlog Item that was planned for during the Sprint but was never started. It just goes back to the Product Backlog. The team should still find out why and discuss this during their Retrospective.

3. Explore What To Do with the Undone Work

The key question to answer in this step is "Who will do the Undone Work and when?" There are several approaches to performing the Undone Work but let's first explore the effects of Undone Work by running through a scenario.

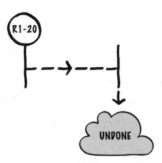

Figure 10.2 Undone Work resulting from an imperfect Definition of Done

In Figure 10.2, the teams completed—according to their Definition of Done—twenty Product Backlog Items. But there is a lot of Undone Work (e.g. stability test and customer documentation) due to their weak Definition of Done. The teams continue working on items for another two Sprints.

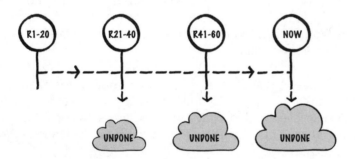

Figure 10.3 Undone Work piling up

In Figure 10.3, the teams completed—according to their weak Definition of Done—sixty Product Backlog Items in three Sprints. The amount of Undone Work has grown enormously, causing a *false* sense of progress. The Product Owner gets excited about the product's market potential and decides that there are enough features. *Now* is the right time to ship the product.

Figure 10.4 Undone
Work causes risk
and delay

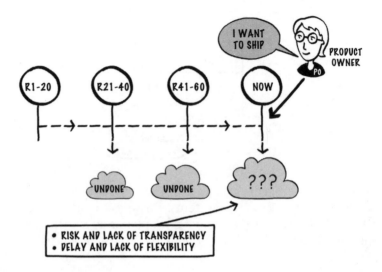

But... they can't ship the product. Though the teams are "done," their weak Definition of Done resulted in vast amounts of accumulated Undone Work. This Undone Work causes delay and a lack of transparency, with major risks hiding in it.

Delay—Undone Work causes a lack of flexibility for the Product Owner—you can't directly respond to market needs and changes due to the inflexible pile of Undone Work-in-progress. The pain caused is aggravated by the fact that the effort to complete the Undone Work is hard to predict.

Risk—Undone Work causes a *lack of transparency*. It delays realization of risks. For example, if performance testing is left Undone, then the risk of a non-performing system stays hidden until close to release... where it hurts most if the risk becomes reality.

Dealing with Undone Work

The best way and *only good way* to cope with Undone Work is to prevent it by having a strong Definition of Done. When this isn't *yet* possible, then the following are three temporarily-needed ways of dealing with Undone Work.

Release Sprints—One or several Sprints before the release where the Teams do *not* work on new features but instead perform the Undone Work.

Figure 10.5 bad idea: doing Undone Work in release Sprints

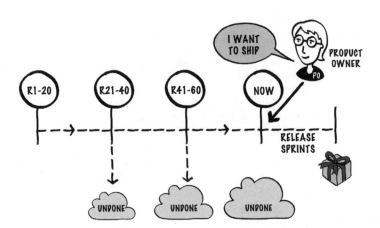

Release Sprints are a *terrible idea* but are sometimes a necessary evil until the Teams expand their Definition of Done. The most common usage of release Sprints is to deal with corporate bureaucracy around deploying. The deployment bureaucracy will eventually need to be resolved but it might take time to change that.

Don't do testing or bug fixing in release Sprints. If the teams have the ability to do these in release Sprints, then they should also be able to do them during normal Sprints. So, instead expand the Definition of Done.

Undone Department Finalizes—A department with specialized people who perform the Undone Work after the Teams are "done" with all the items for a release.

Figure 10.6 bad
idea: doing Undone
Work via an Undone
Department

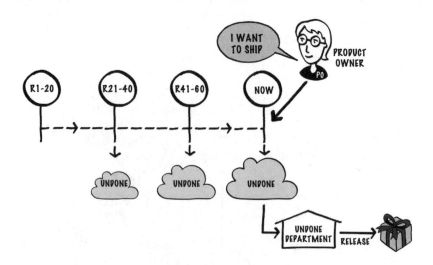

Most Undone departments are relics from ancient times, a temporary band-aid until the Teams expand their Definition of Done. The most common usage of Undone departments is to do testing that hasn't yet been automated or cannot yet be performed by the Teams due to their limited scope. Undone departments are frequently managed with traditional project management techniques or Kanban, inasmuch as Scrum in an Undone department doesn't make sense.

The goal of every LeSS adoption is for the teams to ship every Sprint or more often. To that end, eliminate all Undone departments—they cause additional hand-off, delay, interruptions, risk, and reduced learning. The perceived benefits of specialized functional groups aren't worth it.

Pipelining to Undone Department—At the end of *each* Sprint, the Teams hand off the Undone work to an Undone department so that the Undone Work doesn't accumulate.

Figure 10.7 bad
idea: pipelining the
Undone Work

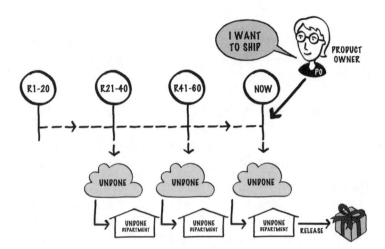

Pipelining might seem like a good idea, but it's another terrible one and is usually a short-term quick fix for limited-scope teams; remove it by expanding the Definition of Done and having true product-wide feature teams. Pipelining is most commonly used when (1) the Teams still have a component-scope and thus some testing is hard to fit inside the Teams, and (2) the testing requires special equipment that is hard to share across teams. The latter is more often than not an excuse by the specialized department so they need not think about how the teams could share the equipment.

Pipelining never works well. The Undone department will require work from the Teams when performing the Undone Work. That will interrupt the Teams in their next Sprint, causing continuous conflict between the Undone department and the Teams.

In our experience, pipelining is always an excuse for not breaking up specialized functional groups or expanding Teams' scope. As product groups improve, pipelining should disappear.

4. Create First Improvements for Expanding the Definition of Done

The key question to answer in this step is "What prevents us from expanding the Definition of Done?" *The Definition of Done defines the product group's current agility* and the Undone Work highlights the improvement opportunities. What improvements can we do?

Consider these common improvements:

> **Automation**—Much Undone Work was traditionally manual work and must be automated.

> **Harmonization**—Product groups have often solved the same problem many ways (e.g. four similar testing frameworks). Having all teams maintain tests in many similar but different technologies is rarely useful, and thus Teams need to agree on a standard.

> **Environment**—Some environments are hard to use or share (e.g. test equipment). Use might need to be improved and sharing must be agreed within the Teams. Alternatively, reduce dependency on environments by increasing virtualization.

> **Parallelization**—Sometimes Teams assume that certain work must be done in sequence (e.g. start testing after all code is done). This assumption is frequently incorrect and work can be parallelized by being done differently.

> **Cross-functionality**—Some Undone Work requires skills that aren't yet in the Teams (e.g. technical writing). Increasing cross-functionality is done either by cross-training or by adding people with the needed skills. One common action is to move people from the Undone department into the Teams.

Review the Undone Work and brainstorm improvements for expanding the Definition of Done. When the teams will work on these improvements, then these items go in the Product Backlog.

Guide: Evolve the Definition of Done

The Definition of Done is multi-faceted and requires close monitoring and needs to evolve. The perfection goal of the Definition of Done is for the *organization* to be capable of shipping the product every Sprint or more often.

Different roles view the Definition of Done from different perspectives:

Managers—While there is an imperfect Definition of Done, the Definition of Done is *the major tool* for monitoring and managing organizational change. Expanding the Definition of Done leads to organizational changes and strategic decisions and are usually the responsibility of managers.

For example, imagine a product group that consists of five development sites, of which two have a specialized system-validation group because of the high cost of test equipment. Expanding the Definition of Done could lead to building system-validation skills in all sites, abandoning the separate system-validation groups, and figuring out how to share the test equipment across multiple geographic locations. Far from a simple change!

Managers need to encourage teams to improve and expand their team Definition of Done. Having teams expand their own Definition of Done makes it easier to expand the product Definition of Done later.

Avoid unilaterally expanding the Definition of Done, especially not without insight from Go See. The result won't be pretty.

Guide: Go See, p. 125

Teams—Every Sprint is an inspect–adapt improvement cycle, and the Definition of Done provides a source for finding improvements in a Team's working methods. Every team can expand their Definition of Done independently beyond the product-level Definition of Done.

For example, in the previously mentioned system-validation example, one Team can improve by learning about system validation or by exploring different ways of sharing the expensive test equipment.

Product Owner—A weak Definition of Done causes risk and delay, which hampers the Product Owner from maximizing the value and from deciding when to ship. A good Product Owner invests in improvements so that the organization's agility increases.

For example, in the previous system-validation example, the Product Owner probably painfully experiences the delays caused by system validations and can improve the situation by investing in test equipment or discussing with teams what Product Backlog Items they need in order to improve their Definition of Done.

Scrum Masters—Not expanding the Definition of Done is a sign of not improving. Scrum Masters are responsible for building teams that are self-managing and continuously improving, and Scrum Masters are responsible for helping the organization to improve.

For example, in the previous system-validation example, when the Teams aren't discussing how to improve their Definition of Done, you would ask questions such as "What is preventing my teams from improving their system validation skills?"

The Definition of Done and how well the Team can achieve that are vital information to gauge the health of the Scrum implementation.

Expansion of the Definition of Done is often decided in:

Management discussions and meetings—The key question for managers to ask themselves is "How to expand the Definition of Done?" Improving the organization's capability to deliver is the main responsibility of managers and the Definition of Done is a key tool for that.

Retrospectives—Both team-level and Overall Retrospectives result in improvement items. These might improve the lives of the team members, or improve the output and its quality, or work towards expanding the Definition of Done. The product-level Definition of Done is shared across all Teams but each Team is encouraged to improve on that.

Guide: Communities, p. 295

Communities—Community discussions are a perfect place for analyzing organizational behavior and systemic problems. This also makes them great for figuring out ways to expand the Definition of Done. Especially the community of Scrum Masters is a good place for this as they have the responsibility to change the organization together with managers by ensuring the discovered problems are removed... together.

Is an organization with a perfect Definition of Done *done* with improving? No, improvements won't ever be done. They never stop. Further improvement can be made:

> Have shorter Sprints.

> Release many times during a Sprint.

> Expand the Definition of Done beyond potentially shippable, and include market success in the Definition of Done. In this case, an item is not done until you have a measurement about how customers are using it. The Lean Startup framework refers to this as *validated learning*.

LeSS Huge

There are no Huge-specific rules or guides. One shared Definition of Done is applicable for the whole product, across all Requirement Areas.

LeSS Sprint

Contents

a multi-site overall PBR workshop in LeSS

PRODUCT BACKLOG
REFINEMENT

I don't necessarily agree with everything I say.
—Marshall McLuhan

ONE-TEAM SCRUM

First, notice the chapter order: *Product Backlog Refinement* (PBR) is before *Sprint Planning*. But PBR does *not* happen *just* before Sprint Planning, but rather well before—usually "mid-Sprint" in some prior Sprint. The chapters are organized this way because from the viewpoint of the flow of requirements, the ball starts rolling with PBR.

For a Product Backlog item to be chosen during Sprint Planning, it needs to be small enough and understood enough by the Team for the Team to judge that the item can realistically be "done" in the Sprint. Therefore, ongoing PBR is needed each Sprint to prepare and refine items to be ready for *future* Sprints. Activities include clarifying and detailing, splitting, and estimating. In the true spirit of empirical process control, Scrum doesn't say how to do PBR though suggests the Team spend no more than 10% of their Sprint capacity on it. It usually happens mid-Sprint.

Refinement of items is *not* done separately by the Product Owner or a "Product Owner team" or a separate group of business analysts or product managers or UX/UI designers—doing so would increase the wastes of handoff, inventory/WIP, and more. And it would reduce empathy and understanding by the Team of the customers and users. Rather, the *whole Team* does this work—and not a subset of the Team (such "our BA experts" or "our UX experts"), as in Scrum there are no sub-groups dedicated to a particular domain such as analysis or UX. The *Scrum Guide* explains:

[PBR] is an ongoing process in which the Product Owner and the Development Team collaborate on the details of Product Backlog items. ... Scrum recognizes no sub-teams in the Development Team, regardless of particular domains that need to be addressed like testing or business analysis; there are no exceptions to this rule.

LeSS Product Backlog Refinement

When scaling, these principles relate to Product Backlog refinement:

Whole-product focus—If each team only separately refined different items (a local optimization), the effects would be to limit domain knowledge, reduce agility, and make coordination difficult. Ways to combat this are key.

Customer-centric—In a traditional organization, so-called requirements are often technical or functional tasks for siloed groups, rather than true customer goals. Therefore, during adoption of LeSS, many developers will be unfamiliar with the full customer requirements and their language and domain—let alone working together with them to solve their problems rather than extracting their preconceived solutions.

Lean thinking & queuing theory—In the old organization several functional groups are often involved in understanding and defining requirements, and handing them off—business and UX analysts, UI designers, product managers, etc. That generates many wastes and many queues stuffed with intermediate WIP documents. But it looks *locally efficient* and the true costs and problems are not grasped. Then a so-called Scrum or agile adoption is done in which these dynamics remain, but under new labels such as "Product Owner team," "story writing team," and so on. But the wastes and queues remain.

• LeSS Rules •

Product Backlog refinement is done per team for the items they are *likely* going to implement in the future. Do multi-team PBR to increase shared understanding and exploit coordination opportunities when having closely related items or a need for broader input/learning.

The Product Owner shouldn't work alone on Product Backlog refinement; she is supported by the multiple Teams working directly with customers/users and other stakeholders.

All prioritization goes through the Product Owner, but clarification is as much as possible directly between the Teams and customer/users and other stakeholders.

Guide: Product Backlog Refinement Types

Product Backlog Refinement (PBR) in LeSS is a workshop where teams clarify upcoming items with users and stakeholders, split big items, and (re)estimate items. The precise pattern of Product Backlog Refinement depends on the following forces:

> Items are not preassigned to specific teams, since that would reduce agility and learning, and increase key-team fragility. And it's often desirable for *a group of teams to refine a set of items* together without yet deciding which team will implement which item, because that broadens knowledge, enhances coordination, and increases agility.

> Having all teams refine all items might take too much effort and can lead to boring refinement meetings. It is also hard to keep everyone interested in the clarification when a team knows they aren't the team who will implement the item.

These forces are resolved by having different types of PBR in different situations. There are four types of PBR meetings:

Overall PBR—Whole-product-focused PBR that is held before multi-team or single-team PBR. The overall PBR is to explore which teams might refine which items, and also to increase learning and alignment.

Multi-team PBR—PBR where *all* members of two or more teams are refining a set of items together without yet deciding which of these teams will implement which item.

Single-team PBR—PBR where all members of one team refine items they are likely to implement. This is the same as in Scrum.

Initial PBR—PBR done when adopting LeSS and held only once in the life of a product. In initial PBR, all teams together create the first Product Backlog and refine enough items to start the first Sprint.

The table below clarifies the different refinement meetings.

	Overall PBR	Multi-team PBR	Single-team PBR	Initial PBR
members from	all teams	2+ teams	1 team	all teams
includes Product Owner?	definitely	depends	rarely	definitely
includes customers/users?	rarely	probably	probably	definitely
select which teams work on which items?	yes (prefer *set of items with group of teams*)	no	done already	no
level of clarification	lightweight	in-depth	in-depth	in-depth
length	shortish	0.5–1 day	0.5–1 day	at least 2 days
typical frequency	every Sprint	most Sprints	most Sprints	once

It's common for a product group with 2–3 teams to have only one PBR meeting where the Product Owner, users, and all members of all teams together do in-depth refinement on all items: effectively, an overall and multi-team PBR meeting combined.

For a product group with three or more teams, there is usually a combination of overall PBR followed up with multi-team and single-team PBR. Avoid single-team PBR unless it is absolutely certain that a specific team will implement specific items. In general, prefer multi-team PBR with *a group of teams to refining a set of items*. Figure 11.1 shows a common PBR pattern.

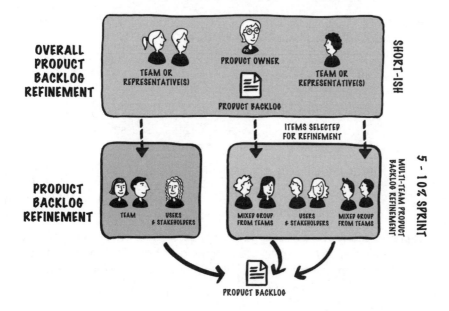

Guide: Overall PBR

In overall PBR it's decided whether further in-depth refinement is done by (1) ideally, a group of teams that refine a set of items, or (2) single teams. Sometimes it's obvious which teams will best refine the items from their past work or their latest interests, and then overall PBR could perhaps be skipped.

Overall PBR is "short and sweet." e.g. an hour if a two-week Sprint. Attendees include the Product Owner and either representatives from all teams or entire teams—*representatives* are more likely in larger groups. Basic activities:

> discuss direction and vision with the Product Owner

> discuss items to be refined

> identify the teams and items for later in-depth team PBR

> > to increase learning and agility and to reduce "key team" fragility, prefer a *set of items with a group of teams* rather than "team-A handles [X, Y, Z]": also leads to *multi-team PBR*

> identify strongly related items that suggest opportunities to cooperate and coordinate; also leads to *multi-team PBR*

In overall PBR the group may also:

> split a big item, which generates discussion and learning

Guide: Scaling Estimation, p. 269

> estimate items, which likewise generates discussion and learning, and also helps *synchronize* estimates across teams

> clarify an item, though not in-depth

> > for example, the clarification may be timeboxed ("10 minutes") or "content boxed" ("two examples")

Representatives? Recurring advice in LeSS is that when there are representatives at any meeting, *rotate those over time*. This increases perspectives, strengthens multiple skills in team members, and reduces the "special people" weaknesses.

Items chooser? During overall PBR let the teams (not the Product Owner) decide which items they will take onward to multi-team or single-team PBR. This fosters self-organizing and reduces work for the Product Owner. And as mentioned, prefer *a set of items with a group of teams* rather than "team-A handles [X, Y, Z]."

Guide: Multi-Team PBR

In multi-team PBR, all members of two or more teams refine a set of items together without yet deciding which team will implement which item. Thereby they defer the decision of team-to-item until some future

Sprint Planning. Organizational *agility*—easily responding to change—increases, and the broader whole-product knowledge fosters self-organized coordination. Who's there? In addition to all the team members, important attendees include customers/users and related stakeholders. When done, multi-team PBR usually replaces single-team PBR.

Naturally, simply having two or three teams refine items in the same room doesn't magically increase shared understanding and so on. So multi-team PBR *must* include a set of *"mix it up"* techniques, such as:

1. **Team mixing**—Start by forming temporary mixed groups with people from each team. For example, two teams re-form into two mixed groups.

   > After all following steps, consider forming new mixed groups for the next cycle, to increase diversity and interactions.

2. **Rotation refinement**—Start with each mixed group refining different (or identical!) items separately at different work areas in the same room. For example, at different whiteboards, tables, or around different computer projectors. After a "30-minute" time-box, all groups rotate to the next work area (and its related item under refinement), leaving one or two people behind to bring the incoming group up to speed on understanding the current refinement. Those left behind will typically include the customers/users or other stakeholders best able to help the group refine an item.

3. **Diverge–merge cycles**—Groups spend some time working separately in different areas of the room for refinement on different (or identical) items, and then spend time all together to share insights, ask questions, and seek other coordination opportunities.

Why multi-team PBR?

> **Increased organizational agility**
> Multi-team PBR increases the number of teams that can implement a set of items. Looked at another way, it *delays the decision* of which team will implement which item. Consequently, the Product Owner can change the order of items in more ways—in response to forces of change—without the rigid constraint that "only team-A can implement X." Increased agility!

> **Increased whole-product focus and knowledge**
> The teams doing multi-team PBR together gain broader domain knowledge from (1) exposure to more varied items and (2) exposure to the people and knowledge in other teams. This increases their ability to understand, see, and focus on the *whole*.

> **Improved coordination**
> Multi-team PBR educates teams *in detail* about what other teams know and are doing. That enhances coordination and the ability to share work.

Guide: Multi-Site PBR

Overall or multi-team PBR might be multi-site. *General* multi-site tips are in "Guide: Cross-Team Meetings" on page 299. This guide focuses on tips related to PBR.

Splitting

Guide: Splitting, p. 260

When splitting a big item, it often helps to sketch a tree-like diagram on a whiteboard. Similarly, in a multi-site meeting use a shared-space *mindmap* drawing tool (e.g. in a browser), since these are optimized for creating tree-like structures. People at different sites can simultaneously both see and modify the mindmap.

Clarifying

Specification by example[1] (SbE) is a great technique for a group to clarify and learn about an item by discussing *examples*. SbE has long been encouraged in LeSS. How to do this in a multi-site PBR? Use a shared-space *spreadsheet* (e.g. in a browser) because many examples naturally fit a table format. And people at all sites can modify it easily.

Estimating

Guide: Scaling Estimation, p. 269

Guide: Tools for Large Product Backlogs, p. 210

First, avoid so-called "agile" planning tools, because they tend to focus people's attention on the tool rather than on one another, and because physical tools such as cards tend to energize and engage people better. Second, any estimation technique is possible in LeSS, but this tip assumes a "planning poker" technique, since it's so popular.

---

1. See the books *Bridging the Communication Gap*, and *Specification by Example*.

Webcams with physical planning-poker cards or hands—In the multi-site meeting, people use big cards with big numbers on them so they're visible through the webcam. A variation is to use fist-and-fingers signals to represent different estimation values.

Shared chat—Everyone has a device with a shared chat tool. When the moderator says "show your number," then everyone enters a number.

Guide: Initial PBR

A product group adopting LeSS needs, before their first Sprint, a Product Backlog with enough *understood items* for the teams to get going. This *initial* PBR preparation in LeSS is called—*cleverly*—**initial PBR**. Aside: This guide could have been in the *Adoption* chapter, but much is relevant to general PBR, so it's here.

Why Bother?

An existing product group adopting LeSS might ask, "Why bother to do this? We already have a backlog, and our people already understand the requirements." Actually, those two assumptions may not be true, and there are other reasons for initial PBR:

> **Existing "backlog" isn't a useful LeSS Product Backlog.**
> When we coach a group starting a LeSS adoption we ask, "Do you have an existing backlog?" Invariably the answer is, "Oh yes, we have our JIRA/Rally/... list!" Caution! We worked with a group that had an original JIRA "backlog" of 508 items. After a two-hour activity, it distilled into a LeSS Product Backlog of *23 items from those 508 inputs*! Why? Most of the old "items" were functional tasks assuming single-function teams (analyze, design, test, ...), component tasks assuming component teams, and so on, all predicated on the assumption of the old organization. They didn't make sense in the new feature-team structure of LeSS.

> **People don't understand re-formed items.**
> Building on the prior point, the items need to be expressed in a true customer-centric end-to-end manner, and understood this way. Due to prior siloed teams, there's a lot of learning the nascent feature teams need for these newly cast items.

> **Limited knowledge of customer-centric view.**
> Even if the old items were previously expressed in a customer-centric way, the prior siloed-specialists focus on narrow tasks, and so don't understand the full customer-centric view.

> **No estimates for re-formed items, poor or insufficient estimates.**
> Newly cast items need new estimates. And even if the items didn't need reformation, the estimates often came from some other group rather than from the newly formed feature teams. And the Product Owner may need estimates for most or all items to support longer-term planning.

> **New broader production definition.**
> The *What is Your Product* guide (p. 157) explains that in a LeSS adoption the product scope may become broader. So several existing backlogs may need to be transformed into a new broader one. And this change implies creating and communicating a new broader product vision, lots of knowledge gaps, and many people unfamiliar to each other who will soon be delivering together.

> **No shared product vision.**
> Whether it's a new broader product or not, it's common—due to the traditional siloed groups—that few people know the product vision, if there even is one! Initial PBR is an opportunity to form, communicate, and start aligning on a common vision.

Basics

Preconditions? (1) The Product Owner is identified. (2) The feature teams and their members have been decided. (3) There's enough detailed information that can be "brought into the room" to sufficiently refine many items ready for Sprint #1. That "bringing in" is ideally users/customers and related stakeholders, but can also include existing documents or backlogs.

Duration? Often two days or longer.

Attendees? "Everybody"! Product Owner, all team members of all teams, customers, users, domain experts, product managers, Scrum Masters, and supporting managers.

Location? Even for a multi-site group, hold initial PBR at one site all together in a large workshop room.

Objectives

The basic objective of initial PBR is to sufficiently refine enough items so all teams can be productive in the first Sprint, implementing items until "done" and creating a shippable product.

Other objectives: (1) establish shared vision and understanding, (2) generate ideas for innovation, (3) identify early major goals, and (4) plan longer term. These objectives are more or less important depending on the current state of the group and product. For example, in a long-stable, single-site, small group working on a mature product, those objectives could already have been met. Quite the opposite of a two-year-old product experiencing explosive growth in a hot market, with three young sites.

Basic Objective: Sufficiently Refine Enough Items

Meeting this objective usually consumes most of the time in initial PBR.

How? Because all the teams are together, study the *Multi-Team PBR* guide for ideas of how they can work together. In the spirit of empirical process control, LeSS doesn't dictate how to refine items, though popular techniques include *agile modeling* and *specification by example*.

How many? What about the number of items to get ready for the first Sprint? As explained in the *Splitting* guide (p. 260), aim for items small enough that one team can do about *four* items per Sprint. So if there are five teams, that means preparing at least 20 (4 x 5) items in initial PBR. *But wait!...* in most situations we observe that it takes on average *two Sprints* for items to go from vague and unexamined to clearly ready for implementation. In that case, then during initial PBR, the group needs to get about *40* items ready: enough to prime the pump for early Sprints, while in Sprint #1 the teams are starting to refine items for later Sprints.

Objective: Establish Shared Vision and Understanding

Every PBR meeting is an opportunity to establish vision and increase shared understanding. But initial PBR is the first time the *entire* group may be focused on this. For example, in the prior traditional organization, vision may have been the sole domain of product managers, while programmers/testers/etc. were just expected to implement according to marching orders. Not so in the new LeSS group.

How? First, for these kinds of activities, a skilled *workshop facilitator* is invaluable! Any technique is possible, but we suggest the collaborative, fun, and fast techniques described in the books *Innovation Games* and *Gamestorming*.

Objective: Generate Ideas for Innovation

As with visioning, any and every PBR meeting is an opportunity to *ideate*—to generate innovative ideas. But initial PBR is the ideal first step to set the tone of engaging everyone in innovation.

How? Once again, any technique is possible; we suggest starting with *Innovation Games* and *Gamestorming*.

Figure 11.2 impact mapping in initial PBR

Objective: Identify Early Major Goals

As with innovation, every kind of PBR meeting is a time to consider new or alternate goals. But initial PBR is the natural time and place to start doing so and to practice new techniques.

How? Two techniques that we often recommend are related to understanding or creating goals are *impact mapping* and *story mapping*. Not surprisingly, they both have excellent books that we suggest you study and apply: *Impact Mapping* and *User Story Mapping*.

Objective: Plan Longer Term—Repeatedly

First and foremost, there's a good reason why Scrum does not formally include the notion of "release planning." Why? Because a key perfection goal is to *ship at least every Sprint*. It's a big idea in agile development and confers many benefits. And so it's also stressed in LeSS: *aim to ship at least every Sprint*. Then all the complexities of big-batch planning fall away, and there's powerful agility to respond to change.

But of course there are circumstances—most common in large-scale development—when planning longer term is important, usually to *synchronize dates* with (1) *internal groups* (e.g. a campaign with Marketing), (2) *customers* (e.g. organize deployment of new radio towers), and (3) *events* (e.g. a trade show). Then, initial PBR is the time and place to start.

Here's a key point about agile planning in the longer term:

> Planning the scope of items for a date is sometimes necessary.
> But don't plan items to specific Sprints. That kills agility.

How? Crucially, regardless of technique, a related question is, "How often?" Every Sprint is a chance to learn and adapt. *Initial* PBR is just the first time to plan longer term; *at every subsequent PBR meeting, every Sprint* can and probably should be used to *re-plan longer term* if it's important.

A key element in planning longer term to synchronize dates will be some kind of *estimation* done during initial PBR. The upcoming "Guide: Scaling

Estimation" on page 269 expands the topic, but here's a key point:

> **Choose the simplest technique that matches the
> purpose and that fosters discussion and learning.**

A second key element of planning longer term is *order*, often of larger *goals or themes*. Naturally, LeSS doesn't prescribe the technique, though the techniques of *Identify Early Major Goals* are suggested, including *impact mapping* and *story mapping*.

Architectural Design & Initial PBR

Guide: Multi-Team
Design Workshop,
p. 301

The results of initial PBR could imply some significant architectural change that should be considered by the teams before Sprint #1. Is this discussed and resolved during initial PBR? No. PBR is for the customer-perspective understanding and learning, it isn't for technical design. Instead, after initial PBR organize one or more *design workshops* for teams to explore the design.

Guide: Splitting

Large-scale is a world of gigantic requirements, so we always hear this: "Our group can't possibly fit our requirements into two-week Sprints. There is no way they can be made smaller while still being customer-centric." We'll invite the person to tell us their largest and most *impossible* item that could *never* be split into small customer-oriented items, and together at a whiteboard we'll start splitting. It usually takes about five minutes. So it's not actually that difficult, though it's different; with a little learning you too can become a *Certified Split Master*!

Why split big items?

> > Delivering high-value or high-risk elements early increases benefits and feedback and reduces risks. Related is that small items increase visibility and control for the Product Owner about what's really important and what's next.

> Customer-centric "vertical" splitting helps divide and parallelize valuable work over the multiple teams—teams that can still do all the activities in the Definition of Done.

> An item has to be completely doable well within a Sprint so that some increment is *done* each Sprint and WIP is lowered.

In this guide you'll start learning to split requirements.

How to Learn?

Seeing fully explained examples of splitting helps learning. Telling stories helps. So the upcoming example tells the true story of splitting an item. Many more examples—worth learning for mastery of this art—are available. Use these resources to become a *Certified Split Master*:

> The LeSS book *Practices for Scaling Lean & Agile Development* has a 20-page section (p. 247) called *Try... Split Product Backlog Items*, with many detailed examples.

> That section is also online at the *less.works* website in the guide also named *Splitting Big Items*.

> The book *Fifty Quick Ideas to Improve Your User Stories* has a 30-page guide on learning to split.

> Richard Lawrence's online *"Patterns for Splitting User Stories"* and *"How to Split a User Story poster"*

How to Split?

One key to learning how to split is to understand *splitting perspectives*, and then learn how to split by them. The table below describes some of them.

use case	the major work flows or cases of use; CRUD use cases	**configuration**	a varying configuration, such as type of operating system
scenario	a *specific* sequence of steps within a use case	**user role, persona**	Attacker, Defender, power user, novice
type	varying types or kinds of things, such as types of trades	**data format**	XML, comma delimited, ...

external integration	with several external elements, such as trading exchanges	data part	a subset of the many elements of the data: may be useful
operation/message	a system operation/ message, e.g. HTTP GET, SWIFT MT304	non-functionals	moderate vs. high throughput, with or without recovery, …
I/O channel	an input or output channel, such as GUI or command line	stub	a fake simple implementation of something

The following example will help you learn to split with perspectives.

Splitting Example: Process Kenya-Market Custody Transactions

This example is from a large securities trading product for the item "Process Kenya-Market Custody Transactions." The context was that this work was previously being done semi-manually, but as the volume in this market grew, the trading group wanted to fully automate it.

The setting was a PBR session that included team members and some hands-on users who knew a lot about the requirements because they'd been involved in the semi-manual processing.

"At Least Four Items per Sprint" on page 268

Can we stop splitting?—Of course, if the item is already estimated as small enough so that 4-ish similar items would fit in one Sprint for one team, no need to split further. And as new split items are defined, they need estimation to decide if further splitting is warranted. In this example, the original item was estimated as very big.

Perspective: Split by use cases—On talking with users in the PBR session it became clear that this requirement involved "handling a transaction." Transactional requirements usually split into major *use cases*,[2] and so did this one: (1) **settle a trade**, (2) **handle a corporate action (such as a stock split) on an unsettled trade**, and (3) some others.

---

2. "Use cases" is the term and model the users knew and used.

The users wanted to talk about and elaborate *all* the use cases. We asked them to pause and said, "Let's do gradual clarification. Which of these use cases is performed most often?" They said, "*Settling a trade* is by far the most common case and we should do it first, since that will quickly reduce costs and errors." So we decided

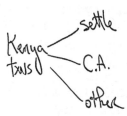

to focus on "settle a trade" first. We didn't bother to discover all the possible use cases. Instead we sketched a tree on a whiteboard to show the split's major sub-items:

> settle a trade

> handle a corporate action on an unsettled trade

> **everything else for handling Kenya-market transactions**

This **partial splitting** with an "everything else" placeholder is important when splitting. It reduces over-processing and WIP, and focuses the group on small-batch development. This big item will be in the Product Backlog as a placeholder for future discovery.

Where to focus next? Splitting direction—What led us to the choice of focusing on "settle a trade"? What's the next direction to focus on? Guides for choosing:

> **split for value or impact**—e.g. to increase revenue or market share or to reduce costs.

> **split for learning about**

> **domain**—e.g. unfamiliar derivative

> **technology**—e.g. unfamiliar protocol

> **size** of the overall item

> **split for risk mitigation**—e.g. split to clarify and deliver an item that prevents a fine, or split to create or evaluate new technology

> **split for progress**—sometimes just getting *something* developed builds confidence that the requirement can be tackled

Can we stop?—People were immediately sure it was still a big item, so we carried on.

Split by type—We asked, "Are there different types of trades to settle?" Answer, "Yes, buys and sells." That suggests buy/sell might be a good way to split further, but we first had to ask an important question when splitting...

Does the splitting reduce the effort?—Just because one can theoretically split a requirement into "settle a buy" and "settle a sell," that doesn't mean that it *splits the effort or work involved*. Sometimes the exact same code handles these variations identically. So then it isn't *useful* to split that way because it doesn't reduce the effort. There-

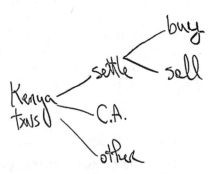

fore we asked, "Are the logic, business rules, handling, and so forth the same for settling a buy versus a sell?" The experts replied, "Oh no, they're quite different." Good! Then we know that splitting by type of trade is useful. Now we had:

> settle a trade
>> settle a buy
>> settle a sell
> handle a corporate action on an unsettled trade
> everything else for handling Kenya-market transactions

Where to focus next?—Automating this requirement was motivated by the goal of reducing the cost and errors of manual handling. If the costs are equal for different types of transactions, then the *frequency* of a transaction type points to where the most benefit is.

We asked, "What's the percentage of buy trades?" Answer, "80%." So we focused further on "settle a buy".

Can we stop?—"*Settle a buy* is small?" Answer, "No, it's still big."

Open questions and discovery of variations—Up to this point we were using our experience during the splitting discussion, such as, "Now that we guess there are use cases, is that true and if so, what are some?" But it's also important to ask open questions because experience doesn't always guide you to a skillful next step.

When asking open questions during a splitting discussion, we were especially trying to learn about the *variations* within the requirement. That's because *finding variations or alternatives is the key to discover a splitting and deeper understanding.*

So we asked, "Tell us about *settle a buy*." We discovered there were two major *types* of settlement processes: *Free of Payment* and *Delivery versus Payment*, each with different requirements. Therefore, the split was:

> > ...settle a buy
>
> > > settle a buy with Free of Payment
> >
> > > settle a buy with Delivery versus Payment

We then discovered that *settle a buy with Free of Payment* was more beneficial to deliver first, because of high frequency. And it was still big.

Time for more open questions: "Tell us about *settle a buy with Free of Payment?*" We then discovered that what initiates this use case is an incoming SWIFT message, and depending on the characteristics of the message, there were varying processing steps. This can be considered splitting on *types* of (or characteristics of) messages. In conversation we then discovered these sub-items:

> > ...settle a buy with Free of Payment
>
> > > settle a buy with Free of Payment; all party details already embedded in the incoming SWIFT message ("complete")
> >
> > > settle a buy with Free of Payment; some party details not in the incoming SWIFT message ("incomplete")

For the latter *incomplete* variation, it would be necessary to write lots of code to retrieve and fill in the missing party details. But in the *complete* case, there wasn't much to do. And at that point the group felt that *settle a buy with Free of Payment; all party details* was probably small enough to not require further splitting.

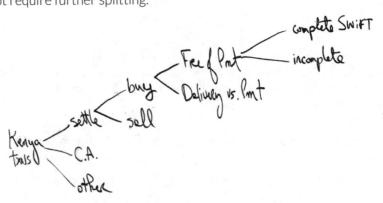

Now, what was actually recorded in the Product Backlog?

> settle a buy with Free of Payment; complete SWIFT message
> settle a buy with Free of Payment; incomplete SWIFT message
> settle a buy with Delivery versus Payment
> settle a sell
> handle a corporate action on an unsettled trade
> everything else for handling Kenya-market transactions

Ancestors—Notice that all the intermediate "ancestors" are expunged from the backlog. That's a nice and simple approach, but sometimes you want to keep some ancestor information. In that case, see "Guide: Dealing with Parents" on page 204.

Done for now!

Split into Thin End-to-End Items

Consider this new sub-item we discovered: *settle a buy with Free of Payment; complete SWIFT message.* It's a complete end-to-end "vertical" customer-centric feature, but *thin*. It can be connected to just a few acceptance tests. This illustrates a *critical key point* about splitting:

Split into thin end-to-end "vertical" requirements.

DO NOT SPLIT ITEMS INTO INTERNAL DESIGN STEPS!

What's that about *steps*? Developers think of development in terms of internal-design logical algorithm steps. For example, for *settle a buy*:

1. identify the SWIFT message type
2. parse the message
3. retrieve the trade associated with the message from a database
4. ...

Don't split by internal-design-algorithm processing steps; e.g. don't define an item for the step "identify the SWIFT message type." Why not?

> You can't add customer-centric automated acceptance tests since no customer-centric end-to-end functionality is implemented.

> Since it can't be used in production, it's WIP with its classic problems: no usable value, hidden defects and risks, and no feedback.

> It introduces component-team-like dynamics and problems. What do we mean?

   Frequently—especially in architectures created when there are or were component teams—*one processing step is associated with one software component*, such as the step "identify message" associated with a component *MessageIdentifier*. When that's true the following can happen…

   Suppose each processing step is defined as a separate item; e.g. an item for "identify the SWIFT message type", and so forth. Then there's a tendency to define and do "all" the changes for "all" the variations of a customer requirement that involve the component associated with the step. For example, "Do all the work in the *Mes-*

sageIdentifier component to identify all the message types, so we only need to touch it once."

This leads back to component-team dynamics and problems in the organization, even if there are apparently feature teams, since they are working on single-component tasks hidden under the label of "processing step" requirements.

In contrast, "settle a buy with Free of Payment; complete SWIFT message" is complete. It's very thin and it isn't all possible variations of "settle a buy," but it's one complete flow. It can be integrated, delivered, used, provide value, and give feedback. And the automated acceptance tests never need to be changed.

A Last and First Resort? Fail First

Sometimes the surprising place to split is with *error* (failure) scenarios. Once, we were involved in implementing the 3G telecom standard HSDPA for a product. The team started the splitting by trying to simplify a success scenario. They discussed:

> *Make an HSDPA call in the simplest possible network configuration, ignoring all error cases.*

But they discovered that even this was too big. Thus, instead of looking at success scenarios, they started splitting from a failure perspective—there are many in a telecom network. They first split for the simplest possible failure scenario and then gradually worked down the stack, implementing more failure scenarios. After two Sprints, the cumulative failure scenarios had put enough stuff in place for them to work on the simplest *success* scenario.

Why was this useful? By splitting on failure cases they gradually built up functionality while still focusing on a customer perspective. Plus, they were addressing some risks early and increasing learning. Of course, having only failure cases does not (usually) deliver usable value.

At Least Four Items per Sprint

How small to split items? Naturally, they need to be smaller than a Sprint so that there's an *increment*. But "almost as big as an entire

Sprint" also isn't desirable. Why is that? Owing to the high variability inherent in R&D, it's quite likely that one big item won't get fully done. Then, *nothing* will be delivered "done" by the team. And then there is no benefit delivered, weak feedback, and less learning and adaptation.

So here's a guideline that influences splitting size: *In a Sprint, one team should select at least four items.*

Why four? It strikes a balance between too big or small. Why not two?

> With big items there's an increased chance one won't get done, because of variability or availability of a constrained resource (such as lab equipment).

> Following on from the last point: If there are lots of half-done (WIP) items at the end of Sprint, the Product Owner has—realistically—fewer choices in the next Sprint since wrapping up the WIP items is almost always compelled.

> Big items tend to promote sloppy waterfall-like practices, and they tend to overwhelm teams with myriad details.

Why not ten? In the large-scale world, "10 items per team" *might* be OK, but can lead to these disadvantages: (1) the overhead of so much splitting, (2) the overhead of managing and understanding an exploding large Product Backlog with myriad teeny-weeny items, (3) difficulty of remaining end-to-end centric, and (4) reinforcement of the old tendency for an item to be done by one person rather than "whole team together" with a shared responsibility.

Guide: Scaling Estimation

In big groups, estimation issues include the straightforward problem of synchronizing the units of estimation across teams and the more pernicious problem of disconnection between the *purpose* of estimates and the effort and techniques used.

Match Estimation Effort with Purpose

Big traditional groups push Taylorist "best estimation practices" onto groups, ignoring context and assuming "better" estimates are always better regardless of cost and drawbacks.

> Estimates don't need to be "accurate" or "precise";
> they need to be *useful*, and usefulness depends on purpose.

For example, the most frequent reason to try improving estimation "accuracy" (reducing variation to actual effort) is increased predictability. But let's reconsider *predictability* in an *agile* world. Even with impossible-to-achieve 100% "accurate" estimates (a contradiction of terms), predictability can't be assured, because new items *must* emerge. We sometimes remind our clients, "the only products that might be without change are those without customers." Thus we want *responding to change over following a plan*.

So why estimate?

ROI prioritization—If you want to get more bang for your bucks, you need estimates of *bang* and *bucks*.

Synchronizing dates—with...

> **internal groups**—e.g. for a roll-out campaign with Marketing

> **customers**—e.g. when delivering new equipment to a telecom operator, they need to organize a deployment project

> **events**—e.g. a trade show

Guide: Customer Collaborations over..., p. 187

Evaluate risks when there are "release promises"—In the unfortunate case that (apparently) fixed-scope and date release promises are still being made, estimation (and *re*-estimation) helps determine risks and the need for adaptation. A variant of big release promises is playing chicken in the market of **constrained** or **fixed-price** outsourcing projects, especially with fixed-scope projects. Estimates are used for profit feasibility and to evaluate on-going risks to profit and delivery.

Learn by exploring or by exposing differences—Estimating *together* increases learning about items, including where to focus attention for further clarification or splitting. And when people disagree about estimates, there's more learning. Notice that in this case it's the *estimating, not the estimate*, that's beneficial.

The Relative Effort of Specific Techniques

LeSS is driven by empirical process control, so no specific estimation technique is prescribed. Use anything from Planning Poker to Parametric Models. Most importantly:

> **Choose the simplest technique that matches the purpose and that fosters discussion and learning.**

Synchronizing Relative-Point Estimation Units Across Teams

Naturally, LeSS doesn't say what estimation unit to use, but relative (story) points are hugely popular. Why use them in a large-scale context? One reason is that they're relatively fast and easy to create, while simultaneously revealing differences and opportunities for learning. And all that increases the chance of *updating* estimates—something rarely done in large groups with many items if the estimation unit or technique is burdensome. Why update? That's valuable input to more learning and to empirical process control of product and processes.

Why *not* use relative points? Using a non-relative unit such as *person-days* eliminates the synchronization problem explored next. And a different unit may be widely understood or used, meaning less re-education or unit transformation. Also, some groups *abuse and distort* relative estimates (e.g. linking them to person days, using them to naively compare teams, linking them to targets and bonuses) and then they become meaningless and dysfunctional.

There's a problem scaling when points are used: They are *relative*—"5" has no absolute independent meaning. Two teams can define "5" differently. If estimates are used for decision-making or progress evaluation, then there are problems due to inconsistency. In contrast, if the group has a common agreement or synchronization on the size of points, then there are benefits:

> a consistent estimate of size—aids prioritization for ROI and increases flexibility of distributing items across teams; and

> a product-level velocity—aids forecasting.

How to synchronize?

Calibrate against done items—One simple approach is for teams to calibrate or compare against a set of *already done items* in the Product Backlog. For this to work well, there should be many such items, to increase the chance that some or many will be familiar to people.

Synchronize in multi-team or overall PBR—When two or more teams do PBR together and do estimation with points together, there's alignment across teams for a common meaning of relative points. Similarly, in overall PBR (with a couple of representatives from all teams), when estimation is done together, then points are synchronized.

LeSS Huge

In LeSS Huge, PBR is handled for each Requirement Area just as in the smaller LeSS framework. So, for example, an "overall" PBR session is for one requirement area, not the entire product.

There are no PBR rules specific to LeSS Huge.

Contents

Sprint Planning One in LeSS

SPRINT PLANNING

The only place that work and motion are the same thing
is the zoo where people pay to see the animals move around.
—Taiichi Ohno

ONE-TEAM SCRUM

Sprint Planning covers two distinct topics that boil down to *what* and *how*. *Topic one* focuses on selection of items and discussion of lingering questions, which should be short due to prior Product Backlog refinement to clarify items. *Topic two* focuses on initial design and a plan of work for items to get "done." The items and tasks make up the Sprint Backlog. Although the Product Owner decides the order of items, solely the Team decides how much to select. Selected items aren't a scope commitment or promise—they're a *forecast* the Team deems realistic.

LeSS SPRINT PLANNING

When scaling, these principles relate to Sprint Planning:

Whole-product focus—When there are multiple teams there's an increased chance of each going in a different direction and not working together. And that's reinforced or reduced in how planning is done.

Empirical process control & continuous improvement—Especially at scale with myriad different contexts and the need to improve, *how* Sprint Planning meetings are done in LeSS must be left up to the teams.

More with less—The traditional view of planning at scale is that it involves lots of complexity and dependency management. But planning in LeSS is simple, because feature teams handle the coordination.

• LeSS Rules •

Sprint Planning consists of two parts: Sprint Planning One is common for all teams; Sprint Planning Two is usually done separately for each team. Do multi-team Sprint Planning Two in a shared space for closely related items.

Sprint Planning One is attended by the Product Owner and Teams or Team representatives. They together tentatively select the items that each team will work on during the next Sprint. The Teams identify opportunities to work together and final questions are clarified.

Each Team has its own Sprint Backlog.

Sprint Planning Two is for Teams to decide how they will do the selected items. This usually involves design and the creation of their Sprint Backlogs.

Guide: Sprint Planning One

What else happens in Sprint Planning One (SP1) in LeSS, besides a focus on *what*? Before answering, a reminder: In earlier Product Backlog refinement, a guideline is a *group of teams with a set of items*. This increases the shared understanding and agility of the teams, and implies that during SP1 it's not obvious or constrained which Team will do what.

Guide: Overall PBR, p. 251

So the Teams and Product Owner need to decide the division of items. The Teams also need to identify opportunities to work together, and discuss how. And because this is complex work with many teams and items, SP1 is a time for the Product Owner and Teams to talk and on-the-spot adapt their decisions about priorities and division.

Duration? In a two-week Sprint, a maximum of two hours for SP1 and two hours for SP2. Use proportional durations for other Sprint lengths.

Who Goes?

By Sprint Planning One (SP1) there should be virtually no more questions about coming items, as they were previously clarified in Product Backlog refinement. Then who is needed? Just the Product Owner and the Teams or their representatives. But especially if it's early in the adoption of LeSS, there are frequently unresolved minor questions during SP1 owing to the many knowledge gaps in the young teams. Then consider inviting other experts who can help answer on-the-spot for small questions, e.g. product managers, users/customers, and so on. Aim to improve so this stop-gap measure isn't needed.

How many Team members? The range is from everyone down to one representative from each Team. Note that the Scrum Master is not a Team member and not a representative. Balance the number of Team members against the number of potential handoff problems if there are only a few representatives; consider also the need to create a sense of inclusion, and meeting room size. If there are representatives, rotate them over time.

Include at least one Scrum Master to coach for *ideas* on how do Sprint Planning in LeSS and to help improve it.

Picking Items

Pre-meeting division? Should the group decide before or during SP1 about the division of items to teams? Probably *during*. Why? This "decide as late as possible" approach defers the decision until there's the most information, which leads to the most informed choice. It also increases organizational agility because more options are kept open, and encourages whole-product focus since teams will need a broader view.

Product Owner decides? Should the Product Owner decide division of items to teams? Probably *not*; prefer to let the teams decide. Why? It reduces the Product Owner's effort, supports self-organization, increases agility and learning when a team chooses less familiar items, and invites a greater sense of ownership by teams in the product. Especially for newly formed teams, the freedom and encouragement to decide for themselves reinforces the messages of self-managing, trust rather than micro-management, putting decision making where the knowledge is, and valuing learning.

Competing for an item? What if different teams are competing for an interesting item? What a great problem! The teams are engaged. Then, a skilled Scrum Master offers decision-making ideas to the teams, ranging from arm wrestling to the Product Owner breaking a tie. That said, we recommend that the Product Owner can ultimately override which teams work on which items (probably in the context of some critical or risky item choices). And of course, the Product Owner can't decide the amount of items a team selects. All *that* said, *if she feels the need to direct teams to items, it probably signals deeper problems.*

Scenario

Here's an *example* SP1, pointing to techniques and purpose.

1. **Put cards on table**—The Product Owner uses cards for the coming items and puts them on the table in Product Backlog order. Team members discuss, decide, pick, and perhaps swap items.

2. **Spread high-order items?**—Consider this case: Assume team-A takes items with order [1, 2, 3, 4] and team-B takes [5, 6, 7, 8]. During the Sprint, team-A drops item-4 (the reason isn't relevant). Result? The high-order item-4 hasn't been done, even though (perhaps) team-B could have done it. If that's a meaningful problem, then try spreading high-priority items across teams. It's not a neat solution because it can compete with the goal of a team wanting to pick related items.

3. **Diverge to clarify?**—Ideally, items are ready for implementation without lingering questions. But sometimes there are some. If there are only two teams, then talking together is workable. If there are *seven* teams, answering serially in one big group can get slow. Then an alternative is for teams to "diverge"—people in each team go to a different area and write questions to clarify. The Product Owner, people from other teams (especially those involved in *multi-team Product Backlog Refinement* for the items), or others move around and help. Write answers to clarify and so any absent team members can read later.

4. **Find opportunities to work together**—Because the teams have shared work, have shared code, need to create one integrated product, and some may be working on strongly related items, SP1 and SP2 are times to discuss and identify opportunities for shared work and coordination. Prefer handling this in a *multi-team SP2* (see next guide). A complement or alternative is this: Near the end of SP1 discuss together.

Multi-site—Use video, and offer items, using a virtual shared space. If questions, the simplest solution is to just talk together. If there are many teams and lots of items to discuss, try a diverging technique such as a chat tool with one window per item.

Sync up after all of Sprint Planning?—After SP1 and all SP2 meetings, some groups like to hold a short sync-up session with people from all teams, to learn and adapt regarding new issues—for example, that a team dropped an item during SP2.

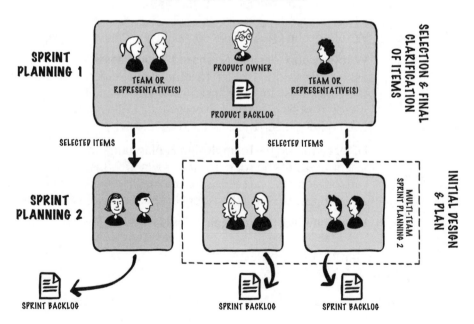

Guide: Multi-Team Sprint Planning Two

The simple case for Sprint Planning Two (SP2) is doing it separately and more-or-less in parallel by each team, with all team members. Key topics include design discussions, and creating a plan expressed in the Sprint Backlog. In a two-week Sprint, use a maximum duration of two hours.

Guide: Multi-Team PBR, p. 252

An often preferable alternative is **multi-team Sprint Planning Two** with two or more teams in the same room. This will be of interest to the same group that previously did together *multi-team Product Backlog Refinement* (PBR) for related items. Generally, do multi-team SP2 with teams with strongly related—in requirements or designs—items and, being together, can enhance discussion, design, coordination, and handling of shared work.

Multi-team SP2 dovetails with but is different from multi-team PBR. The latter is the teams together in mixed groups clarifying items, whereas multi-team SP2 is the teams doing their separate SP2 in a shared space so they can coordinate instantly.

Scenario—Here's an *example* multi-team SP2.

1. **Whole-group Q&A**—Clear some fog and create some paths.
2. **Whole-group design & shared work session**—For common designs, discuss and sketch together, or with merge-diverge workshop patterns. Identify tasks common to multiple teams, and decide how to cooperate. Note! All of SP2 is only (for example) two hours, so keep this short and timeboxed.
3. **Diverge for single-team design & planning**—Teams move to different areas of the room for their own SP2. Instantly coordinate with other teams via the *"just scream"* technique, an advanced variation of "just talk." This phase should be the majority of SP2.

Guide: Just Talk, p. 287

4. **When needed, merge again**—For issues that concern all teams.

"Opportunity for Shared Work" versus "Dependencies between Teams"

What is shared work? Suppose two or more teams have items that all require a common task. That's common or shared work.

A group still with a traditional mindset will speak of "dependencies between teams" and "managing the team dependencies." But LeSS cuts the Gordian Knot on this problem and perspective.

> The are no dependencies between teams.
> There are only opportunities for shared work.

How is shared work handled? In multi-team SP2, suppose that Teams A and B discover they have a shared task X. In discussion, it's *decided* that Team A plans to do it, and they add the task to their Sprint Backlog. Simple! If later in the Sprint it's *discovered* that Team B needs X first, then Team B will do task X instead and will just talk with team A to inform them, adapting with simple agility.

See or finding *opportunities for shared work* is easy for a self-organizing group of feature teams in multi-team SP2. But it's a big mindset and practice change for groups used to dealing with "dependencies between teams" arising from strict task ownership—as is common with individual code ownership, component teams, tasks assigned by project managers, or a separate "team" that manages the dependencies and coordinates.

Guide: No Software Tools for Sprint Backlog

The Product and Sprint Backlogs are *separate*, with different purposes. The Product Backlog is for managing items, while the Sprint Backlog is for a Team to manage themselves. It's not for the Product Owner or for external tracking. The *Scrum Guide* emphasizes that the *Sprint Backlog belongs solely to the Team*. So each

Guide: Tools for Large Product Backlogs, p. 210

Team needs to be able to choose their own unique tool and change it. Therefore, *don't use the same tool for Product Backlog and Sprint Backlogs*.

And although it's likely that a digital tool will be used for the Product Backlog, for the Sprint Backlogs we recommend this:

> **Don't use any software tool for Sprint Backlogs;**
> **just use physical visual management, probably cards on a wall.**

Why? For these reasons:

> **Increased interaction with team and information**—If one watches closely—as we have many times—the behavior of teams, comparing and contrasting teams that use "cards on a wall" for their Sprint Backlog versus a software tool, it is easy to see a night-and-day difference in the amount of interaction and collaboration of a Team acting as a *team*, rather than as a group of individuals. *Cards on walls encourage teams, cards in computers encourage individuals.* Also, the simplicity, ease of use and change, and panoramic visualization lead to teams that actively and eagerly work with the information in their Sprint Backlog on a wall. We see the opposite in practice when teams use a software tool.

> **Increased interaction during SP2**—Only using "cards on a wall" implies—and we recommend—that *no computers are used during SP2*. We observe that *computers kill collaboration during SP2*.

> **Prevention of tracking and micro-management**—Watch what happens if teams put their Sprint Backlog information in a software tool: Habituated temptations return for managers to start tracking teams, comparing teams, and micro-managing. Even the Product Owner may start micro-managing Sprint Backlogs. We've seen this dysfunction in almost every case where tools were used, and bet many of you have as well.

LeSS Huge

Sprint Planning is held per Requirement Area. No special rules.

Guide: Product Owner Team Meeting

Each Area Product Owner is relatively autonomous in decision making, so there's the risk of losing whole-product focus or alignment between areas in the choice of themes and items. A countermeasure is to hold—before the next Sprint—a Product Owner Team meeting. Area Product Owners share their particular situation and upcoming goals, and they discuss opportunities to align. Also, the one Product Owner can provide high-level guidance.

This meeting can also be used to discuss the results of the previous Sprint Review meetings in each Requirement Area, as input to planning.

Include some team representatives for more learning and feedback, and at least one Scrum Master to support reflection and improvement.

Contents

Open Space for coordination in LeSS

COORDINATION & INTEGRATION

1. Write down the problem. 2. Think really hard. 3. Write down the solution.
—*The Feynman algorithm, described by Murray Gell-Mann*

ONE-TEAM SCRUM

Spontaneous and instant interaction by team members towards their shared goal. Continuous integration of all work as the product gradually grows during the Sprint. Those are the essential characteristics of coordination and integration of a good one-team Scrum. You can hear a good team by the continuous buzz that the collaboration creates. You can almost hear their integration!

How does Scrum support this? The core elements are critical: self management, shared responsibility, shared goal, and empirical process control. And the secondary practices help: Sprint Planning, Sprint Backlog, and the Daily Scrum. These help create the buzz of great teams.

How to create this same spontaneous self-organized coordination and integration with *multiple* teams? That's the challenge in LeSS adoptions.

LeSS COORDINATION & INTEGRATION

Why *coordination* and *integration*? Because when you are integrating continuously, the coordination and integration channels strongly overlap: integration requires coordination, and coordination results in integration.

When scaling, principles related to coordination include:

Large-Scale Scrum is Scrum—In a one-team product group, the Team handles its own internal coordination. With multiple teams, the "internal" coordination responsibility extends across the teams since they all share a common goal to create a shippable increment. But most teams are unfamiliar with how to coordinate and integrate with others—they only know how to do it within their team, and previously a separate management group handled larger coordination.

Systems Thinking & Whole-product focus—Traditional silo teams are not responsible for the whole product, neither coordinating to ship it nor thinking about the system as a whole working together. Teams new to LeSS will be challenged to *see the whole*.

Empirical process control & Continuous improvement towards perfection—Coordination techniques need to be especially situational and customizable in large groups. Why? Because organizational and product contexts are quite complex and variable. And to increase a sense of ownership and engagement by the teams in coordination techniques, they need to define and refine them.

• LeSS Rules •

Cross-team coordination is decided by the teams. Prefer decentralized and informal coordination over centralized coordination.

Each Team has its own Daily Scrum.

Guide: Just Talk

After working in big groups for years, and observing tons of techniques for coordination across multiple teams, we've discovered the one technique that by far seems to work best. Here are the steps:

1. You realize a *need to coordinate* with team B;

2. stand up;

3. walk to team B;

4. say, "Hey! We need to talk."

We call it *just talk*.

This might sound like just a silly joke but we mean it. Why? A pattern we've seen is that *the more formal coordination methods in place, the less coordination happening*, because people feel it's important to use the "correct" channel for coordination. For example, you realize there's a coordination issue and then recall that tomorrow afternoon is a Scrum-of-Scrums meeting. So rather than just dealing with the coordination issue now, you decide to wait and bring it up then.

Accepting that the best way to coordinate between teams is to *just talk* leads to reframing the problem of coordination. The problem isn't "what coordination methods should we use?" but instead "how do the teams know they need to coordinate and talk?" How do they discover a need to talk *now*, and with *whom?*

> The problem with large-scale coordination isn't
> *what* coordination technique to use, but realizing
> that you need to coordinate and whom to talk with.

The upcoming guides each cover a coordination experiment that has a primary specific purpose and a secondary effect of creating a web of informal coordination links and information sharing. It is that informal web of information sharing that lets team members realize that they need to coordinate and just talk.

For example, a traveler is a person who travels between teams every Sprint to be at the place where he is most needed. The primary purpose is to share and teach his specific knowledge, but the secondary effect is that he brings practices from team to team and creates informal links between teams.

The main coordination guides:

> just talk
> communicate in code
> communities
> cross-team meetings
> open space
> component mentors
> travelers
> scouts
> leading teams

Before exploring how to communicate in code, we first explore what foundation is needed for a coordination-friendly environment.

Guide: Coordination-Friendly Environment

How to broadly and informally allow information to flow so teams realize this need? What's a coordination-friendly environment?

> teams owning coordination
> prefer decentralized and informal coordination
> feature teams with common aim
> whole-product focus
> friendly physical and technical environments

Teams Own the Coordination

In LeSS, the coordination and integration is owned by the teams, rather than by a separate group such as the "project management team" or "integration team." Meaning? Each team is responsible to coordinate with other teams to ensure one integrated product increment that can ship at least once per Sprint. Why is this important?

> - puts responsibility for coordination & integration decisions and actions with the people doing the hands-on work
> - supports the teams owning their processes—and then improving
> - reduces delays and handoff
> - reduces organizational complexity—no special roles needed

Prefer Decentralized over Centralized Coordination

Centralized coordination techniques are scheduled meetings with people from all teams together, such as Scrum of Scrums, Town Hall meetings, or a project status meeting (often re-badged with an agile label, but no different). Some weaknesses? They increase bottlenecking of information, handoff, delay, "it's not my problem" behaviors, and... can be incredibly boring!

Decentralized coordination techniques don't require a central meeting or group, and encompass networks of people interacting. For example, teams working in a shared space and talking, or multi-site teams discussing through a chat tool. They avoid bottlenecks, handoff, delay. But a few drawbacks: getting an overview—to see if issues are falling through the cracks—is more difficult; and information about the overall system is less broad and less consistently shared.

In favor of decentralized methods, they underpin more *emergent behavior* for coordination, and in LeSS *this emergence is encouraged*. Why? In large systems centralized and prescribed methods of coordination can inhibit (1) empirical process control and continuous improvement, and (2) teams having a sense of owning these processes.

No false dichotomies: Both approaches help, but prefer decentralized.

> **Promote bottom-up *emergent behaviors* for coordination. Decentralized techniques support this.**

Feature Teams with Common Aim

With component teams, the dependencies between teams are asynchronous, and the teams don't have a common aim. Feature F might require the work from component teams A and B. This Sprint team A works on their part of F, as it's the highest priority work for them. But team B works on their part a few Sprints later and then tries to integrate their work with team A. That won't work, so team B attempts to coordinate with team A. That causes a conflict as team A now has a different focus, so the coordination attempt is an interruption for them. This frames the situation between teams as "a bothersome interruption due to a dependency" and makes it difficult.

With feature teams and shared code, there will be team interactions all related to common aims. For example, in the same Sprint, feature teams working on different items modify common code and have some common or shared work. All this common work and its coordination is *related and synchronized within the same Sprint*. The feature teams keenly care about working together because coordination benefits all teams working towards a common increment.

Whole-Product Focus

Teams cooperating need a *common aim*. In contrast, teams planning their own separate Sprints into the future, each with its own "team backlog" leads to the teams focusing on their separate part rather than the whole product. This makes coordination between teams harder. Don't do that. Increase whole-product focus so that teams share aims for a common product increment at the end of a common Sprint.

Many elements of LeSS promote a whole-product focus: one Product Owner, one Product Backlog, one Sprint, one Sprint Planning One, one Sprint Review, and one integrated product increment.

Environments: Physical & Technical

Physical:

> The best for teams cooperating is when all teams are physically together—no separate cubicles or offices. Each team works at a table together in their own space, with lots of flat surfaces for visual management around them.

> To achieve as much co-location as possible, reduce the number of floors, buildings, and sites.

> For larger multi-team meetings in LeSS, and for design workshops with vast whiteboard areas, some large minimal-furniture meeting rooms are needed; we especially like those with floor-to-ceiling whiteboard panels or whiteboard paint.

> Regular travel by team members between sites (or buildings) is important for high-bandwidth interaction, learning, and real friendships or partnerships that have high levels of trust and understanding.

> Share cross-team spaces for relaxing, learning, and serendipitous sharing. Coffee area, lunch spaces with big shared tables, libraries with lazy chairs and lots of books that everyone can freely take.

> Provide collaboration goodies. Stools for pairing. Post-it notes for reminding. A4-size whiteboards for pair-session sketching. Whiteboard cling sheets for instant team discussion anywhere. Anything physical and *throwable* that encourages cooperation.

Technical:

> Shared *information* spaces, such as a wiki, Google docs, and so on. Especially because of the flood of information in a large group, the best-utilized we've seen have someone playing the (part-time) role of *librarian* who cares about and works on the discoverability: organizing, highlighting, and tagging information.

> Shared *communication* spaces, such as discussion groups, mailing lists, notification tools, video tools, and chat—especially group chat (e.g. Slack).

> Shared and social *coding* spaces, so that people can code together when apart in time or space, such as Screenhero (screen sharing), and "social coding" tools (e.g. GitHub/GitLab) that make it easier to communicate about code.

Guide: Communicate in Code

What do teams need to coordinate about? Often, *integration*. For example, teams might have shared work in a component. Traditionally, they would try to discover this *before making changes* so that they can manage their dependency, avoid code duplication, and avoid merge conflicts.

This leads to a key insight: *Coordination channels reflect integration lines*! But when continuously integrating, we can turn this around and we can *discover coordination needs via the integration lines*.

> Traditionally *coordination supported integration*,
> but we can also have *integration support coordination*.

The practice of discovering coordination needs through continuously integrating code is called *communicate in code*. How to do that? Here's an example. As a team member, I pull others' changes into my local copy *many* times a day. Each time, I quickly check all changes and when I discover another team working on the same component at the same time,

I'll *just talk* to them about how we can work together to benefit from one another's work.

A related simple practice is to add notifications in the version control system so that I can subscribe to changes in a particular component or file that interests me.

Warning: Avoid Branching!

Communicate in code makes *branching* even more *evil* than it already was. Why? Because especially at scale…

> When you branch, not only are you delaying integration, you are impeding coordination and cooperation between teams.

You can't communicate in code without continuously integrating.

Guide: Integrate Continuously

At every group we visit, we ask "Are you doing continuous integration?" And the answer invariably is "Oh yes! We've installed Jenkins!" (or equivalent build tool). But in that very same group, how are developers *behaving*? We see

> developers waiting *days* before checking in code;
> developers working on separate branches (or local Git repositories).

You can have Jenkins build systems *out the wazoo*, but *if developers **delay** pushing their code together, they aren't integrating continuously.*

> Continuous integration implies *integrating continuously*!
> Continuous integration is a *developer behavior*, not a tool.

That's why this guide is called *integrate continuously* and not "continuous integration" (CI), to emphasize the big idea: CI is a developer behavior, not a build system.

So what does CI really imply?

> **Continuous integration is...**
> a developer behavior to keep a working system by small
> changes growing the system by integrating very frequently on
> a "mainline" supported by a CI system with automated tests.

Some elaboration:

A developer behavior—CI is a *practice* that developers do "all the time." But since basic-behavior change is hard, there's endemic fake CI. And CI behavior is also inhibited by policies: Many large groups establish the policy "thou shalt not break the build" and even shame people who break it. What's the consequence? Delay integrating, of course! Then there's the *illusion* of a passing build. The CI policies and CI police end up hurting developers rather than helping them. Solution? Drive out fear by eliminating blaming and shaming, do test-driven development with constant refactoring for clean code, encourage frequent integration, and a stop-and-fix culture when a build breaks. Then CI becomes a practice that quickly informs developers about problems and the need to coordinate. *If developers say that CI is hurting them rather than helping them, there's something wrong.*

By small changes—*Large* changes to a stable system *will* destabilize and break it in large ways. The larger the change, the more time it takes—often superlinearly more—to get the system stable again. So avoid large changes. Instead, split each change into small changes—the lean thinking concept of small batches. Each micro-change integrates in the system easily.

Growing the system—*Growing* a system implies nurturing it and evolving it. With CI behavior, a developer continuously integrates his work. He does not wait for the whole feature to be complete. Rather, whenever a small amount of work can be integrated without breaking the system, he integrates it.

Very frequently—How frequent is "continuous"? Um... *continuously*. How close can a large group get to integrating *everything every second*, as a perfection vision? Maybe that's not achievable, but that's the direction, and it's limited by these variables:

> **People's skill to split large changes**—An expert in test-driven development (TDD) can usually split down to a *five-minute* cycle of change to the next stable state. Really!

> **Speed of integration**—Faster if (1) micro-small batch size (such as one five-minute TDD cycle), (2) modern fast version-control tools, and (3) elimination of delay policies such as "review the code before checking in."

> **Duration of feedback cycle**—Shorter requires (1) fast tests running on fast computers, (2) parallelization, and (3) multi-step staged execution of test subsets that fail fast.

> **Ability to work on the "mainline"**—Not on branches.

Guide: Communities

In a cross-functional-team organization, the group still has to attend to cross-team concerns including functional and other skills, standards, tools, and designs. The go-to solution is to create *communities*.

A community is a group of volunteers from the teams who share an interest or topic and have the passion to deepen their knowledge or take action through discussion and interaction with peers. Participation in communities is *completely voluntary*.

A community isn't a team and doesn't implement items. Typically, a community is for a functional practice (e.g. design and architecture) but can exist for any interest, such as infrastructure tooling, communication, Scrum Masters, and so forth. The scope of a community may be just a few teams (e.g. in one LeSS Huge Requirement Area), a product, a site, or the enterprise.

Communities ought to be *dynamic*. Anyone can start a community. And when there is no more passion in the community or it is working dysfunctionally, then it will *die*—sometimes a slow lingering death!

Aims and Authority of Communities

There are roughly two major aims for a community:

> **Learning**
Communities focus on sharing knowledge, learning, and improving skills. *Communities of Practice*, such as clean-code community and test community, fall into this category.

> **Cross-team agreements**
There are product-level or enterprise-level cross-team concerns that must be taken care of. Examples are architectural guidelines, UI standards, or test automation practices. Another less obvious example of a cross-team agreement is the architecture community's speculation about architectural evolution that should guide the individual teams' design decisions.

Many communities fulfill both aims, and often will. For example, a *test* community might propose a recommendation for test automation agreement.

On communities that produce *agreements*: Can communities make decisions that the teams must adopt? No.

> **Communities cannot make decisions for the teams, but they can produce something that the teams *decide* to adopt.**

Thus, if a community wants its output to be adopted, then it had *better ensure a broad participation from all the teams.*

Tips for Communities

A flourishing community benefits from proactive organization and attention. Good communities

> have a **community coordinator** with passion for the concern and desire to cultivate a strong community that cares; preferably someone who is an active hands-on practitioner;

> actively try to recruit participation from most teams;

> are visible and easily discoverable so that everyone knows the current communities and knows how to join;

> preferably focus on concrete problem-solving goals— they make learning practical and concrete;

> have agreed how they work and make decisions;

> might have a Scrum Master who helps them work and improve, and who facilitates community meetings or workshops;

> use wiki, discussion groups, group chat;

> meet regularly; and

> are strongly encouraged within the organization; everyone knows that it is OK and indeed *expected* for them to join communities and spend effort in community activities.

Here are a few ways to drive a stake through the heart of a community and destroy it:

> Forgo a community coordinator or the coordinator doesn't care (this often happens if the person was *assigned*).

> Hold frequent meetings just for the sake of meeting.

> Have mostly members that are not in feature teams.

> Regard the community as secondary so that participation is downgraded because "we're too busy to participate."

Recommended communities—We notice that certain communities almost always need to exist and flourish for a successful group. These include *human interface*, *design/architecture*, and *test*.

Activities and outputs—A community is not a team and doesn't implement items. What do they do or produce?

> **Teaching**—e.g. returning to their feature teams and teaching their team members about the framework design ideas.

> **Organizing education or coaching**—e.g. organizing a course on modern human interface (HI) design.

> **Proposing guidelines or standards**—e.g. proposing HI guidelines.

> **Identifying work**—e.g. "we need a much faster message bus."

> **Investigating**—e.g. holding a *spike* to learn something.

> **Learning & sharing**—e.g. organizing a lightning talk session where community members share information with each other.

> **Design workshopping**—e.g. getting together at a whiteboard to discuss and sketch ideas for a framework design.

Guide: Handling Special Items, p. 207

A community can identify the need to investigate something. Big investigations should go through the product backlog, but smaller ones can go directly through the community. Investigation and other activities might also generate follow-on work, such as "make the new framework." This is not done by a community—they aren't a team. When the follow-on work can be handled by a regular feature team, record it in the Product Backlog so that work flows to feature teams in one consistent way.

Company-wide communities—In addition to communities within one group, there's often a need for communities that span the company—for example, for cross-product consistent user experience. The traditional organizational structure for handling that concern is a separate single-function group, but in a cross-functional organization the alternative is a company community of feature-team members from different product communities, such as the various community coordinators.

Guide: Culture Follows Structure, p. 64

Fake communities—Traditional large groups are structured as single-function teams, such as architecture, test, and so forth. Most organizations are implicitly optimized to avoid changing the status quo manager and specialist positions and power structures. Consequently, we've see *fake communities* that are just the old single-function teams relabeled the "architecture community" and so on, giving the superficial impression that something has changed when nothing has changed. Sad.

Guide: Cross-Team Meetings

Naturally, by **cross-team meeting** we mean an event with people from at least two teams, either all team members or representatives. In LeSS, cross-team meetings are further classified as *multi-team, overall,* and *other.* There are guides (or sub-guides) for most specific cases of them in LeSS; this guide summarizes them, with examples and a few tips.

multi-team meeting	overall meeting	other
all members from at least two teams	**people from all teams, representatives, or all**	**participants vary**
multi-team Product Backlog Refinementp. 252	Sprint Planning One p. 276	community meetings
multi-team Sprint Planning Two p. 280	overall Product Backlog Refinement p. 249	Open Space p. 305
multi-team design workshop p. 301	Sprint Review p. 316	architecture learning workshops p. 303
	Overall Retrospective p. 317	

Large Meetings

Facilitator—Most meetings are more effective with a skilled facilitator, but especially *big* meetings or workshops. A Scrum Master is a good candidate facilitator, but don't just ask her to "facilitate the meeting," as skillful facilitation needs education and preparation—especially in the case of *large-group facilitation* skills.

Diverge–merge cycles—Being all together in a meeting or workshop can increase common understanding, alignment, and reduce information scatter. That's good. But especially in a big group, drawbacks include many people not engaged or drowned out, and less diversity and quantity of ideas. So use a cyclic diverge–merge meeting pattern whereby teams or mixed groups are sometimes (e.g. for 30 minutes) diverged in separate areas of the room, and sometimes all together in common activity or discussion. Merging is important, but remember:

> **Centralization destroys energy; decentralization creates it.**

Multi-Site Meetings

Many LeSS groups have multi-site development, so we've coached and observed *too* many multi-site cross-team meetings.

Tips:

> *Seeing*, **a precondition for empathy**—Cooperation is connected to trust and empathy. To cultivate that, we need to engage our senses—we need to *see* our colleagues. And to make that happen...

> **Free ubiquitous video tools**—We've seen clients in these contrasting cases: (1) Required to use an expensive video conferencing system in a special room. (2) Use a free and ubiquitous video tool and a cheap video projector. The results of ubiquitous video tools are night-and-day in terms of use and engagement.

> **"Cloud" shared-document tools**—Observe, "I'll update the Excel sheet and put it in the shared folder" *versus* "Here's a link to the shared Google Sheet we can all see and edit while we talk." Second case is *much* better.

> **Diverge–merge**—See the previous section on this technique. In this case, the natural diverged-phase groups are each separate site, which sucks but is the art of the possible in this case.

Guide: Multi-Team Design Workshop

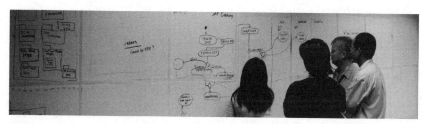

When several teams want to collaborate on the *speculative* design of features, components, or large-scale architectural elements, hold a multi-team **design workshop** with **agile modeling**.

When?—A multi-team design workshop can and often *should* happen in multi-team *Sprint Planning Two* for items that are about to be implemented. But when the novelty or complexity of the upcoming items is high, or to leisurely generate more alternatives when options and creativity are important then hold a design workshop in a prior Sprint. This is less desirable since there is more potential for waste but might be needed because Sprint Planning Two is short and timeboxed. A prior-Sprint multi-team design workshop is likely when applying *Take a Bite*.

Guide: Multi-Team Sprint Planning Two, p. 280

Guide: Take a Bite, p. 202

What?—For everything! A design workshop can be for speculative design of human interfaces (HI), data models, algorithms, objects, or large-scale components, services, interactions, and "architecture."

Who?—Per definition, a multi-team design workshop is all members from two or more teams. An important and common variation is an **Architecture Community design workshop**, a community meeting that is likely to include representatives from many teams.

How?—With **agile modeling**, which implies a group together creating simple "barely good enough" models that foster creativity, conversation, visualization, and quick change. The agile modeling credo?

> We model *to have a conversation.*

The tools of agile modeling? First and foremost, *avoid software tools*. Those tend to kill collaboration, flow, and idea generation. Focus on simple physical tools, including sticky notes and whiteboards.

Tips for a design workshop:

> **Vast "whiteboard" spaces**—*Workshop success is proportional to the amount of whiteboard space*! And instead of standard whiteboards, cover all wall space with sheets of special plastic "whiteboard like" material, such as "Wizard Wall" sheets.

> **Multi-site modeling**—In this case, software tools are hard to avoid. Combined with video conferencing, one technology is collaborative-sketching "whiteboard" apps on tablets or browsers. Another approach we've used for two-site design workshops is physical whiteboards, each viewable with a webcam, combined with diverge–merge cycles.

> **Recording**—The important aspects of agile modeling are the conversations, creativity, and growing alignment, not the sticky notes or whiteboard sketches. If the group wants to remember or share their results from a design workshop, they can take photos or videos.

Models are not documentation—Agile modeling is for speculative "barely good enough" models to inspire next steps (such as coding), not long-lived documentation, so keep it simple. If the group wants to create some documentation, then apply the next guide...

this is for conversation & speculation, not for documentation

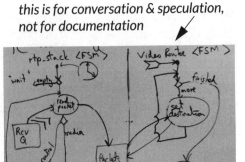

Guide: Current-Architecture Workshop

A cross-team *current-architecture **learning** workshop* is for educating about the existing in-the-code architecture. That learning is especially important to groups recently adopting LeSS and moving from component teams to feature teams and shared code. How come? Because in the former case most people know little about the overall architecture or the more granular architecture of other components. That knowledge is important for feature teams to work together. These workshops are often initiated by the Architecture Community or by component mentors.

Tips:

> **Learn as-is architecture**—Ensure participants grasp that this workshop is to educate people about current *as-is* architecture; the focus is on learning and teaching. Use *design workshops* for *might-be*.

> **Sketch different architectural views**—Visualize multiple views by using the 4+1 architectural view model, including a *logical view* of the large components, a *deployment view* of hardware, networking, and processes, and so on.

> **Play-act scenarios**—Help people learn and remember—in a fun energetic way—key scenarios of execution by people playing component roles and "tossing the ball" of control between them.

> **Create technical memos**—Sketch out summaries of unusual or noteworthy architectural elements or design decisions, such as "our use of the Drools rules engine, and why" or "FSMs: our dominant theme—what and why."

> **Hold Q&A sessions, video recorded**—In addition to diverging for creating the 4+1 architectural views and technical memos, also regularly merge all together and hold Q&A sessions for each view and memo, discussing both what and *why*. Video record these.

Most importantly, people learn while together, and secondarily, an effortless digital record is created for others to watch later on.

Guide: Component Mentors

Feature teams have to work in unfamiliar areas of code. How to help them learn these areas?… especially in cases where a software component is delicate or fragile. Help them with a **component mentor** who…

> is a regular feature-team member, but reserves mentoring time,

> holds current-architecture learning workshops to teach others about the component,

> finds and mentors targeted developers in many teams to learn more about the component,

> teaches while pair- or mob-programming,

> creates a component community,

> organizes or participates in design workshops when there will be a major impact on the component,

> does code reviews and gives improvement feedback,

> evangelizes for people to improve the code and add tests,

> monitors the long-term health of the component, and

> finds and mentors other mentors.

Guide: Integrate
Continuously, p. 293
Does NOT approve code commits—Component mentors do *NOT* do approval. They are teachers and mentors of the component. They are not a *quality gate*, as that would introduce *dramatically delayed integration*—and hence impede coordination and cooperation. In a feature-team shared-code organization there is an *optimistic* policy of people committing code and integrating it without delay. That said, there are two common code-contribution cases:

> **Direct commit**—People commit and push to the central shared repository (or "head of trunk") without delay. This is the default

optimistic behavior. And when *wacky code* is discovered, a mentor *teaches*, which will be less and less frequent as the mentor's teaching and improving takes hold.

> **Pull request**—The component mentor is not a *gate*, but there are times—such as when someone is changing unfamiliar code—when a developer will *voluntarily* create a "pull request" for code for the mentor to review and provide feedback on it before merging it.

Naturally, people don't only do direct commits or pull requests; they'll use direct commits for more familiar code, and pull requests for the unfamiliar. Best of both worlds.

Does NOT handle component bugs—A seductive local optimization is to route component bugs to a component mentor. They'll get done so fast and skillfully! ... And then you have no component mentors.

Share the mentoring—Especially in the early phase of transitioning to shared code and feature teams, a mentor can become overburdened. Add more mentors and share the work.

Guide: Open Space

Institute regular **Open Space**[1] meetings for learning, coordination, and more. Open Space is a meeting technique with self-organization baked in. Steps:

1.Together create an agenda of parallel sessions on burning-issue topics.

2.Conveners host the sessions and people participate as desired. The Law of Two Feet is mandated: If you're not learning or contributing, move somewhere else.

Some uses of Open Space in LeSS:

> as a regular (e.g. bi-weekly) meeting for learning and cooperation
> **Tip:** Have *food and coffee* while *opening the space*

---

1. For more on Open Space, check out Harrison Owen's book *Open Space Technology*.

> > as the format for an Overall Retrospective to analyze situations and design improvement experiments

> > as a "quarterly" one-day meeting for deeper learning and strengthening social networks

> > as the format for a community meeting

Meetings Similar to Open Space?

Open Space is part of a family of popular collaborative meeting processes worth trying. These include *World Café*, *Lean Coffee*, and its much more fun cousin... *Lean Beer*.

Guide: Travelers

We worked with a product group that had a couple of experienced technical experts. This group created feature teams with dedicated members but could not decide in which team to add the most scarce experts whose knowledge was critical to all teams. (Aside: This siloed knowledge was a weakness exposed by the LeSS adoption.) So the two key experts temporarily became **travelers**.

Travelers work as a normal team member in the team for one Sprint. They have a shared responsibility for all of the work of the team. Importantly, they have a secondary goal of reducing the dependency on them, usually by teaching. Note that the teams who do not have a traveler with them this Sprint are on their own and need to figure out how to achieve their goals without the constant support of the expert.

To underline this last point: a traveler *avoids* helping other teams during the Sprint. That's an important behavior to spur the dynamic of a team focusing on *learning* from the traveler visiting for the Sprint, as well as eliminating the need for scarce expertise.

Having a "bottleneck" expert as traveler during the early stage of a LeSS adoption is an obvious case. But anyone can be a traveler; some people love to work that way. Larger groups, especially can benefit from travelers because they bring lots of *informal information* and *create relationships* between teams—elements that tend to get weaker and weaker in larger and larger groups. Travelers can strengthen a network of informal coordination channels and increase the consistency of some knowledge or practice across teams.

Caution: In LeSS a dominant quality of each team is *long-lived and stable membership*, because of the long time it takes for a team to jell and move towards high performance. The idea of some travelers in LeSS is not meant to be used to mutate an organization into a matrix-management structure with short-lived "project teams." Ow!

When and how do travelers decide what team to visit for the Sprint? Probably in Sprint Planning One. And this is a self-organizing group, so the traveler and the teams make the decision, not the Product Owner.

Travelers could be temporary or "permanent," but note: To be a traveler requires that there's a team willing to accept an incoming visitor for a Sprint. Travelers can't force themselves on a team. So the overall group will self-regulate the degree of travelers, and one can't be a "permanent" traveler if teams aren't accepting visitors any longer. And therefore either then, or really at any time, a traveler can find a home.

Guide: Scouts

A simple technique for teams working together is to send a **scout**—not the Scrum Master—to other teams to learn something, and then to report back. It's a simple way to learn when there's a need to just talk, and whom to talk with.

The most likely time and place for a scout to roam is to the Daily Scrum of other teams, as a silent observer. What teams? Probably the ones with whom they did multi-team Sprint Planning Two or multi-team Product Backlog Refinement.

Guide: Maybe Don't Do Scrum of Scrums

A Scrum of Scrums meeting is a Daily-Scrum-like meeting between team representatives—not Scrum Masters or managers—that's commonly held three times per week.

Scrum of Scrums is a formal centralized meeting and *thus not preferred*.

That said, sometimes Scrum of Scrums works really well and then... keep it! But most often teams new to scaling feel they *must* do it owing to misinformation about scaling, and they keep doing it, even though it isn't really useful. If so, drop it and focus on other coordination methods.

Guide: Leading Team

A **leading team** is a team that has additional responsibilities in the delivery of a feature or a set of related features. The team refines and implements feature items, but additionally focuses on the big picture of the set of features together. Usually the leading team's responsibility focus is on (1) education, and (2) coordination (often with external groups).

Guide: New Area for Giant Requirement, p. 223

Education—A leading team is more connected to a set of features than are the other teams, perhaps because of their background expertise or because they were the first team to work in this area. As other teams eventually join their effort on a large set of related features, these incoming teams need education (e.g. about the domain and evolving solution), and the leading team plays that teaching role. For example, during multi-team Product Backlog Refinement they explain the background or details of items they've worked on, to help teams understand new ones. Or they hold a current-architecture learning workshop related to major new elements.

Coordination—For the big feature or set of features, the leading team often takes up coordination responsibilities with *external groups* such as (1) an external group creating a component or (2) undone departments. In contrast, coordination between internal teams is as much as possible left to the teams themselves. A closer look:

> **coordination with external component groups**—Big products often have some components created—at least when first adopt-

ing LeSS—by another group. So some work needs to be coordinated. Instead of many teams doing it ad hoc or a separate management group doing it, the leading team does it. Although coordination is handled by the leading team, *clarification* should go directly between a specific team and the external group, to avoid more handover waste.

> **coordination with Undone department**—Leading teams take feature responsibility end-to-end until the feature is shippable in the product. With a weak Definition of Done, coordination and support to the Undone department during the final activities is needed, to make the feature truly shippable. Notice that the leading team is taking on a responsibility traditionally handled by project or release managers.

Guide: Mix and Match Techniques

Many of the techniques covered in this chapter can *reinforce* each other, used together. Some examples:

JUST TALK   SCOUT   OPEN SPACE

TRAVELER   COMMUNITIES   COMPONENT MENTOR

Component Community—The component mentor becomes the community coordinator for a component community. The community has a discussion list for build failures, code reviews, etc. They meet regularly and every now and then have...

Component-Community Open Space—The component community discovered a lot of discussion and training needs and decides to organize an Open Space. Of course, not just the community is invited but everyone is welcome. Topics are raised, discussions held. They discover the need for a...

Multi-Team Design Workshop with Component Mentor—Component mentors anticipate lots of changes in the component and organize a design workshop. During this session a component mentor identifies what teams to offer joining as he is a...

Component Mentor Traveler—The component mentor's specialized knowledge limits the ability of many new feature teams to make changes in the component. He became a traveler to help the teams that need him most. Traveling can get lonely, so he also decided to join the...

Traveler Community—All the travelers form their own community to share their experiences joining a team for one Sprint, share gossip, and learn from each other. Eventually they decide to organize a...

Traveler Community Open Space—Which of course also welcomes non-travelers! Several people from the **Communities community** also join so they can learn about the practice of community open spaces and share that information with other teams.

> The more combined, the more powerful they become.

LeSS HUGE

Guide: Integrate Continuously, p. 293

Most previous guides apply to LeSS Huge. Some, such as *Integrating Continuously*, are intrinsically cross-Requirement-Area practices. There are no special LeSS Huge rules.

Building on the previous *Just Talk* guide, take inspiration from its motivation and approach to encourage *informal decentralized* communication across Requirement Areas.

Contents

Sprint Review Bazaar in LeSS

REVIEW & RETROSPECTIVE

A constitution should be short and obscure.
—Napoléon Bonaparte

ONE-TEAM SCRUM

At the heart of Scrum is empirical process control for both the *product* and *how it's created*. Create a small shippable slice of the product, then inspect what and how, and adapt both. In essence, that's the purpose of the Sprint Review and Retrospective.

In the **Sprint Review** the users/customers and other stakeholders learn with the Product Owner and Team. Users hands-on explore the new items. Everyone explores what's going on in the market and with users. And last but not least, they discuss what to do in the future. In the **Sprint Retrospective** the Team reflects on their experience and explores how to easily deliver an amazing product increment that improves the environment, and makes lives better—including their lives. They create an experiment to try in the next Sprint, aiming towards this impossible perfection.

LeSS SPRINT REVIEW & RETROSPECTIVES

The upcoming guides cover Review and Overall Retrospective, but not single-team Retrospectives. Related principles when scaling:

Customer-centric—*"Why would we want to include users/customers in every Sprint Review?"* Old groups aren't used to learning together across silos. We've met far too many teams that *never* met a user and were afraid to include users in reviews, as that would mean real transparency.

Transparency—Executives *espouse* the salutary benefit of transparency, but watch what happens when painfully true transparency is enabled in a group new to LeSS. Ouch! Many groups are opaque and afraid to reveal the actual messy state of affairs. It's hard to get over that.

Continuous improvement towards perfection—We've had clients that once a *year* held a *postmortem* to create heavenly improvements for next year's fantasy. And worked in many big groups that said "Things are basically good enough." There's no *intrinsic* desire for improvement.

Empirical process control—Many large-scale organizations have a centralized process or PMO group tasked with improvement, based on a Taylorist culture of pushing "improvements" onto teams. There's no sense of empowerment or engagement. The notion of empirical process control for the product and how it's created *every Sprint* is a million miles away from their habits.

Whole-product focus and Systems thinking—Big groups with silo teams don't have the attitude and behavior of looking at the whole, being responsible for the whole, and thinking about the system.

• LeSS Rules •

There is one product Sprint Review; it's common for all teams. Ensure that suitable stakeholders join to contribute the information needed for effective inspection and adaptation.

Each Team has its own Sprint Retrospective.

An Overall Retrospective is held after Team Retrospectives to discuss cross-team and systemwide issues and to create improvement experiments. Attended by Product Owner, Scrum Masters, Team representatives, and managers (if any).

Guide: Adapt the Product Early and Often

If your entire company is *nine* people, we hope you won't do something as dumb as creating an annual plan of scope and schedule, and trying to march on-plan towards a big-batch end-date for user acceptance testing. But the bigger the product group, the more likely that institutionalized dumbness exists, for reasons packed in a can of worms that we won't open. The upshot is that when a large group transitions to LeSS, there's a chance they'll carry the baggage of *predictive planning* and *inspection for acceptance* into the Sprint Review, which becomes an event to see if the group is *on schedule* and if the items will be *accepted*.

Don't do that. Instead, try *agility* and *learning together*. In the Sprint Review seek new information about profit drivers, strategic customers, business risks, competitors, new problems and opportunities, in order to adapt and decide the product direction for next Sprint. And *discuss together* about the new items—everyone learning something. Repeat forever. This is a major mindset and behavior change for large groups.

Sprint Review & Retrospectives in LeSS

LeSS SPRINT REVIEW & RETROSPECTIVE

SPRINT REVIEW

TEAM RETROSPECTIVE

OVERALL RETROSPECTIVE

Guide: Review Bazaar

A Sprint Review *bazaar* is analogous to a science fair: A large room has multiple areas, each staffed by team representatives, where the items developed are explored and discussed together with users, teams, etc. The opening photo in this chapter shows an example.

Note! The bazaar is not the whole Review. There's also the critically important post-bazaar discussing and *deciding what to do next*.

For a bazaar, the macro-level steps for the Sprint Review are (1) diverge for a bazaar-style exploration of items, and (2) merge for all-together discussion with the Product Owner towards next steps. Reserve lots of time for the critical second step.

Example bazaar-phase steps:

1. Prepare different areas for exploring different sets of items. Include devices that are running the product. Team members are at each area to discuss with users, people from other teams, and other stakeholders. Learning happens both ways! Include paper feedback cards to record noteworthy points and questions.

2. Invite people—including other team members—to visit any area.

3. Start a short-duration timer (e.g. 15 minutes) during the exploration. The timer creates a cadence move-on to another area.

4. While people hands-on explore the items and discuss together, record noteworthy points on cards.

   > Tip: Avoid *demos*, as they don't engage users and don't provoke deep feedback. Rather, encourage hands-on use by users. Team members can answer questions or guide.

5. At the end of the short cycle, invite people to rotate or remain for another cycle. These mini-cycles help a more broad and diverse exploration of all items.

After the bazaar come the major all-together discussion steps:

1. People sort their feedback and question cards so that the Product Owner sees important ones first.

2. While all together, the Product Owner leads discussion of the feedback cards, as shown in Figure 14.1.

3. The Product Owner leads discussion on the market and customers, upcoming business, market feedback about the product, and broadly, what's going on outside.

4. Most importantly for the entire Review, there's a discussion—and perhaps a decision—about the direction for the next Sprint.

Figure 14.1 Product Owner leading feedback-cards discussion

Multi-site—How to hold a bazaar when multiple sites are involved? One approach is to replicate it at each site (time zones permitting), but ensure that all feedback and questions get to the Product Owner. For the all-together discussions after the bazaar, try video conferencing tools.

Another or complementary option for the bazaar is for people to play with features on devices wherever they are. To record feedback, rather than using cards, consider digital tools such as a chat window for each item.

Guide: Overall Retrospective

"We can't do continuous delivery because of the deployment policies." "We have too many sites." "Our code is crap." "Requests from government regulators take ages before we hear about them." "We're going too slow." "The users aren't participating." "HR won't let us." "The vendors aren't involved."

These, and many more, are statements we've heard over the years in groups adopting LeSS. One thing they all have in common is they relate to all-team concerns and/or the overall *system*—spanning everyone and everything from concept to cash.

The time and place to deal with these systemic concerns—and to think about improving the system towards perfection—is the Overall Retrospective. Who's there? The Product Owner, team representatives, Scrum Masters, and managers. Why? They're all part of the *system*, with interest in improving it. They (1) discuss and learn about some aspects of the system, (2) create a systemic improvement experiment for the next Sprint, and (3) reflect on the results of the last retrospective experiment and use that to learn and adapt.

One of the LeSS principles is *continuous improvement towards perfection*. We once visited a huge group that was considering a LeSS adoption and a manager said, "We're making a profit and have a stable customer base. Why should we bother to improve?" Ow! We've learned that dealing with this attitude is one of the harder challenges with early adoptions, because in the prior system so many people have been so disconnected from the customers and business results. Connecting teams with real customers and users, and engaging them in product ownership, are key steps to cultivating an intrinsic desire to improve towards *perfection*. And what is that? Well, there isn't one answer, but there are examples:

Guide: Organizational Perfection Vision, p. 66

> The product is awesomely popular and profitable, defect-free, and features are created with ease.

> The organization has agility; it can easily change direction with almost no friction or cost—it can *turn on a dime for a dime*.

> Everyone has great breadth and depth of knowledge, cares deeply about the customers and product, and are happy in the work.

That should keep the group improving for awhile!

Some Overall Retrospective tips:

> Reflect on the results of the last experiment.

> As emphasized in the following guide, focus on the *system*.

> Hold the Overall Retrospective early in the next Sprint, since the last day of the Sprint includes the Review and Team Retrospective meetings, and so people can be bored or burned out for meetings on that day.

> Include at least two major steps: (1) the analysis of something systemic, and (2) the design of a systemic improvement experiment.

> Create only *one* new experiment; be focused, and follow through.

> Remember that, especially in large-scale systems, an experiment can involve many weeks or months of support and activity, so the new experiment may be strongly related to a prior one.

Multi-site—Try a multi-site Overall Retrospective with video and diverge–merge cycles. For example, (1) each site separately does *5-Whys* analysis or systems modeling for a concern, (2) each site shares results, (3) sites separately brainstorm countermeasures, (4) sites together share these and pick an experiment. Also, as some issues are site specific (e.g. environment and culture), try site-level retrospectives. Figure 14.2 shows an example.

Figure 14.2 multi-site Overall Retrospective, during a diverge phase

Multi-team Retrospectives—A Retrospective involving all team members from two or more Teams is another option in LeSS. Some teams might want to do that when, for example, they've been working closely together. But this doesn't replace an Overall Retrospective, where the focus is on the system.

Guide: Improve the System

It's instinctive for all of us to fall into the thinking mistake of *local* concerns and optimization. In an Overall Retrospective signs of that include—perhaps this will be a surprise—collecting results of the Team-level Retrospectives as the starting point of "overall" analysis. But this bottom-up approach misses an important insight of *systems thinking*: *the system is not the sum of its parts.* So *beware of bottom-up.* Of course, this doesn't literally mean ignoring an important escalated issue coming from all the teams. Those need attention. We mean something subtler:

> **Understand & improve the system by focusing on the *system*.**

What's the *system*? Everyone and everything from concept to cash, and all its dynamics in time and space. People, organizational design, physical and technical environments, and more are part of the system—and all related and interacting.

The first step of **systems thinking** is "simply" recognizing that there is a *whole system*, with elements that *influence* one another within a whole. These influences can have *delays*, create *reinforcing cycles*, and have *unintended* or *hidden* consequences, with a *cascade* of new influences.

In a way, "recognize there's a *system*" seems a trivial idea without use. But that's not true, because we Homo sapiens haven't evolved brains for *"What's the nonlinear delay dynamics in our organization?"* We evolved for *"I'll have chocolate, now."* And this local perspective is reinforced in big old organizations with single-specialized groups, as this causes the loss of system perspective. The *Business Analysis* group is concerned with *their* tasks and being *locally* efficient, and they don't know—nor are expected to know—other perspectives. In short, there's biology, structure, culture, and conditioning to see the *part*, not to *see the whole*.

Understand—How to apply systems thinking? How to understand the system, or more correctly, how to discuss and think about a *model* of the system? With a **systems model**, also known as a *causal loop diagram*. Now, superficially a systems model uses a specific visual-modeling language or notation, but first let's step back and consider what's going on in this session:

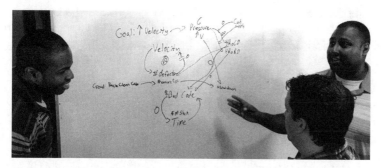

At a surface level they're drawing a diagram in some notation, though that's not very important. But the content and focus is. They're thinking about and discussing the system and its dynamics, they are *system thinking*. Furthermore—and not to be underestimated—they are demonstrating the credo of good modeling:

We model to have a conversation.
The output is shared understanding, not the model.

While the group is in an Overall Retrospective sketching a systems model together, they're exploring each other's understanding of the *as-is* system and their beliefs. They're taking complex and invisible notions in each other's minds, and making them visible... "Oh! Now I *see* what you are thinking about the current system. Is that true?"

Understand More During Early Adoption—This guide has emphasized using systems modeling during retrospectives, but it's also useful during "Step 0: Educate Everyone" when getting started with a LeSS adoption.

Guide: Getting Started, p. 59

Action—The Overall Retrospective includes a second major step to design a systemic improvement experiment: action! Systems modeling can be used in this step too. For example, the group can speculate about a future *to-be* system model and discuss and explore its consequences. And they can discuss and model the dynamics of introducing a particular change experiment into the as-is system. What might happen? We can't predict the future, but we can think about its scenarios. Besides the obvious action experiment, notice that something subtler can and will happen: people's minds have changed as they learn a better model of the system, and that itself can "organically" lead to improved behaviors or decisions in the future, unrelated to any specific action.

First Steps in Learning to Systems Model

There's a non-trivial language for systems modeling, since systems are non-trivial. But the basics aren't complicated, and good enough for lots of useful discussion. The basics:

> **variable**—A thing expressed as a measurable quantity, such as velocity (rate of delivery) of features, and code quality.

> **causal link**—Influence between variables, such as saying if number of features increases then waste increases, and vice versa.

>> **Note!** Thinking about interactions and causal relationships is the *critical focus* needed in systems thinking. And doubly so for large-scale systems, because the time and space are vast, and the interaction dynamics between the myriad parties are usually full of *hidden* but crucial facts and forces.

> **opposite effect**—A causal link can have an opposite effect, such as if the percentage of weak developers goes up, then code quality goes down, and vice versa

The sketch in Figure 14.3 shows notation for variables, and direct and opposite causal links.

Tip: Sketch a systems model on a whiteboard with sticky notes for the variables—to make moving them easy.

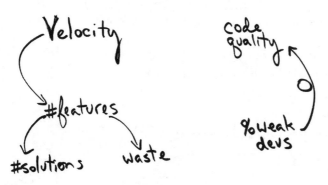

Figure 14.3 causal links, variables, and opposite effects

Some other useful concepts and related notation:

> **delay**—One key reason for flawed beliefs of how a system behaves is that influences can have delays. Causes and effects are not close in time—nor close in space in large-scale development. And delayed consequences, such as information loss, can be hidden in the interaction effects between groups. So people have trouble seeing and learning these dynamics. For example, managers are pushed to increase velocity, and do the *quick fix* of hiring many low-cost (and it turns out in this case, weak) developers. In the short run this quick fix gives the appearance of increasing velocity. But there is a long-term delayed consequence of reduced code quality, leading to a slower velocity *eleven* months later.

> **belief**—Another key practice in systems modeling is to discuss beliefs. It's one thing to sketch, claim, imply, or assume "managers can evaluate developers without looking in depth at their code," but it's another to recognize that could be belief, not fact. *We model to have a conversation*, so systems modeling is a time to discuss and become conscious of our beliefs, make them *visible*, and critique them.

Almost *every* causal link or variable is an opportunity to examine and discuss beliefs. Is *Velocity* a good variable to include? What does measuring it lead to? Do weak developers create bad code? What do you mean by "more features means more waste?"

The sketch in Figure 14.4 includes notation for delays, which are visualized with double lines through a causal link, and some informal notes capturing discussions. Of course, the notation doesn't really matter as long as the group has a common understanding.

This example model isn't meant to be "insightful," it's meant to illustrate that *we model to have a conversation*!

Figure 14.4 delays and informal notes to clarify the discussion

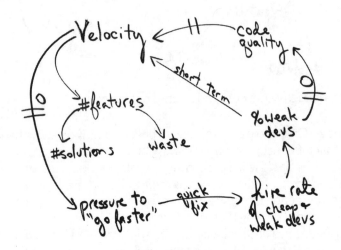

Learn—Learn more about systems thinking and modeling here:

> *Systems Thinking* chapter in the first LeSS book, *Scaling Lean & Agile Development: Thinking & Organizational Tools for Large-Scale Scrum*, by Larman & Vodde. This chapter is also online at *less.works*.

> *The Fifth Discipline* by Senge, an important classic.

> *Thinking in Systems*, by Meadows & Wright

> *Systemantics*, by Gall.

LeSS Huge

• LeSS Huge Rules •

There are no LeSS Huge rules for reviews and retrospectives. The catch-all statement *"All Sprint LeSS rules apply for each Requirement Area"* implies a Sprint Review and Overall Retrospective for each separate Requirement Area. But there's no requirement for meetings that span the entire product.

Guide: Multi-Area Reviews & Retrospectives

Review—Although not required, a multi-area Review spanning from two up to all areas (full product) is certainly possible when the group feels the need.

Why isn't a product-level Sprint Review mandated in LeSS Huge? After all, avoiding one can reduce focusing on and seeing the whole. First, a group *can* hold a product-level review. But each area is often different enough that no great insights come from one—at least not every Sprint. And especially at Huge scale, in addition to gathering the entire Product Owner Team and representatives from many teams, the complexity of a product-level review could involve people at 10 sites worldwide, so can be a real pain to set up and run. There needs to be a compelling reason, and if there is, it's probably not compelling for every Sprint.

Retrospective—Similarly, there's no rule requiring a product-level *Retrospective*, but there may indeed be a good reason to hold a multi-area Retrospective since *improving the system* is key, and the organizational system spans the areas. A multi-area Retrospective is more likely when areas aren't working well together, or several areas have similar problems. It's also useful for teams from different Requirement Areas working together at the same physical site, to improve relationships and knowledge sharing.

More or LeSS

What's Next?

Now this is not the end. It is not even the beginning of the end.
But it is, perhaps, the end of the beginning.
—Winston Churchill

Congratulations, you've made it to the end of the beginning. What's next? We hope it's hands-on practice to solidify the ideas in this book.

Don't forget to experiment. The other two LeSS books—*Scaling Lean & Agile Development* and *Practices for Scaling Lean & Agile Development*—are catalogs of experiments to try out.

While writing this book, we created the 3-day *Certified LeSS Practitioner* course, which covers this book and additional experiments, stories, case studies, and examples. These courses are taught by Certified LeSS Trainers based on their hands-on LeSS experience. In addition, every year there is a LeSS Conference for sharing experiences.

We keep updating the LeSS site at *less.works*. You can test your LeSS understanding by trying the *online test*. We'll keep adding more content, videos, case studies, and other learning material.

The LeSS site also has a growing collection of experience reports. Each has interesting knowledge and ideas to try: a wealth of learning.

If you want to write up your experience and share it, let us know! We are constantly looking for experiences to learn from and new ideas to try out. If you've been involved with an existing case study, the site allows for Certified LeSS Practitioners to share their perspective in an experience report. There are always perspectives to learn from.

With these learning resources, we sincerely hope to maximize your joy for creating products that have a impact. To achieve more with LeSS.

15. What's Next?

RECOMMENDED READINGS

In this book, we decided not to include an extensive bibliography. Instead we list all the recommended readings that we mentioned throughout the book. In the previous two LeSS books, *Scaling Lean & Agile Development* and *Practices for Scaling Lean & Agile Development*, you can find more extensive bibliographies.

Adzic, G., 2011. *Specification by Example: How Successful Teams Deliver the Right Software*, Manning Publications

Adzic, G., 2012. *Impact Mapping: Making a Big Impact with Software Products and Projects*, Provoking Thoughts

Adzic, G., Evans, D., 2014. *Fifty Quick Ideas to Improve Your User Stories*, Neuri Consulting

Balle, M., Balle F., 2009. *The Lean Manager: A Novel of Lean Transformation*, Lean Enterprise Institute

Deemer, P., Benefield, G., Larman, C., Vodde, B., 2012. *The Scrum Primer*, at *scrumprimer.org* and at *less.works*.

Gall, J., 2003. *Systemantics, The Systems Bible: The Beginner's Guide to Systems Large and Small*, General Systemantics

Gray, D., Brown, S., Maconufo, J., 2010. *Gamestorming: A Playbook for Innovators, Rulebreakers, and Changemakers*, O'Reilly Media

Hackman, R., 2002. *Leading Teams*, Harvard Business Press

Hamel, G., 2007. *The Future of Management*, Harvard Business Review Press

Hohmann, L. 2006. *Innovation Games: Creating Breakthrough Products Through Collaborative Play*, Addison-Wesley

James, M., 2010, *The Scrum Master Checklist*, at *scrummasterchecklist.org*

Kimsey-House, H., Kimsey-House, K., 2011. *Co-active Coaching: Changing Business, Transforming Lives*, Nicholas Brealey America

Laloux, F. 2014. *Reinventing Organizations*, Nelson Parker

Larman, C., Vodde, B., 2008. *Scaling Lean & Agile Development: Thinking and Organizational Tools for Large-Scale Scrum*, Addison-Wesley

Larman, C., Vodde, B., 2010. *Practices for Scaling Lean & Agile Development: Large, Multisite, and Offshore Product Development with Large-Scale Scrum*, Addison-Wesley

Larman, C., Vodde, B., 2011, *Feature Team Primer*, at *featureteams.org*

Larman, C., Fahmy, A., 2013, *How to Form Teams in Large-Scale Scrum? A Story of Self-Designing Teams*, at *http://www.scrumalliance.org/community/articles/2013/2013-april/how-to-form-teams-in-large-scale-scrum-a-story-of*

Lawrence, R. 2009. *Patterns for Splitting User Stories*, at *http://agileforall.com/patterns-for-splitting-user-stories/*

Lencioni, P., 2002. *The Five Dysfunctions of a Team: A Leadership Fable*, Jossey-Bass

LeSS site, at https://less.works

McGregor, D., 1960. *The Human Side of Enterprise*, McGraw-Hill Education

Meadows, D., Wright, D. [editor], 2008, *Thinking in Systems: A Primer*, Chelsea Green Publishing

Ohno, T., 1988. *Workplace Management*, Productivity Press

Owen, H., 2008. *Open Space Technology: A User's Guide*, Berret-Koehler Publishers

Patton, J., 2014. *User Story Mapping: Discover the Whole Story, Build the Right Product*, O'Reilly Media

Pfeffer, J., Sutton, R., 2006. *Hard Facts, Dangerous Half-Truths and Total Nonsense: Profiting from Evidence-Based Management*, Harvard Business Review Press

Schein, E., 2013. *Humble Inquiry: The Gentle Art of Asking Instead of Telling*, Berret-Koehler Publishers

Schwaber, K., 2013. *The Scrum Guide*, at *scrumguides.org*

Schwarz, R., 2002. *The Skilled Facilitator: A Comprehensive Resource for Consultants, Facilitators, Managers, Trainers, and Coaches*, Jossey-Bass

Senge, P. 2006. *The Fifth Discipline: The Art & Practice of the Learning Organization*, Doubleday

Vodde, B., 2011. *Specialization and Generalization in Teams*, at *http://www.scrumalliance.org/community/articles/2011/january/specialization-and-generalization-in-teams*

APPENDIX A: RULES

The LeSS Rules are the definition of the LeSS Framework. They are things we consider a must. Why? This is explained in the *Why LeSS* description on *less.works*.

LeSS FRAMEWORK RULES

The LeSS framework applies to products with 2–"8" teams.

• LeSS Structure •

> Structure the organization using real teams as the basic organizational building block.

> Each team is (1) self-managing, (2) cross-functional, (3) co-located, and (4) long-lived.

> The majority of the teams are customer-focused feature teams.

> Scrum Masters are responsible for a well-working LeSS adoption. Their focus is towards the Teams, Product Owner, organization, and development practices. A Scrum Master does not focus on just one team but on the overall organizational system.

> A Scrum Master is a dedicated full-time role.

> One Scrum Master can serve 1–3 teams.

> In LeSS, managers are optional, but if managers do exist, their role is likely to change. Their focus shifts from managing the day-to-day product work to improving the value-delivering capability of the product development system.

> Managers' role is to improve the product development system by practicing Go See, encouraging Stop & Fix, and "experiments over conformance."

> For the product group, establish the complete LeSS structure "at the start"; this is vital for a LeSS adoption.

> For the larger organization beyond the product group, adopt LeSS evolutionally by using Go and See to create an organization where experimentation and improvement is the norm.

• LeSS Product •

> There is one Product Owner and one Product Backlog for the complete shippable product.

> The Product Owner shouldn't work alone on Product Backlog refinement; he is supported by the multiple Teams working directly with customers/users and other stakeholders.

> All prioritization goes through the Product Owner, but clarification is as much as possible directly between the Teams and customer/users and other stakeholders.

> The definition of product should be as broad and end-user-/customer- centric as is practical. Over time, the definition of product might expand. Broader definitions are preferred.

> There is one Definition of Done for the whole product, common for all teams.

> Each team can have its own stronger Definition of Done by expanding the common one.

> The perfection goal is to improve the Definition of Done so that it results in a shippable product each Sprint (or even more frequently).

• LeSS Sprint •

> There is one product-level Sprint, not a different Sprint for each Team. Each Team starts and ends the Sprint at the same time. Each Sprint results in an integrated whole product.

> Sprint Planning consists of two parts: Sprint Planning One is common for all teams, whereas Sprint Planning Two is usually done separately for each team. Do multi-team Sprint Planning Two in a shared space for closely related items.

> Sprint Planning One is attended by the Product Owner and Teams or Team representatives. Together, they tentatively select the

items that each team will work on during that Sprint. The Teams identify opportunities to work together, and final questions are clarified.

> Each Team has its own Sprint Backlog.

> Sprint Planning Two is for Teams to decide how they will do the selected items. That usually involves design and the creation of their Sprint Backlogs.

> Each Team has its own Daily Scrum.

> Cross-team coordination is decided by the teams. Prefer decentralized and informal coordination over centralized coordination. Emphasize Just Talk and informal networks through communicating in code, cross-team meetings, component mentors, travelers, scouts, and open spaces.

> Product Backlog Refinement (PBR) is done per team for the items they will likely do in the future. Do multi-team and/or overall PBR to increase shared understanding, and exploit coordination opportunities when having closely related items or a need for broader input/learning.

> There is one product Sprint Review; it is common for all teams. Ensure that suitable stakeholders join to contribute the information needed for effective inspection and adaptation.

> Each Team has its own Sprint Retrospective.

> An Overall Retrospective is held after the Team Retrospectives to discuss cross-team and systemwide issues and to create improvement experiments. In attendance are Product Owner, Scrum Masters, Team Representatives, and managers (if any).

LeSS Huge Framework Rules

LeSS Huge applies to products with "8+" teams. Avoid applying LeSS Huge to smaller product groups as its principles will result in more overhead and local optimizations. All LeSS rules apply to LeSS Huge unless otherwise stated. Each Requirement Area acts like the basic LeSS framework.

• LeSS Huge Structure •

> Customer requirements that are strongly related from a customer perspective are grouped in Requirement Areas.

> Each Team specializes in one Requirement Area. Teams stay in one area for a long time. When there is more value in other areas, teams might change Requirement Area.

> Each Requirement Area has one Area Product Owner.

> Each Requirement Area has between "4–8" teams. Avoid violating this range.

> LeSS Huge adoptions, including the structural changes, are done with an evolutionary incremental approach.

> Remember each day: LeSS Huge adoptions take months or years, infinite patience, and sense of humor.

• LeSS Huge Product •

> Each Requirement Area has one Area Product Owner.

> One (overall) Product Owner is responsible for product-wide prioritization and for deciding which teams work in which Area. He works closely with Area Product Owners.

> Area Product Owners act as Product Owners towards their teams.

> There is one Product Backlog; every item in it belongs to exactly one Requirement Area.

> There is one Area Product Backlog per Requirement Area. This is conceptually a more granular view into the one Product Backlog.

• LeSS Huge Sprint •

> There is one product-level Sprint, not a different Sprint for each Requirement Area. It ends in one integrated whole product.

> The Product Owner and Area Product Owners synchronize frequently. Before Sprint Planning they ensure that the Teams work on the most valuable items. After the Sprint Review, they further enable product-level adaptations.

Appendix B: Guides

INDEX